QUALITY OF LIFE,
BALANCE OF POWER
AND NUCLEAR WEAPONS

Quality of Life, Balance of Power and Nuclear Weapons

A Statistical Yearbook
for Statesmen and Citizens
2011

Alexander V. Avakov

Algora Publishing
New York

Library of Congress Cataloging-in-Publication Data —

Avakov, Aleksandr V. (Aleksandr Vladimirovich), 1954-
   Quality of life, balance of power and nuclear weapons: a statistical yearbook for
statesmen and citizens / Alexander V. Avakov.
      p. cm.
   Includes bibliographical references and index.
   ISBN 978-0-87586-819-6 (soft: alk. paper) — ISBN 978-0-87586-820-2 (hard cover:
alk. paper) — ISBN 978-0-87586-821-9 (ebook: alk. paper) 1. Economic indicators. 2.
Social indicators. 3. Quality of life—Statistics. 4. Armed Forces—Appropriations and
expenditures—Statistics.. 5. Nuclear weapons—Statistics. 6. Health status indicators. I.
Title.

   HC59.3.A83 2008
   306.09'0511021—dc22
                              2008003446

Printed in the United States

TABLE OF CONTENTS

3. DEVELOPED MARKET ECONOMIES   145

INTRODUCTION

This statistical annual presents fundamental data in three sections: (1) Quality of Life, (2) Balance of Powers, (3) Developed Market Economies since 1960.

The advantage of this yearbook is that it contains data generally not available elsewhere. Sections 1 and 2 give statistics for 232 countries. By comparison, the World Bank and *Encyclopedia Britannica* provide statistical data for a maximum of about 160 countries. The actual number of countries in World Bank statistical tables is even smaller. The CIA *World Factbook* gives data for about 230 countries, but that data is limited in scope and is imprecise. Other statistical publications are even less satisfactory. I managed to increase the number of countries tallied by writing proprietary software utilizing statistical regressions, selecting data which, first of all, is important and, second, is relatively reliable, offering high correlation coefficients for these regressions.

Section 1 concentrates on data that reflect the quality of life. First, I focused on major economic and demographic indicators. In addition to data about the quality of life as measured strictly in economic terms, I sought to produce a methodologically rigorous estimate of a human rights index. The latter measures civil and political rights as well as socioeconomic rights. I also computed an integrated economico-political quality-of-life index.

In Section 2, the book deals with major indicators of the balance of power. In addition to data about each country's economic power, military personnel and military expenditures, it includes data about nuclear delivery systems and provides the number of nuclear warheads of all nuclear powers. This is based on information from reputable sources. Among others, it includes estimates of the Israeli nuclear arsenal which usually do not appear in the press. I also give a rough account of countries possessing, pursuing or capable of acquiring other weapons of mass destruction. Chances are that if the American public were more familiar with these statistics, some Middle East foreign policy failures might have been avoided.

It should also be underscored that many official estimates, for example estimates of Russian military expenditures distributed by US and British intelligence communities, are methodologically flawed. Such estimates claim to give a picture of the military expenditures of the countries of the world at market exchange rates; at the same time, they apparently cite Russian military expense figures at purchasing power parity, thus inflating these numbers in comparison to those of other countries. Such deceptive practices of the Anglo–American intelligence services are counterbalanced by presenting two different tables, showing military expenditures estimates both at market exchange rates and at purchasing power parities. Members of the US Congress and others who care about the foundations of power politics in the nuclear age will find facts that speak for themselves in this section.

In Section 3, I give data on the hot topic of health care. It seems that public health expenditures as a share of total health expenditures has a stronger correlation with the comparative level (and the rates of improvement) of the main health care indicators than the absolute level (measured as a percent of GDP) of total health expenditures. It is also worth noting that, as the data demonstrates, the US has the lowest public health expenditure of developed market economies and is increasingly lagging behind other countries by main health care indicators. The recent legislation that was intended to provide greater access to health care for people in the US was furiously attacked by opponents who suspected it would entail some sort of tax increase that would hurt the economy. I therefore also try to shed light on modern ideological debates about the share of taxation in GDP and its influence on rates of growth. Surprisingly enough, the empirical data for the developed market economies does not seem to support the popular idea that low taxes are strongly correlated with higher rates of growth; depending on how the data is analyzed, the correlations are either low or even the reverse of what is commonly believed.

SOURCES

The sources are shown in the form: XX(Source), or XX(Source)W, or XX(Source A/SourceB), where XX is a year, W after (Source) means that data is weighted against the World Bank data for the U.S., and (Source) (or Source A or Source B) is one of the following:

WB	The World Bank (1)
E	Encyclopedia Britannica
CIA	Central Intelligence Agency
CALC(CIA)	Calculated using data of the Central Intelligence Agency
UN	United Nations Development Programme
GPI	Global Peace Index
USAID	U.S. Agency for International Development
FH	Freedom House
IISS	International Institute for Strategic Studies
SIPRI	Stockholm International Peace Research Institute
BULL	Bulletin of the Atomic Scientists
UCS	Union of Concerned Scientists
WIKI	Wikipedia
REG	Regression
EST	Estimate
PRIN1(EQL)	Principal Component 1 of Economic Quality-of-Life Indicators
PRIN1(PQL)	Principal Component 1 of Political Quality-of-Life Indicators
PRIN1(EPQL)	Principal Component 1 of Economico-Political Quality-of-Life Indicators
POP*GPC	Obtained by multiplication of Population by GDP Per Capita at Market Exchange Rates
POP*GPCPPP	Obtained by multiplication of Population by GDP Per Capita at Purchasing Power Parities
GDP*MILGDP+MILAID	Obtained by multiplication of GDP at Market Exchange Rates by Percent of Military Expenditures as Share of GDP plus Foreign Military Aid
GDPPPP*MILGDP+MILAID	Obtained by multiplication of GDP at Purchasing Power Parities by Percent of Military Expenditures as Share of GDP plus Foreign Military Aid

REGIONS

AFR	Africa
CPA	Centrally Planned Asia
DME	Developed Market Economies
EEU	Eastern Europe
LAM	Latin America
MEA	Middle East
SAS	South Asia
SEA	South-East Asia and Pacific
USR	Former U.S.S.R.

ABBREVIATIONS

OBS	Number of Countries Observed
GPC	Gross National Income at Market Exchange Rates Per Capita
INFMRT	Infant Mortality
LIFEXP	Life Expectancy
GPCPPP	Gross Domestic Product at Purchasing Power Parities Per Capita
EQLX	Economic Quality-of-Life Index
SCINTX	Societal Integration Index
CPRX	Civil and Political Rights Index
HDX	Human Development Index
GINI	Gini Coefficient of Income Inequality
PQLX	Political Quality-of-Life Index
EPQLX	Economico-Political Quality-of-Life Index
POP	Population
GDPPPP	Gross Domestic Product at Purchasing Power Parities
GDP	Gross National Income at Market Exchange Rates
ARMY	Armed Forces Personnel
MILGDP	Military Expenditures as Share of GDP
MILAID	Foreign Military Aid
MILXPP	Military Expenditures at Purchasing Power Parities plus Foreign Military Aid
MILEXP	Military Expenditures at Market Exchange Rates plus Foreign Military Aid
GPCxx	Gross National Income Per Capita at Market Exchange Rates, Year xx
GRPCMER	Growth Rates of GNI Per Capita at Market Exchange Rates
GPCPPPxx	Gross Domestic Product Per Capita at Purchasing Power Parities, Year xx
GRPCPPP	Growth Rates of GDP Per Capita at Purchasing Power Parities
INFMRTxx	Infant Mortality, Year xx
DRIM	Decrease Rates of Infant Mortality
LIFEXPxx	Life Expectancy, Year xx
GRLE	Growth Rates of Life Expectancy
HLTGDP	Total Health Expenditures as Percent of GDP
PUBHLT	Public Health Expenditures as Percent of Total Health Expenditures
TAXGDPxx	Taxes as Share of GDP, Year xx

1. QUALITY OF LIFE

TABLE 1.1 GROSS NATIONAL INCOME AT MARKET EXCHANGE RATES PER CAPITA, 2008					
OBS	REGION	COUNTRY	GPC	RANK	SOURCE
1	DME	Monaco	195,717	1.0	08(E)
2	DME	Liechtenstein	125,110	2.0	(REG)
3	MEA	Qatar	88,990	3.0	08(E)
4	DME	Norway	87,070	4.0	08(WB)
5	DME	Bermuda	86,265	5.0	07(E)
6	DME	Luxembourg	84,890	6.0	08(WB)
7	DME	Switzerland	65,330	7.0	08(WB)
8	DME	Jersey	63,400	8.0	08(E)
9	DME	San Marino	60,925	9.0	08(E)
10	DME	Denmark	59,130	10.0	08(WB)
11	MEA	UAE	57,094	11.0	08(E)
12	DME	Guernsey	55,212	12.0	07(E)
13	DME	Sweden	50,940	13.0	08(WB)
14	DME	Netherlands	50,150	14.0	08(WB)
15	DME	Ireland	49,590	15.0	08(WB)
16	DME	Faeroe Islands	48,436	16.0	08(E)
17	DME	Finland	48,120	17.0	08(WB)
18	DME	United States	47,580	18.0	08(WB)
19	LAM	Cayman Islands	46,729	19.0	07(E)
20	DME	Austria	46,260	20.0	08(WB)
21	DME	United Kingdom	45,390	21.0	08(WB)
22	DME	Isle of Man	44,988	22.0	07(E)
23	DME	Andorra	44,910	23.0	07(E)
24	DME	Belgium	44,330	24.0	08(WB)
25	SEA	Macao	42,730	25.0	08(E)
26	DME	Germany	42,440	26.0	08(WB)
27	DME	France	42,250	27.0	08(WB)
28	DME	Canada	41,730	28.0	08(WB)
29	DME	Australia	40,350	29.0	08(WB)
30	DME	Iceland	40,070	30.0	08(WB)
31	DME	Falkland Islands	39,903	31.0	(REG)
32	LAM	Virgin Islands, Brit.	39,509	32.0	(REG)
33	MEA	Kuwait	39,244	33.0	07(E)
34	DME	Japan	38,210	34.0	08(WB)
35	LAM	Virgin Islands, US	38,019	35.0	06(E)
36	SEA	New Caledonia	37,630	36.0	08(E)
37	DME	Gibraltar	36,783	37.0	(REG)
38	DME	Italy	35,240	38.0	08(WB)
39	SEA	Singapore	34,760	39.0	08(WB)
40	DME	Greenland	33,477	40.0	07(E)
41	SEA	Brunei	32,263	41.0	07(E)
42	DME	Spain	31,960	42.0	08(WB)
43	SEA	Hong Kong	31,420	43.0	08(WB)
44	DME	Greece	28,650	44.0	08(WB)

OBS	REGION	COUNTRY	GPC	RANK	SOURCE
		TABLE 1.1 GROSS NATIONAL INCOME AT MARKET EXCHANGE RATES PER CAPITA, 2008			
45	DME	New Zealand	27,940	45.0	08(WB)
46	LAM	Martinique	27,824	46.0	07(E)
47	SEA	Guam	24,747	47.0	05(E)
48	DME	Israel	24,700	48.0	08(WB)
49	LAM	Aruba	24,523	49.0	07(E)
50	AFR	Reunion	24,226	50.0	07(E)
51	EEU	Slovenia	24,010	51.0	08(WB)
52	MEA	Cyprus	23,692	52.0	07(WB)
53	LAM	Guadeloupe	23,053	53.0	06(E)
54	SEA	French Polynesia	22,509	54.0	07(E)
55	LAM	Bahamas	21,701	55.0	07(E)
56	SEA	Korea, South	21,530	56.0	08(WB)
57	DME	Portugal	20,560	57.0	08(WB)
58	LAM	Neth. Antilles	19,557	58.0	08(E)
59	MEA	Saudi Arabia	18,718	59.0	08(E)
60	MEA	Oman	17,884	60.0	08(E)
61	SEA	Taiwan	17,542	61.0	08(E)
62	DME	Malta	17,219	62.0	07(WB)
63	EEU	Czechia	16,600	63.0	08(WB)
64	LAM	Trinidad & Tobago	16,540	64.0	08(WB)
65	LAM	Puerto Rico	15,399	65.0	08(E)
66	AFR	Equatorial Guinea	14,980	66.0	08(WB)
67	SEA	Northern Mariana Is.	14,579	67.0	05(E)
68	LAM	Guiana, French	14,556	68.0	07(E)
69	EEU	Slovakia	14,540	69.0	08(WB)
70	USR	Estonia	14,270	70.0	08(WB)
71	LAM	Antigua & Barbuda	13,620	71.0	08(WB)
72	EEU	Croatia	13,570	72.0	08(WB)
73	MEA	Bahrain	13,353	73.0	07(E)
74	EEU	Hungary	12,810	74.0	08(WB)
75	LAM	Barbados	12,572	75.0	07(E)
76	EEU	Poland	11,880	76.0	08(WB)
77	USR	Lithuania	11,870	77.0	08(WB)
78	USR	Latvia	11,860	78.0	08(WB)
79	MEA	Libya	11,590	79.0	08(WB)
80	LAM	St. Kitts & Nevis	10,960	80.0	08(WB)
81	LAM	Turks & Caicos Is.	10,645	81.0	(REG)
82	AFR	Seychelles	10,290	82.0	08(WB)
83	LAM	Mexico	9,980	83.0	08(WB)
84	USR	Russia	9,620	84.0	08(WB)
85	LAM	Chile	9,400	85.0	08(WB)
86	MEA	Turkey	9,340	86.0	08(WB)
87	LAM	Venezuela	9,230	87.0	08(WB)
88	SEA	Palau	8,650	88.0	08(WB)

OBS	REGION	COUNTRY	GPC	RANK	SOURCE
	TABLE 1.1 GROSS NATIONAL INCOME AT MARKET EXCHANGE RATES PER CAPITA, 2008

OBS	REGION	COUNTRY	GPC	RANK	SOURCE
89	LAM	Uruguay	8,260	89.0	08(WB)
90	SEA	Samoa, American	8,089	90.0	05(E)
91	EEU	Romania	7,930	91.0	08(WB)
92	LAM	Brazil	7,350	92.0	08(WB)
93	AFR	Gabon	7,240	93.0	08(WB)
94	LAM	Argentina	7,200	94.0	08(WB)
95	LAM	Anguilla	6,973	95.0	(REG)
96	SEA	Malaysia	6,970	96.0	08(WB)
97	SEA	Cook Islands	6,815	97.0	(REG)
98	AFR	Botswana	6,470	98.0	08(WB)
99	EEU	Montenegro	6,440	99.0	08(WB)
100	AFR	Mauritius	6,400	100.0	08(WB)
101	MEA	Lebanon	6,350	101.0	08(WB)
102	LAM	Panama	6,180	102.0	08(WB)
103	USR	Kazakhstan	6,140	103.0	08(WB)
104	DME	St. Pierre & Miquelon	6,110	104.0	(REG)
105	LAM	Costa Rica	6,060	105.0	08(WB)
106	AFR	South Africa	5,820	106.0	08(WB)
107	LAM	Grenada	5,710	107.0	08(WB)
108	EEU	Serbia	5,700	108.0	08(WB)
109	LAM	St. Lucia	5,530	109.0	08(WB)
110	EEU	Bulgaria	5,490	110.0	08(WB)
111	USR	Belarus	5,380	111.0	08(WB)
112	LAM	St. Vincent	5,140	112.0	08(WB)
113	LAM	Suriname	4,990	113.0	08(WB)
114	LAM	Jamaica	4,870	114.0	08(WB)
115	LAM	Dominica	4,770	115.0	08(WB)
116	LAM	Cuba	4,688	116.0	07(E)
117	LAM	Colombia	4,660	117.0	08(WB)
118	SEA	Niue	4,558	118.0	(REG)
119	EEU	Bosnia	4,510	119.0	08(WB)
120	LAM	Dominican Rep.	4,390	120.0	08(WB)
121	MEA	Algeria	4,260	121.0	08(WB)
122	AFR	Namibia	4,200	122.0	08(WB)
123	EEU	Macedonia	4,140	123.0	08(WB)
124	LAM	Peru	3,990	124.0	08(WB)
125	SEA	Fiji	3,930	125.0	08(WB)
126	EEU	Albania	3,840	126.0	08(WB)
127	USR	Azerbaijan	3,830	127.0	08(WB)
128	LAM	Belize	3,820	128.0	08(WB)
129	AFR	Mayotte	3,751	129.0	02(E)
130	MEA	Iran	3,654	130.0	07(WB)
131	SEA	Nauru	3,650	131.0	08(E)
132	LAM	Ecuador	3,640	132.0	08(WB)
133	SAS	Maldives	3,630	133.0	08(WB)

OBS	REGION	COUNTRY	GPC	RANK	SOURCE
\multicolumn{6}{l}{TABLE 1.1 GROSS NATIONAL INCOME AT MARKET EXCHANGE RATES PER CAPITA, 2008}
134	LAM	El Salvador	3,480	134.0	08(WB)
135	AFR	Angola	3,450	135.0	08(WB)
136	USR	Armenia	3,350	136.0	08(WB)
137	MEA	Jordan	3,310	137.0	08(WB)
138	MEA	Tunisia	3,290	138.0	08(WB)
139	SEA	Marshall Islands	3,270	139.0	08(WB)
140	USR	Ukraine	3,210	140.0	08(WB)
141	AFR	Cape Verde	3,130	141.0	08(WB)
142	CPA	China	2,940	142.0	08(WB)
143	SEA	Tuvalu	2,889	143.0	08(E)
144	SEA	Thailand	2,840	144.5	08(WB)
145	USR	Turkmenistan	2,840	144.5	08(WB)
146	SEA	Samoa, Western	2,780	146.0	08(WB)
147	LAM	Guatemala	2,680	147.0	08(WB)
148	SEA	Wallis & Futuna	2,599	148.0	(REG)
149	MEA	Morocco	2,580	149.0	08(WB)
150	SEA	Tonga	2,560	150.0	08(WB)
151	LAM	Montserrat	2,542	151.0	(REG)
152	AFR	Swaziland	2,520	152.0	08(WB)
153	USR	Georgia	2,470	153.0	08(WB)
154	SEA	East Timor	2,460	154.0	08(WB)
155	MEA	Iraq	2,444	155.0	07(E)
156	SEA	Micronesia	2,340	156.0	08(WB)
157	SEA	Vanuatu	2,330	157.0	08(WB)
158	EEU	Kosovo	2,185	158.0	07(E)
159	LAM	Paraguay	2,180	159.0	08(WB)
160	MEA	Syria	2,090	160.0	08(WB)
161	AFR	St. Helena	2,085	161.0	(REG)
162	SEA	Indonesia	2,010	162.0	08(WB)
163	SEA	Kiribati	2,000	163.0	08(WB)
164	AFR	Congo, Rep.	1,970	164.0	08(WB)
165	SAS	Bhutan	1,900	165.0	08(WB)
166	SEA	Philippines	1,890	166.0	08(WB)
167	MEA	Egypt	1,800	167.5	08(WB)
168	LAM	Honduras	1,800	167.5	08(WB)
169	SAS	Sri Lanka	1,780	169.0	08(WB)
170	CPA	Mongolia	1,680	170.0	08(WB)
171	MEA	Gaza Strip	1,484	171.5	06(E)
172	MEA	West Bank	1,484	171.5	06(E)
173	USR	Moldova	1,470	173.0	08(WB)
174	LAM	Bolivia	1,460	174.0	08(WB)
175	LAM	Guyana	1,420	175.0	08(WB)
176	AFR	Western Sahara	1,313	176.0	(REG)
177	SEA	Solomon Islands	1,180	177.0	08(WB)
178	AFR	Nigeria	1,160	178.0	08(WB)
179	AFR	Cameroon	1,150	179.0	08(WB)

OBS	REGION	COUNTRY	GPC	RANK	SOURCE
		TABLE 1.1 GROSS NATIONAL INCOME AT MARKET EXCHANGE RATES PER CAPITA, 2008			
180	AFR	Djibouti	1,130	180.5	08(WB)
181	AFR	Sudan	1,130	180.5	08(WB)
182	AFR	Lesotho	1,080	182.5	08(WB)
183	LAM	Nicaragua	1,080	182.5	08(WB)
184	SAS	India	1,070	184.0	08(WB)
185	CPA	Korea, North	1,033	185.0	08(E)
186	AFR	San Tome & Principe	1,020	186.0	08(WB)
187	SEA	Papua New Guinea	1,010	187.0	08(WB)
188	AFR	Ivory Coast	980	188.5	08(WB)
189	SAS	Pakistan	980	188.5	08(WB)
190	AFR	Senegal	970	190.0	08(WB)
191	MEA	Yemen	950	191.5	08(WB)
192	AFR	Zambia	950	191.5	08(WB)
193	SEA	Tokelau	915	193.0	(REG)
194	USR	Uzbekistan	910	194.0	08(WB)
195	CPA	Vietnam	890	195.0	08(WB)
196	AFR	Mauritania	867	196.0	07(WB)
197	AFR	Kenya	770	197.0	08(WB)
198	AFR	Comoros	750	198.0	08(WB)
199	USR	Kyrgyzstan	740	199.5	08(WB)
200	CPA	Laos	740	199.5	08(WB)
201	AFR	Benin	690	201.0	08(WB)
202	AFR	Ghana	670	202.0	08(WB)
203	LAM	Haiti	660	203.0	08(WB)
204	CPA	Cambodia	600	204.5	08(WB)
205	USR	Tajikistan	600	204.5	08(WB)
206	AFR	Mali	580	206.0	08(WB)
207	CPA	Burma	578	207.0	08(E)
208	AFR	Chad	530	208.0	08(WB)
209	SAS	Bangladesh	520	209.0	08(WB)
210	AFR	Burkina Faso	480	210.0	08(WB)
211	AFR	Tanzania	440	211.0	08(WB)
212	AFR	Uganda	420	212.0	08(WB)
213	AFR	CAR	410	214.0	08(WB)
214	AFR	Madagascar	410	214.0	08(WB)
215	AFR	Rwanda	410	214.0	08(WB)
216	AFR	Guinea	403	216.0	07(WB)
217	SAS	Nepal	400	217.5	08(WB)
218	AFR	Togo	400	217.5	08(WB)
219	AFR	Gambia	390	219.0	08(WB)
220	SAS	Afghanistan	385	220.0	07(E)
221	AFR	Mozambique	370	221.0	08(WB)
222	AFR	Niger	330	222.0	08(WB)
223	AFR	Sierra Leone	320	223.0	08(WB)
224	AFR	Zimbabwe	312	224.0	08(E)

TABLE 1.1 GROSS NATIONAL INCOME AT MARKET EXCHANGE RATES PER CAPITA, 2008					
OBS	REGION	COUNTRY	GPC	RANK	SOURCE
225	AFR	Eritrea	300	225.0	08(WB)
226	AFR	Malawi	290	226.0	08(WB)
227	AFR	Somalia	288	227.0	08(E)
228	AFR	Ethiopia	280	228.0	08(WB)
229	AFR	Guinea-Bissau	250	229.0	08(WB)
230	AFR	Liberia	170	230.0	08(WB)
231	AFR	Congo, Dem. Rep.	150	231.0	08(WB)
232	AFR	Burundi	140	232.0	08(WB)

TABLE 1.2 INFANT MORTALITY, RATE PER 1,000 LIVE BIRTHS, 2008					
OBS	REGION	COUNTRY	INFMRT	RANK	SOURCE
1	DME	San Marino	1.20	1.0	08(WB)
2	DME	Liechtenstein	1.76	2.0	08(WB)
3	DME	Iceland	1.90	3.5	08(WB)
4	DME	Luxembourg	1.90	3.5	08(WB)
5	SEA	Singapore	2.30	5.5	08(WB)
6	DME	Sweden	2.30	5.5	08(WB)
7	DME	Japan	2.50	7.0	08(WB)
8	DME	Finland	2.70	8.0	08(WB)
9	DME	Norway	2.90	10.0	08(WB)
10	DME	Portugal	2.90	10.0	08(WB)
11	EEU	Slovenia	2.90	10.0	08(WB)
12	SEA	Hong Kong	2.93	12.0	08(CIA)
13	DME	Andorra	3.00	14.0	08(WB)
14	DME	Ireland	3.00	14.0	08(WB)
15	DME	Italy	3.00	14.0	08(WB)
16	EEU	Czechia	3.10	16.0	08(WB)
17	DME	France	3.30	17.5	08(WB)
18	DME	Greece	3.30	17.5	08(WB)
19	DME	Austria	3.40	19.5	08(WB)
20	DME	Monaco	3.40	19.5	08(WB)
21	MEA	Cyprus	3.50	21.5	08(WB)
22	DME	Spain	3.50	21.5	08(WB)
23	LAM	Anguilla	3.54	23.0	08(CIA)
24	DME	Israel	3.60	24.0	08(WB)
25	DME	Denmark	3.70	25.5	08(WB)
26	DME	Germany	3.70	25.5	08(WB)
27	DME	Belgium	3.90	27.0	08(WB)
28	DME	Netherlands	4.00	28.5	08(WB)
29	DME	Switzerland	4.00	28.5	08(WB)
30	SEA	Macao	4.30	30.0	08(CIA)
31	USR	Estonia	4.40	31.0	08(WB)
32	DME	Guernsey	4.53	32.0	08(CIA)
33	SEA	Korea, South	4.73	33.0	08(WB)
34	DME	Falkland Islands	4.79	34.0	(REG)
35	LAM	Cuba	4.80	35.0	08(WB)
36	DME	Australia	4.90	37.0	08(WB)
37	DME	New Zealand	4.90	37.0	08(WB)
38	DME	United Kingdom	4.90	37.0	08(WB)
39	DME	Gibraltar	4.91	39.0	08(CIA)
40	DME	Jersey	5.01	40.0	08(CIA)
41	EEU	Croatia	5.10	41.0	08(WB)
42	EEU	Hungary	5.40	42.0	08(WB)
43	SEA	Taiwan	5.45	43.0	08(CIA)
44	SEA	Brunei	5.50	44.5	08(WB)
45	DME	Malta	5.50	44.5	08(WB)
46	DME	Isle of Man	5.62	46.0	08(CIA)
47	DME	Canada	5.70	47.0	08(WB)

OBS	REGION	COUNTRY	INFMRT	RANK	SOURCE
		TABLE 1.2 INFANT MORTALITY, RATE PER 1,000 LIVE BIRTHS, 2008			
48	EEU	Poland	5.80	48.0	08(WB)
49	SEA	Malaysia	5.92	49.0	08(WB)
50	USR	Lithuania	6.10	50.0	08(WB)
51	EEU	Serbia	6.30	51.0	08(WB)
52	DME	Faeroe Islands	6.46	52.0	08(CIA)
53	SEA	Guam	6.55	53.0	08(CIA)
54	EEU	Slovakia	6.60	54.0	08(WB)
55	DME	United States	6.70	55.0	08(WB)
56	SEA	Northern Mariana Is.	6.72	56.0	08(CIA)
57	AFR	Reunion	6.80	57.0	08(E)
58	LAM	Montserrat	6.86	58.0	08(CIA)
59	EEU	Montenegro	6.90	59.0	08(WB)
60	DME	St. Pierre & Miquelon	7.04	60.0	08(CIA)
61	MEA	UAE	7.05	61.0	08(WB)
62	LAM	Cayman Islands	7.10	62.0	08(CIA)
63	SEA	New Caledonia	7.19	63.0	08(CIA)
64	LAM	Chile	7.20	64.0	08(WB)
65	LAM	Martinique	7.30	65.0	08(E)
66	LAM	Virgin Islands, US	7.53	66.0	08(CIA)
67	SEA	French Polynesia	7.70	67.0	08(CIA)
68	DME	Bermuda	7.87	68.0	08(CIA)
69	USR	Latvia	7.90	69.0	08(WB)
70	LAM	Guadeloupe	8.60	70.0	08(E)
71	LAM	Puerto Rico	8.65	71.0	08(CIA)
72	SEA	Samoa, American	8.69	72.0	08(CIA)
73	EEU	Bulgaria	8.80	73.0	08(WB)
74	LAM	Bahamas	8.90	74.0	08(WB)
75	MEA	Qatar	9.21	75.0	08(WB)
76	LAM	Dominica	9.30	76.0	08(WB)
77	LAM	Neth. Antilles	9.36	77.0	08(CIA)
78	MEA	Kuwait	9.40	78.0	08(WB)
79	SEA	Nauru	9.43	79.0	08(CIA)
80	LAM	Costa Rica	9.55	80.0	08(WB)
81	MEA	Bahrain	9.60	81.0	08(WB)
82	LAM	Barbados	10.10	82.0	08(WB)
83	MEA	Oman	10.30	83.0	08(WB)
84	EEU	Macedonia	10.46	84.0	08(WB)
85	AFR	Seychelles	10.70	85.0	08(WB)
86	LAM	Antigua & Barbuda	11.02	86.0	08(WB)
87	USR	Belarus	11.28	87.0	08(WB)
88	EEU	Romania	11.60	88.0	08(WB)
89	LAM	Uruguay	11.70	89.0	08(WB)
90	CPA	Vietnam	11.81	90.0	08(WB)

OBS	REGION	COUNTRY	INFMRT	RANK	SOURCE
TABLE 1.2 INFANT MORTALITY, RATE PER 1,000 LIVE BIRTHS, 2008					
91	MEA	Lebanon	11.85	91.0	08(WB)
92	LAM	St. Vincent	11.90	92.0	08(WB)
93	USR	Russia	11.94	93.0	08(WB)
94	LAM	Guiana, French	12.10	94.0	08(E)
95	SEA	Thailand	12.51	95.0	08(WB)
96	EEU	Albania	12.60	96.0	08(WB)
97	EEU	Bosnia	12.70	97.0	08(WB)
98	SAS	Sri Lanka	13.09	98.0	08(WB)
99	LAM	Grenada	13.10	99.5	08(WB)
100	LAM	St. Lucia	13.10	99.5	08(WB)
101	SEA	Palau	13.20	101.0	08(WB)
102	LAM	St. Kitts & Nevis	13.66	102.5	08(WB)
103	USR	Ukraine	13.66	102.5	08(WB)
104	LAM	Aruba	14.26	104.0	08(CIA)
105	MEA	Syria	14.32	105.0	08(WB)
106	LAM	Turks & Caicos Is.	14.35	106.0	08(CIA)
107	LAM	Argentina	14.56	107.5	08(WB)
108	DME	Greenland	14.56	107.5	08(CIA)
109	AFR	Mauritius	15.10	109.0	08(WB)
110	USR	Moldova	15.22	110.0	08(WB)
111	MEA	Libya	15.27	111.0	08(WB)
112	LAM	Mexico	15.30	112.0	08(WB)
113	SEA	Fiji	15.50	113.0	08(WB)
114	LAM	Virgin Islands, Brit.	15.54	114.0	08(CIA)
115	LAM	El Salvador	15.63	115.0	08(WB)
116	LAM	Venezuela	15.80	116.0	08(WB)
117	SEA	Niue	16.00	117.0	94(CIA)
118	LAM	Colombia	16.46	118.0	08(WB)
119	SEA	Tonga	16.70	119.0	08(WB)
120	LAM	Belize	16.87	120.0	08(WB)
121	MEA	Jordan	16.95	121.0	08(WB)
122	CPA	China	17.77	122.0	08(WB)
123	MEA	West Bank	18.21	123.0	08(CIA)
124	LAM	Brazil	18.30	124.5	08(WB)
125	MEA	Tunisia	18.30	124.5	08(WB)
126	AFR	St. Helena	18.31	126.0	08(CIA)
127	MEA	Saudi Arabia	18.40	127.0	08(WB)
128	SEA	Tuvalu	18.97	128.0	08(CIA)
129	LAM	Panama	19.25	129.0	08(WB)
130	SEA	Wallis & Futuna	19.48	130.0	98(CIA)
131	MEA	Egypt	19.75	131.0	08(WB)
132	MEA	Turkey	19.92	132.0	08(WB)
133	USR	Armenia	20.69	133.0	08(WB)
134	LAM	Ecuador	21.10	134.0	08(WB)
135	MEA	Gaza Strip	21.35	135.0	08(CIA)

TABLE 1.2 INFANT MORTALITY, RATE PER 1,000 LIVE BIRTHS, 2008					
OBS	REGION	COUNTRY	INFMRT	RANK	SOURCE
136	LAM	Peru	21.91	136.0	08(WB)
137	SEA	Samoa, Western	22.00	137.0	08(WB)
138	LAM	Nicaragua	22.87	138.0	08(WB)
139	SEA	Cook Islands	23.31	139.0	00(CIA)
140	LAM	Paraguay	23.96	140.0	08(WB)
141	AFR	Cape Verde	24.19	141.0	08(WB)
142	SAS	Maldives	24.20	142.0	08(WB)
143	LAM	Suriname	24.56	143.0	08(WB)
144	LAM	Honduras	25.67	144.0	08(WB)
145	SEA	Philippines	25.72	145.0	08(WB)
146	AFR	Botswana	25.95	146.0	08(WB)
147	LAM	Jamaica	25.99	147.0	08(WB)
148	USR	Georgia	26.46	148.0	08(WB)
149	MEA	Iran	27.06	149.0	08(WB)
150	SEA	Vanuatu	27.14	150.0	08(WB)
151	LAM	Dominican Rep.	27.21	151.0	08(WB)
152	EEU	Kosovo	27.85	152.0	(REG)
153	LAM	Guatemala	28.63	153.0	08(WB)
154	USR	Kazakhstan	28.88	154.0	08(WB)
155	SEA	Marshall Islands	29.53	155.0	08(WB)
156	SEA	Solomon Islands	29.68	156.0	08(WB)
157	SEA	Indonesia	30.73	157.0	08(WB)
158	LAM	Trinidad & Tobago	31.10	158.0	08(WB)
159	AFR	Namibia	31.40	159.0	08(WB)
160	USR	Azerbaijan	31.93	160.0	08(WB)
161	SEA	Micronesia	32.23	161.0	08(WB)
162	MEA	Morocco	32.32	162.0	08(WB)
163	USR	Kyrgyzstan	33.30	163.0	08(WB)
164	CPA	Mongolia	33.50	164.0	08(WB)
165	USR	Uzbekistan	33.66	165.0	08(WB)
166	MEA	Iraq	35.67	166.0	08(WB)
167	MEA	Algeria	35.99	167.0	08(WB)
168	SEA	Tokelau	37.44	168.0	01(CIA)
169	SEA	Kiribati	38.44	169.0	08(WB)
170	AFR	Eritrea	40.78	170.0	08(WB)
171	SAS	Nepal	40.84	171.0	08(WB)
172	CPA	Korea, North	42.00	172.0	08(WB)
173	SAS	Bangladesh	42.89	173.0	08(WB)
174	USR	Turkmenistan	43.10	174.0	08(WB)
175	LAM	Bolivia	45.73	175.0	08(WB)
176	LAM	Guyana	46.50	176.0	08(WB)
177	CPA	Laos	47.50	177.0	08(WB)
178	AFR	South Africa	47.90	178.0	08(WB)
179	AFR	Ghana	51.01	179.0	08(WB)
180	SAS	India	52.30	180.0	08(WB)

OBS	REGION	COUNTRY	INFMRT	RANK	SOURCE
		TABLE 1.2 INFANT MORTALITY, RATE PER 1,000 LIVE BIRTHS, 2008			
181	SEA	Papua New Guinea	52.57	181.0	08(WB)
182	MEA	Yemen	52.64	182.0	08(WB)
183	SAS	Bhutan	53.93	183.0	08(WB)
184	USR	Tajikistan	54.14	184.0	08(WB)
185	LAM	Haiti	54.36	185.0	08(WB)
186	AFR	Senegal	56.90	186.0	08(WB)
187	AFR	Gabon	57.20	187.0	08(WB)
188	AFR	Mayotte	57.88	188.0	08(CIA)
189	AFR	Swaziland	58.80	189.0	08(WB)
190	AFR	Zimbabwe	61.50	190.0	08(WB)
191	AFR	Lesotho	63.10	191.0	08(WB)
192	AFR	San Tome & Principe	63.60	192.0	08(WB)
193	AFR	Togo	63.70	193.0	08(WB)
194	AFR	Malawi	64.70	194.0	08(WB)
195	AFR	Tanzania	66.80	195.0	08(WB)
196	AFR	Madagascar	68.07	196.0	08(WB)
197	CPA	Cambodia	69.31	197.0	08(WB)
198	AFR	Ethiopia	69.43	198.0	08(WB)
199	AFR	Sudan	69.65	199.0	08(WB)
200	CPA	Burma	70.64	200.0	08(WB)
201	AFR	Western Sahara	71.13	201.0	08(CIA)
202	AFR	Rwanda	71.60	202.0	08(WB)
203	SAS	Pakistan	71.91	203.0	08(WB)
204	SEA	East Timor	74.55	204.0	08(WB)
205	AFR	Mauritania	74.60	205.0	08(WB)
206	AFR	Comoros	75.49	206.0	08(WB)
207	AFR	Djibouti	75.95	207.0	08(WB)
208	AFR	Benin	76.28	208.0	08(WB)
209	AFR	Niger	78.72	209.0	08(WB)
210	AFR	Congo, Rep.	79.69	210.0	08(WB)
211	AFR	Gambia	79.90	211.0	08(WB)
212	AFR	Kenya	80.50	212.0	08(WB)
213	AFR	Ivory Coast	80.90	213.0	08(WB)
214	AFR	Cameroon	82.30	214.0	08(WB)
215	AFR	Uganda	84.50	215.0	08(WB)
216	AFR	Equatorial Guinea	89.50	216.0	08(WB)
217	AFR	Guinea	90.17	217.0	08(WB)
218	AFR	Mozambique	90.40	218.0	08(WB)
219	AFR	Zambia	92.00	219.0	08(WB)
220	AFR	Burkina Faso	92.09	220.0	08(WB)
221	AFR	Nigeria	95.80	221.0	08(WB)
222	AFR	Liberia	100.42	222.0	08(WB)
223	AFR	Burundi	101.91	223.0	08(WB)
224	AFR	Mali	102.50	224.0	08(WB)

TABLE 1.2 INFANT MORTALITY, RATE PER 1,000 LIVE BIRTHS, 2008					
OBS	REGION	COUNTRY	INFMRT	RANK	SOURCE
225	AFR	CAR	114.60	225.0	08(WB)
226	AFR	Guinea-Bissau	116.57	226.0	08(WB)
227	AFR	Somalia	119.16	227.0	08(WB)
228	AFR	Sierra Leone	123.38	228.0	08(WB)
229	AFR	Chad	124.02	229.0	08(WB)
230	AFR	Congo, Dem. Rep.	125.79	230.0	08(WB)
231	AFR	Angola	130.25	231.0	08(WB)
232	SAS	Afghanistan	165.00	232.0	08(WB)

OBS	REGION	COUNTRY	LIFEXP	RANK	SOURCE
		TABLE 1.3 EXPECTATION OF LIFE AT BIRTH, AVERAGE BETWEEN MALE AND FEMALE LIFE EXPECTANCY, 2008			
1	DME	Andorra	83.530	1.0	08(CIA)
2	DME	Liechtenstein	82.634	2.0	08(WB)
3	DME	Japan	82.588	3.0	08(WB)
4	SEA	Hong Kong	82.340	4.0	08(WB)
5	DME	Switzerland	82.162	5.0	08(WB)
6	DME	Italy	81.945	6.0	08(WB)
7	DME	San Marino	81.880	7.0	08(CIA)
8	DME	Iceland	81.575	8.0	08(WB)
9	DME	France	81.520	9.0	08(WB)
10	DME	Australia	81.395	10.0	08(WB)
11	DME	Sweden	81.237	11.0	08(WB)
12	DME	Spain	81.088	12.0	08(WB)
13	DME	Israel	81.002	13.0	08(WB)
14	DME	Canada	80.965	14.0	08(WB)
15	DME	Norway	80.741	15.5	08(WB)
16	SEA	Singapore	80.741	15.5	08(WB)
17	SEA	Macao	80.669	17.0	08(WB)
18	DME	Guernsey	80.650	18.0	08(CIA)
19	LAM	Anguilla	80.530	19.0	08(CIA)
20	DME	Luxembourg	80.525	20.0	08(WB)
21	DME	Austria	80.448	21.0	08(WB)
22	DME	Netherlands	80.401	22.0	08(WB)
23	LAM	Cayman Islands	80.320	23.0	08(CIA)
24	DME	New Zealand	80.151	24.0	08(WB)
25	DME	Belgium	80.110	25.0	08(WB)
26	DME	Germany	80.089	26.0	08(WB)
27	DME	Gibraltar	80.060	27.0	08(CIA)
28	DME	Greece	79.963	28.0	08(WB)
29	DME	Monaco	79.960	29.0	08(CIA)
30	DME	United Kingdom	79.903	30.0	08(WB)
31	DME	Ireland	79.857	31.0	08(WB)
32	SEA	Korea, South	79.833	32.0	08(WB)
33	DME	Finland	79.792	33.0	08(WB)
34	MEA	Cyprus	79.661	34.0	08(WB)
35	DME	Jersey	79.650	35.0	08(CIA)
36	DME	Malta	79.641	36.0	08(WB)
37	LAM	Martinique	79.550	37.0	08(E)
38	LAM	Guadeloupe	79.366	38.0	07(E)
39	DME	Faeroe Islands	79.290	39.0	08(CIA)
40	DME	Falkland Islands	79.260	40.0	(REG)
41	DME	Portugal	79.250	41.0	08(WB)
42	LAM	Montserrat	79.150	42.0	08(CIA)
43	DME	Bermuda	79.004	43.0	08(WB)
44	EEU	Slovenia	78.974	44.0	08(WB)
45	LAM	Virgin Islands, US	78.930	45.0	08(WB)
46	LAM	Costa Rica	78.918	46.0	08(WB)

OBS	REGION	COUNTRY	LIFEXP	RANK	SOURCE
		TABLE 1.3 EXPECTATION OF LIFE AT BIRTH, AVERAGE BETWEEN MALE AND FEMALE LIFE EXPECTANCY, 2008			
47	DME	St. Pierre & Miquelon	78.910	47.0	08(CIA)
48	DME	Isle of Man	78.800	48.0	08(CIA)
49	LAM	Cuba	78.721	49.0	08(WB)
50	DME	Denmark	78.700	50.0	08(WB)
51	LAM	Chile	78.614	51.0	08(WB)
52	LAM	Puerto Rico	78.559	52.0	08(WB)
53	DME	United States	78.439	53.0	08(WB)
54	AFR	St. Helena	78.270	54.0	08(CIA)
55	MEA	Kuwait	77.970	55.0	08(WB)
56	SEA	Taiwan	77.760	56.0	08(CIA)
57	MEA	UAE	77.748	57.0	08(WB)
58	LAM	Guiana, French	77.610	58.0	07(E)
59	AFR	Reunion	77.499	59.0	06(E)
60	SEA	Brunei	77.365	60.0	08(WB)
61	EEU	Czechia	77.211	61.0	08(WB)
62	LAM	Virgin Islands, Brit.	77.060	62.0	08(CIA)
63	LAM	Barbados	77.009	63.0	08(WB)
64	EEU	Albania	76.634	64.0	08(WB)
65	SEA	Northern Mariana Is.	76.500	65.0	08(CIA)
66	SEA	Samoa, American	76.450	66.0	08(CIA)
67	LAM	Belize	76.323	67.0	08(WB)
68	SEA	New Caledonia	76.115	68.0	08(WB)
69	AFR	Mayotte	76.074	69.0	08(WB)
70	LAM	Neth. Antilles	76.033	70.0	08(WB)
71	LAM	Uruguay	75.981	71.0	08(WB)
72	MEA	Qatar	75.942	72.0	08(WB)
73	MEA	Oman	75.913	73.0	08(WB)
74	EEU	Croatia	75.912	74.0	08(WB)
75	MEA	Bahrain	75.911	75.0	08(WB)
76	LAM	Panama	75.661	76.0	08(WB)
77	SEA	Guam	75.624	77.0	08(WB)
78	SEA	Wallis & Futuna	75.606	78.0	98(CIA)
79	EEU	Poland	75.533	79.0	08(WB)
80	LAM	Argentina	75.334	80.0	08(WB)
81	LAM	Dominica	75.330	81.0	08(CIA)
82	LAM	Grenada	75.322	82.0	08(WB)
83	LAM	Turks & Caicos Is.	75.190	83.0	08(CIA)
84	LAM	Ecuador	75.135	84.0	08(WB)
85	EEU	Bosnia	75.106	85.0	08(WB)
86	LAM	Mexico	75.065	86.0	08(WB)
87	EEU	Slovakia	74.811	87.0	08(WB)
88	LAM	Aruba	74.689	88.0	08(WB)
89	SEA	French Polynesia	74.487	89.0	08(WB)

TABLE 1.3 EXPECTATION OF LIFE AT BIRTH, AVERAGE BETWEEN MALE AND FEMALE LIFE EXPECTANCY, 2008

OBS	REGION	COUNTRY	LIFEXP	RANK	SOURCE
90	SEA	Malaysia	74.380	90.0	08(WB)
91	CPA	Vietnam	74.371	91.0	08(WB)
92	MEA	Libya	74.329	92.0	08(WB)
93	LAM	St. Lucia	74.320	93.0	08(CIA)
94	MEA	Tunisia	74.302	94.0	08(WB)
95	MEA	Syria	74.225	95.0	08(WB)
96	EEU	Macedonia	74.211	96.0	08(WB)
97	SAS	Sri Lanka	74.127	97.0	08(WB)
98	EEU	Montenegro	74.098	98.0	08(WB)
99	EEU	Hungary	74.009	99.0	08(WB)
100	USR	Estonia	73.973	100.0	08(WB)
101	MEA	West Bank	73.650	101.0	08(CIA)
102	EEU	Serbia	73.637	102.0	08(WB)
103	LAM	Venezuela	73.549	103.0	08(WB)
104	USR	Armenia	73.537	104.0	08(WB)
105	LAM	Bahamas	73.485	105.0	08(WB)
106	EEU	Romania	73.373	106.0	08(WB)
107	EEU	Bulgaria	73.317	107.0	08(WB)
108	LAM	Peru	73.262	108.0	08(WB)
109	AFR	Seychelles	73.163	109.0	08(WB)
110	LAM	Nicaragua	73.142	110.0	08(WB)
111	CPA	China	73.125	111.0	08(WB)
112	MEA	Saudi Arabia	73.119	112.0	08(WB)
113	LAM	Colombia	72.980	113.0	08(WB)
114	LAM	St. Kitts & Nevis	72.930	114.0	08(CIA)
115	MEA	Jordan	72.714	115.0	08(WB)
116	LAM	Antigua & Barbuda	72.690	116.0	08(CIA)
117	LAM	Dominican Rep.	72.571	117.5	08(WB)
118	AFR	Mauritius	72.571	117.5	08(WB)
119	SEA	Cook Islands	72.438	119.0	00(CIA)
120	LAM	Brazil	72.402	120.0	08(WB)
121	MEA	Algeria	72.389	121.0	08(WB)
122	MEA	Gaza Strip	72.340	122.0	08(CIA)
123	USR	Latvia	72.238	123.0	08(WB)
124	LAM	Honduras	72.196	124.0	08(WB)
125	MEA	Lebanon	72.047	125.0	08(WB)
126	MEA	Turkey	71.892	126.0	08(WB)
127	LAM	Paraguay	71.885	127.0	08(WB)
128	SEA	Tonga	71.876	128.0	08(WB)
129	LAM	Jamaica	71.843	129.0	08(WB)
130	SEA	Philippines	71.834	130.0	08(WB)
131	USR	Lithuania	71.822	131.0	08(WB)
132	SEA	Samoa, Western	71.753	132.0	08(WB)
133	LAM	St. Vincent	71.658	133.0	08(WB)
134	SAS	Maldives	71.582	134.0	08(WB)

TABLE 1.3 EXPECTATION OF LIFE AT BIRTH, AVERAGE BETWEEN MALE AND FEMALE LIFE EXPECTANCY, 2008

OBS	REGION	COUNTRY	LIFEXP	RANK	SOURCE
135	USR	Georgia	71.548	135.0	08(WB)
136	MEA	Iran	71.441	136.0	08(WB)
137	MEA	Morocco	71.292	137.0	08(WB)
138	LAM	El Salvador	71.261	138.0	08(WB)
139	AFR	Cape Verde	71.040	139.0	08(WB)
140	SEA	Palau	71.000	140.0	08(CIA)
141	SEA	Marshall Islands	70.900	141.0	08(CIA)
142	SEA	Indonesia	70.793	142.0	08(WB)
143	USR	Belarus	70.633	143.0	08(WB)
144	DME	Greenland	70.530	144.0	08(CIA)
145	LAM	Guatemala	70.335	145.0	08(WB)
146	SEA	Vanuatu	70.292	146.0	08(WB)
147	USR	Azerbaijan	70.178	147.0	08(WB)
148	MEA	Egypt	70.138	148.0	08(WB)
149	EEU	Kosovo	69.418	149.0	08(WB)
150	LAM	Trinidad & Tobago	69.339	150.0	08(WB)
151	SEA	Tokelau	69.240	151.0	05(CIA)
152	LAM	Suriname	69.022	152.0	08(WB)
153	SEA	Tuvalu	68.970	153.0	08(CIA)
154	SEA	Fiji	68.866	154.0	08(WB)
155	SEA	Thailand	68.860	155.0	08(WB)
156	SEA	Micronesia	68.583	156.0	08(WB)
157	USR	Moldova	68.437	157.0	08(WB)
158	USR	Ukraine	68.251	158.0	08(WB)
159	MEA	Iraq	67.930	159.0	08(WB)
160	USR	Russia	67.845	160.0	08(WB)
161	USR	Uzbekistan	67.756	161.0	08(WB)
162	USR	Kyrgyzstan	67.370	162.0	08(WB)
163	CPA	Korea, North	67.156	163.0	08(WB)
164	LAM	Guyana	67.105	164.0	08(WB)
165	USR	Tajikistan	66.747	165.0	08(WB)
166	SAS	Nepal	66.690	166.0	08(WB)
167	CPA	Mongolia	66.569	167.0	08(WB)
168	SAS	Pakistan	66.529	168.0	08(WB)
169	USR	Kazakhstan	66.442	169.0	08(WB)
170	SEA	Solomon Islands	66.255	170.0	08(WB)
171	SAS	Bangladesh	66.145	171.0	08(WB)
172	SAS	Bhutan	66.134	172.0	08(WB)
173	LAM	Bolivia	65.684	173.0	08(WB)
174	AFR	San Tome & Principe	65.531	174.0	08(WB)
175	SEA	Niue	65.388	175.0	94(CIA)
176	AFR	Comoros	65.346	176.0	08(WB)
177	CPA	Laos	64.973	177.0	08(WB)
178	USR	Turkmenistan	64.821	178.0	08(WB)

OBS	REGION	COUNTRY	LIFEXP	RANK	SOURCE

TABLE 1.3 EXPECTATION OF LIFE AT BIRTH, AVERAGE BETWEEN MALE AND FEMALE LIFE EXPECTANCY, 2008

OBS	REGION	COUNTRY	LIFEXP	RANK	SOURCE
179	SEA	Nauru	63.810	179.0	08(CIA)
180	SAS	India	63.718	180.0	08(WB)
181	MEA	Yemen	62.916	181.0	08(WB)
182	SEA	Kiribati	62.850	182.0	08(CIA)
183	AFR	Togo	62.507	183.0	08(WB)
184	CPA	Burma	61.555	184.0	08(WB)
185	AFR	Benin	61.378	185.0	08(WB)
186	LAM	Haiti	61.215	186.0	08(WB)
187	SEA	East Timor	61.121	187.0	08(WB)
188	SEA	Papua New Guinea	61.101	188.0	08(WB)
189	AFR	Namibia	61.014	189.0	08(WB)
190	CPA	Cambodia	60.969	190.0	08(WB)
191	AFR	Gabon	60.444	191.0	08(WB)
192	AFR	Madagascar	60.341	192.0	08(WB)
193	AFR	Eritrea	59.452	193.0	08(WB)
194	AFR	Liberia	58.263	194.0	08(WB)
195	AFR	Sudan	58.148	195.0	08(WB)
196	AFR	Guinea	57.821	196.0	08(WB)
197	AFR	Ivory Coast	57.442	197.0	08(WB)
198	AFR	Mauritania	56.729	198.0	08(WB)
199	AFR	Ghana	56.617	199.0	08(WB)
200	AFR	Gambia	55.932	200.0	08(WB)
201	AFR	Tanzania	55.647	201.0	08(WB)
202	AFR	Senegal	55.595	202.0	08(WB)
203	AFR	Djibouti	55.389	203.0	08(WB)
204	AFR	Ethiopia	55.195	204.0	08(WB)
205	AFR	Botswana	54.241	205.0	08(WB)
206	AFR	Kenya	54.237	206.0	08(WB)
207	AFR	Western Sahara	53.920	207.0	08(CIA)
208	AFR	Congo, Rep.	53.552	208.0	08(WB)
209	AFR	Malawi	53.059	209.0	08(WB)
210	AFR	Burkina Faso	52.988	210.0	08(WB)
211	AFR	Uganda	52.667	211.0	08(WB)
212	AFR	South Africa	51.477	212.0	08(WB)
213	AFR	Niger	51.401	213.0	08(WB)
214	AFR	Cameroon	51.064	214.0	08(WB)
215	AFR	Burundi	50.434	215.0	08(WB)
216	AFR	Equatorial Guinea	50.227	216.0	08(WB)
217	AFR	Rwanda	50.131	217.0	08(WB)
218	AFR	Somalia	49.835	218.0	08(WB)
219	AFR	Chad	48.731	219.0	08(WB)
220	AFR	Mali	48.429	220.0	08(WB)
221	AFR	Nigeria	47.909	221.0	08(WB)
222	AFR	Mozambique	47.894	222.0	08(WB)
223	AFR	Guinea-Bissau	47.823	223.0	08(WB)

TABLE 1.3 EXPECTATION OF LIFE AT BIRTH, AVERAGE BETWEEN MALE AND FEMALE LIFE EXPECTANCY, 2008					
OBS	REGION	COUNTRY	LIFEXP	RANK	SOURCE
224	AFR	Congo, Dem. Rep.	47.645	224.0	08(WB)
225	AFR	Sierra Leone	47.600	225.0	08(WB)
226	AFR	Angola	47.038	226.0	08(WB)
227	AFR	CAR	46.959	227.0	08(WB)
228	AFR	Swaziland	45.765	228.0	08(WB)
229	AFR	Zambia	45.396	229.0	08(WB)
230	AFR	Lesotho	44.995	230.0	08(WB)
231	AFR	Zimbabwe	44.214	231.0	08(WB)
232	SAS	Afghanistan	43.946	232.0	08(WB)

		TABLE 1.4 GROSS DOMESTIC PRODUCT AT PURCHASING POWER PARITIES PER CAPITA, 2008			
OBS	REGION	COUNTRY	GPCPPP	RANK	SOURCE
1	DME	Monaco	151,937	1.0	(REG)
2	DME	Liechtenstein	120,777	2.0	07(CIA)
3	MEA	Qatar	103,500	3.0	08(CIA)
4	DME	Bermuda	82,230	4.0	04(CIA)
5	DME	Luxembourg	78,599	5.0	08(WB)
6	DME	Jersey	63,593	6.0	05(CIA)
7	SEA	Macao	59,430	7.0	08(WB)
8	DME	Norway	58,138	8.0	08(WB)
9	MEA	Kuwait	57,400	9.0	08(CIA)
10	SEA	Brunei	53,100	10.0	08(CIA)
11	LAM	Cayman Islands	51,526	11.0	04(CIA)
12	DME	Guernsey	49,758	12.0	05(CIA)
13	SEA	Singapore	49,284	13.0	08(WB)
14	DME	United States	46,716	14.0	08(WB)
15	DME	Falkland Islands	45,675	15.0	02(CIA)
16	LAM	Virgin Islands, Brit.	45,291	16.0	04(CIA)
17	DME	Ireland	44,200	17.0	08(WB)
18	SEA	Hong Kong	43,924	18.0	08(WB)
19	DME	Andorra	43,500	19.0	07(CIA)
20	DME	San Marino	42,886	20.0	07(CIA)
21	DME	Gibraltar	42,618	21.0	05(CIA)
22	DME	Switzerland	42,536	22.0	08(WB)
23	DME	Faeroe Islands	40,969	23.0	01(CIA)
24	DME	Netherlands	40,849	24.0	08(WB)
25	MEA	UAE	40,000	25.0	08(CIA)
26	DME	Isle of Man	39,048	26.0	05(CIA)
27	DME	Austria	38,152	27.0	08(WB)
28	DME	Sweden	37,383	28.0	08(WB)
29	MEA	Bahrain	37,200	29.0	08(CIA)
30	DME	Iceland	36,775	30.0	08(WB)
31	DME	Denmark	36,607	31.0	08(WB)
32	DME	Canada	36,444	32.0	08(WB)
33	DME	Australia	35,677	33.0	08(WB)
34	DME	Germany	35,613	34.0	08(WB)
35	DME	United Kingdom	35,445	35.0	08(WB)
36	DME	Finland	35,427	36.0	08(WB)
37	DME	Belgium	34,493	37.0	08(WB)
38	DME	Japan	34,099	38.0	08(WB)
39	DME	France	34,045	39.0	08(WB)
40	AFR	Equatorial Guinea	33,873	40.0	08(WB)
41	DME	Spain	31,954	41.0	08(WB)
42	SEA	Taiwan	31,900	42.0	08(CIA)
43	LAM	Martinique	31,274	43.0	(REG)
44	DME	Italy	30,756	44.0	08(WB)
45	DME	Greece	29,361	45.0	08(WB)

OBS	REGION	COUNTRY	GPCPPP	RANK	SOURCE
\multicolumn{6}{|c|}{TABLE 1.4 GROSS DOMESTIC PRODUCT AT PURCHASING POWER PARITIES PER CAPITA, 2008}				

OBS	REGION	COUNTRY	GPCPPP	RANK	SOURCE
46	LAM	Bahamas	28,600	46.5	08(CIA)
47	MEA	Cyprus	28,600	46.5	08(CIA)
48	AFR	Reunion	27,955	48.0	(REG)
49	SEA	Korea, South	27,939	49.0	08(WB)
50	EEU	Slovenia	27,605	50.0	08(WB)
51	DME	Israel	27,548	51.0	08(WB)
52	DME	New Zealand	27,029	52.0	08(WB)
53	DME	Greenland	26,999	53.0	01(CIA)
54	LAM	Guadeloupe	26,853	54.0	(REG)
55	LAM	Aruba	25,102	55.0	05(E)
56	LAM	Trinidad & Tobago	24,748	56.0	08(WB)
57	EEU	Czechia	24,712	57.0	08(WB)
58	MEA	Saudi Arabia	23,920	58.0	08(WB)
59	DME	Malta	23,623	59.0	07(WB)
60	DME	Portugal	23,074	60.0	08(WB)
61	EEU	Slovakia	22,081	61.0	08(WB)
62	AFR	Seychelles	21,530	62.0	08(WB)
63	LAM	Antigua & Barbuda	21,323	63.0	08(WB)
64	USR	Estonia	20,662	64.0	08(WB)
65	MEA	Oman	20,200	65.0	08(CIA)
66	EEU	Hungary	19,330	66.0	08(WB)
67	LAM	Barbados	19,300	67.0	08(CIA)
68	EEU	Croatia	19,084	68.0	08(WB)
69	USR	Lithuania	18,824	69.0	08(WB)
70	LAM	Neth. Antilles	18,822	70.0	04(CIA)
71	SEA	New Caledonia	18,644	71.0	03(CIA)
72	SEA	French Polynesia	18,573	72.0	06(E)
73	LAM	Guiana, French	18,501	73.0	(REG)
74	LAM	Puerto Rico	17,800	74.0	08(CIA)
75	EEU	Poland	17,625	75.0	08(WB)
76	USR	Latvia	17,100	76.0	08(WB)
77	LAM	Virgin Islands, US	17,058	77.0	04(CIA)
78	SEA	Northern Mariana Is.	16,874	78.0	00(CIA)
79	SEA	Guam	16,735	79.0	05(CIA)
80	LAM	St. Kitts & Nevis	16,160	80.0	08(WB)
81	USR	Russia	16,139	81.0	08(WB)
82	MEA	Libya	15,402	82.0	08(WB)
83	LAM	Turks & Caicos Is.	14,838	83.0	02(CIA)
84	AFR	Gabon	14,527	84.0	08(WB)
85	LAM	Mexico	14,495	85.0	08(WB)
86	LAM	Chile	14,465	86.0	08(WB)
87	LAM	Argentina	14,333	87.0	08(WB)
88	SEA	Malaysia	14,215	88.0	08(WB)

TABLE 1.4 GROSS DOMESTIC PRODUCT AT PURCHASING POWER PARITIES PER CAPITA, 2008

OBS	REGION	COUNTRY	GPCPPP	RANK	SOURCE
89	EEU	Romania	14,065	89.0	08(WB)
90	EEU	Montenegro	13,951	90.0	08(WB)
91	MEA	Turkey	13,920	91.0	08(WB)
92	AFR	Botswana	13,392	92.0	08(WB)
93	LAM	Venezuela	12,804	93.0	08(WB)
94	LAM	Uruguay	12,734	94.0	08(WB)
95	LAM	Panama	12,504	95.0	08(WB)
96	EEU	Bulgaria	12,393	96.0	08(WB)
97	USR	Belarus	12,261	97.0	08(WB)
98	AFR	Mauritius	12,079	98.0	08(WB)
99	MEA	Iran	11,666	99.0	08(WB)
100	MEA	Lebanon	11,570	100.0	08(WB)
101	EEU	Serbia	11,456	101.0	08(WB)
102	USR	Kazakhstan	11,315	102.0	08(WB)
103	LAM	Costa Rica	11,241	103.0	08(WB)
104	LAM	Anguilla	10,352	104.0	04(CIA)
105	LAM	Brazil	10,296	105.0	08(WB)
106	SEA	Cook Islands	10,152	106.0	05(CIA)
107	AFR	South Africa	10,109	107.0	08(WB)
108	EEU	Macedonia	10,041	108.0	08(WB)
109	LAM	St. Lucia	9,907	109.0	08(WB)
110	LAM	Cuba	9,500	110.0	08(CIA)
111	DME	St. Pierre & Miquelon	9,251	111.0	01(CIA)
112	LAM	St. Vincent	9,155	112.0	08(WB)
113	LAM	Colombia	8,885	113.0	08(WB)
114	USR	Azerbaijan	8,765	114.0	08(WB)
115	LAM	Dominica	8,696	115.0	08(WB)
116	LAM	Grenada	8,541	116.0	08(WB)
117	LAM	Peru	8,507	117.0	08(WB)
118	EEU	Bosnia	8,390	118.0	08(WB)
119	LAM	Dominican Rep.	8,217	119.0	08(WB)
120	SEA	Samoa, American	8,188	120.0	07(CIA)
121	SEA	Palau	8,100	121.0	08(CIA)
122	MEA	Algeria	8,033	122.0	08(WB)
123	LAM	Ecuador	8,009	123.0	08(WB)
124	MEA	Tunisia	7,996	124.0	08(WB)
125	EEU	Albania	7,715	125.0	08(WB)
126	LAM	Jamaica	7,705	126.0	08(WB)
127	SEA	Thailand	7,703	127.0	08(WB)
128	LAM	Suriname	7,506	128.0	08(WB)
129	USR	Ukraine	7,271	129.0	08(WB)
130	SEA	Niue	7,209	130.0	03(CIA)
131	LAM	Belize	6,941	131.0	08(WB)
132	LAM	El Salvador	6,794	132.0	08(WB)
133	USR	Turkmenistan	6,641	133.0	08(WB)

TABLE 1.4 GROSS DOMESTIC PRODUCT AT PURCHASING POWER
PARITIES PER CAPITA, 2008

OBS	REGION	COUNTRY	GPCPPP	RANK	SOURCE
134	AFR	Namibia	6,343	134.0	08(WB)
135	USR	Armenia	6,070	135.0	08(WB)
136	CPA	China	5,962	136.0	08(WB)
137	AFR	Angola	5,899	137.0	08(WB)
138	SEA	Nauru	5,578	138.0	05(CIA)
139	SAS	Maldives	5,504	139.0	08(WB)
140	AFR	Mayotte	5,467	140.0	05(CIA)
141	MEA	Egypt	5,416	141.0	08(WB)
142	MEA	Jordan	5,283	142.0	08(WB)
143	AFR	Swaziland	4,928	143.0	08(WB)
144	USR	Georgia	4,896	144.0	08(WB)
145	LAM	Guatemala	4,760	145.0	08(WB)
146	SAS	Bhutan	4,755	146.0	08(WB)
147	LAM	Paraguay	4,709	147.0	08(WB)
148	SAS	Sri Lanka	4,560	148.0	08(WB)
149	SEA	Samoa, Western	4,485	149.0	08(WB)
150	SEA	Wallis & Futuna	4,470	150.0	04(CIA)
151	MEA	Syria	4,440	151.0	08(WB)
152	MEA	Morocco	4,388	152.0	08(WB)
153	LAM	Montserrat	4,387	153.0	02(CIA)
154	SEA	Fiji	4,382	154.0	08(WB)
155	LAM	Bolivia	4,278	155.0	08(WB)
156	MEA	Iraq	4,000	156.0	08(CIA)
157	SEA	Vanuatu	3,978	157.0	08(WB)
158	SEA	Indonesia	3,975	158.0	08(WB)
159	LAM	Honduras	3,965	159.0	08(WB)
160	AFR	Congo, Rep.	3,946	160.0	08(WB)
161	SEA	Tonga	3,824	161.0	08(WB)
162	AFR	St. Helena	3,705	162.0	98(CIA)
163	CPA	Mongolia	3,566	163.0	08(WB)
164	SEA	Philippines	3,510	164.0	08(WB)
165	AFR	Cape Verde	3,504	165.0	08(WB)
166	SAS	India	2,972	166.0	08(WB)
167	USR	Moldova	2,925	167.0	08(WB)
168	MEA	Gaza Strip	2,900	168.5	08(CIA)
169	MEA	West Bank	2,900	168.5	08(CIA)
170	SEA	Micronesia	2,830	170.0	08(WB)
171	CPA	Vietnam	2,785	171.0	08(WB)
172	LAM	Nicaragua	2,682	172.0	08(WB)
173	USR	Uzbekistan	2,656	173.0	08(WB)
174	SAS	Pakistan	2,644	174.0	08(WB)
175	SEA	Solomon Islands	2,610	175.0	08(WB)
176	LAM	Guyana	2,542	176.0	08(WB)
177	SEA	Marshall Islands	2,500	177.5	08(CIA)
178	AFR	Western Sahara	2,500	177.5	08(CIA)
179	SEA	Kiribati	2,484	179.0	08(WB)

		TABLE 1.4 GROSS DOMESTIC PRODUCT AT PURCHASING POWER PARITIES PER CAPITA, 2008			
OBS	REGION	COUNTRY	GPCPPP	RANK	SOURCE
180	MEA	Yemen	2,400	180.0	08(WB)
181	EEU	Kosovo	2,354	181.0	07(CIA)
182	AFR	Cameroon	2,215	182.0	08(WB)
183	SEA	Papua New Guinea	2,208	183.0	08(WB)
184	USR	Kyrgyzstan	2,188	184.0	08(WB)
185	AFR	Sudan	2,153	185.0	08(WB)
186	AFR	Djibouti	2,140	186.0	08(WB)
187	CPA	Laos	2,134	187.0	08(WB)
188	AFR	Mauritania	2,100	188.0	08(CIA)
189	AFR	Nigeria	2,082	189.0	08(WB)
190	SEA	Tuvalu	2,064	190.0	02(CIA)
191	USR	Tajikistan	1,906	191.0	08(WB)
192	CPA	Cambodia	1,905	192.0	08(WB)
193	SEA	Tokelau	1,839	193.0	93(CIA)
194	AFR	Senegal	1,772	194.0	08(WB)
195	AFR	San Tome & Principe	1,738	195.0	08(WB)
196	CPA	Korea, North	1,700	196.0	08(CIA)
197	AFR	Ivory Coast	1,651	197.0	08(WB)
198	AFR	Kenya	1,590	198.0	08(WB)
199	AFR	Lesotho	1,588	199.0	08(WB)
200	AFR	Benin	1,468	200.0	08(WB)
201	AFR	Chad	1,455	201.0	08(WB)
202	AFR	Ghana	1,452	202.0	08(WB)
203	AFR	Gambia	1,363	203.0	08(WB)
204	AFR	Zambia	1,356	204.0	08(WB)
205	SAS	Bangladesh	1,334	205.0	08(WB)
206	AFR	Tanzania	1,263	206.0	08(WB)
207	AFR	Guinea	1,204	207.0	08(WB)
208	CPA	Burma	1,200	208.0	08(CIA)
209	LAM	Haiti	1,177	209.0	08(WB)
210	AFR	Comoros	1,169	210.0	08(WB)
211	AFR	Uganda	1,165	211.0	08(WB)
212	AFR	Burkina Faso	1,161	212.0	08(WB)
213	AFR	Mali	1,128	213.0	08(WB)
214	SAS	Nepal	1,112	214.0	08(WB)
215	AFR	Madagascar	1,049	215.0	08(WB)
216	AFR	Rwanda	1,022	216.0	08(WB)
217	AFR	Ethiopia	868	217.0	08(WB)
218	AFR	Mozambique	855	218.0	08(WB)
219	AFR	Malawi	837	219.0	08(WB)
220	AFR	Togo	829	220.0	08(WB)
221	SEA	East Timor	801	221.0	08(WB)
222	SAS	Afghanistan	800	222.0	08(CIA)
223	AFR	Sierra Leone	766	223.0	08(WB)

TABLE 1.4 GROSS DOMESTIC PRODUCT AT PURCHASING POWER PARITIES PER CAPITA, 2008					
OBS	REGION	COUNTRY	GPCPPP	RANK	SOURCE
224	AFR	CAR	736	224.0	08(WB)
225	AFR	Niger	684	225.0	08(WB)
226	AFR	Eritrea	632	226.0	08(WB)
227	AFR	Somalia	600	227.0	08(CIA)
228	AFR	Guinea-Bissau	538	228.0	08(WB)
229	AFR	Liberia	388	229.0	08(WB)
230	AFR	Burundi	383	230.0	08(WB)
231	AFR	Congo, Dem. Rep.	321	231.0	08(WB)
232	AFR	Zimbabwe	200	232.0	08(CIA)

TABLE 1.5 ECONOMIC QUALITY-OF-LIFE INDEX, PRINCIPAL COMPONENT OF THE ECONOMIC QUALITY-OF-LIFE INDICATORS, 2008						
OBS	REGION	COUNTRY	EQLX	RANK	SOURCE
1	DME	Liechtenstein	2.13171	1	PRIN1(EQL)
2	DME	Monaco	1.87473	2	PRIN1(EQL)
3	DME	San Marino	1.82751	3	PRIN1(EQL)
4	DME	Luxembourg	1.78413	4	PRIN1(EQL)
5	DME	Andorra	1.75217	5	PRIN1(EQL)
6	DME	Norway	1.64685	6	PRIN1(EQL)
7	DME	Japan	1.60623	7	PRIN1(EQL)
8	DME	Iceland	1.59581	8	PRIN1(EQL)
9	DME	Switzerland	1.58392	9	PRIN1(EQL)
10	DME	Sweden	1.56564	10	PRIN1(EQL)
11	SEA	Hong Kong	1.56111	11	PRIN1(EQL)
12	SEA	Singapore	1.51932	12	PRIN1(EQL)
13	DME	Italy	1.46683	13	PRIN1(EQL)
14	DME	France	1.45643	14	PRIN1(EQL)
15	SEA	Macao	1.43865	15	PRIN1(EQL)
16	DME	Ireland	1.43369	16	PRIN1(EQL)
17	DME	Guernsey	1.43224	17	PRIN1(EQL)
18	DME	Jersey	1.41226	18	PRIN1(EQL)
19	DME	Finland	1.40609	19	PRIN1(EQL)
20	DME	Austria	1.40411	20	PRIN1(EQL)
21	DME	Netherlands	1.38949	21	PRIN1(EQL)
22	DME	Bermuda	1.36914	22	PRIN1(EQL)
23	DME	Australia	1.35576	23	PRIN1(EQL)
24	DME	Spain	1.34999	24	PRIN1(EQL)
25	DME	Germany	1.33266	25	PRIN1(EQL)
26	DME	Belgium	1.32267	26	PRIN1(EQL)
27	DME	Denmark	1.30871	27	PRIN1(EQL)
28	DME	Canada	1.29611	28	PRIN1(EQL)
29	LAM	Cayman Islands	1.28429	29	PRIN1(EQL)
30	DME	Gibraltar	1.27670	30	PRIN1(EQL)
31	DME	Israel	1.26602	31	PRIN1(EQL)
32	DME	United Kingdom	1.26526	32	PRIN1(EQL)
33	DME	Falkland Islands	1.25932	33	PRIN1(EQL)
34	DME	Greece	1.24956	34	PRIN1(EQL)
35	MEA	Qatar	1.23659	35	PRIN1(EQL)
36	DME	Faeroe Islands	1.20210	36	PRIN1(EQL)
37	DME	Isle of Man	1.18520	37	PRIN1(EQL)
38	MEA	Cyprus	1.18075	38	PRIN1(EQL)
39	EEU	Slovenia	1.17910	39	PRIN1(EQL)
40	DME	United States	1.16889	40	PRIN1(EQL)
41	DME	New Zealand	1.14986	41	PRIN1(EQL)
42	DME	Portugal	1.13485	42	PRIN1(EQL)
43	SEA	Brunei	1.12331	43	PRIN1(EQL)
44	MEA	UAE	1.12147	44	PRIN1(EQL)
45	SEA	Korea, South	1.10146	45	PRIN1(EQL)
46	MEA	Kuwait	1.07493	46	PRIN1(EQL)

TABLE 1.5 ECONOMIC QUALITY-OF-LIFE INDEX, PRINCIPAL COMPONENT OF THE ECONOMIC QUALITY-OF-LIFE INDICATORS, 2008

OBS	REGION	COUNTRY	EQLX	RANK	SOURCE
47	LAM	Martinique	1.04662	47	PRIN1(EQL)
48	EEU	Czechia	0.99252	48	PRIN1(EQL)
49	DME	Malta	0.98539	49	PRIN1(EQL)
50	SEA	Taiwan	0.94603	50	PRIN1(EQL)
51	LAM	Guadeloupe	0.93720	51	PRIN1(EQL)
52	LAM	Virgin Islands, US	0.93587	52	PRIN1(EQL)
53	AFR	Reunion	0.90883	53	PRIN1(EQL)
54	LAM	Virgin Islands, Brit.	0.86990	54	PRIN1(EQL)
55	LAM	Anguilla	0.83904	55	PRIN1(EQL)
56	SEA	New Caledonia	0.82761	56	PRIN1(EQL)
57	LAM	Puerto Rico	0.74471	57	PRIN1(EQL)
58	SEA	Guam	0.74041	58	PRIN1(EQL)
59	EEU	Croatia	0.73794	59	PRIN1(EQL)
60	USR	Estonia	0.72404	60	PRIN1(EQL)
61	MEA	Bahrain	0.71823	61	PRIN1(EQL)
62	SEA	Northern Mariana Is.	0.68591	62	PRIN1(EQL)
63	LAM	Bahamas	0.67541	63	PRIN1(EQL)
64	EEU	Slovakia	0.67539	64	PRIN1(EQL)
65	LAM	Chile	0.66970	65	PRIN1(EQL)
66	SEA	French Polynesia	0.66523	66	PRIN1(EQL)
67	LAM	Neth. Antilles	0.65844	67	PRIN1(EQL)
68	EEU	Poland	0.65594	68	PRIN1(EQL)
69	EEU	Hungary	0.64717	69	PRIN1(EQL)
70	MEA	Oman	0.63056	70	PRIN1(EQL)
71	LAM	Guiana, French	0.61705	71	PRIN1(EQL)
72	LAM	Barbados	0.61558	72	PRIN1(EQL)
73	LAM	Aruba	0.60184	73	PRIN1(EQL)
74	LAM	Cuba	0.57481	74	PRIN1(EQL)
75	DME	St. Pierre & Miquelon	0.53414	75	PRIN1(EQL)
76	DME	Greenland	0.53264	76	PRIN1(EQL)
77	USR	Lithuania	0.53224	77	PRIN1(EQL)
78	LAM	Costa Rica	0.50032	78	PRIN1(EQL)
79	SEA	Malaysia	0.47994	79	PRIN1(EQL)
80	LAM	Antigua & Barbuda	0.46752	80	PRIN1(EQL)
81	USR	Latvia	0.46563	81	PRIN1(EQL)
82	AFR	Seychelles	0.44560	82	PRIN1(EQL)
83	MEA	Saudi Arabia	0.43594	83	PRIN1(EQL)
84	EEU	Montenegro	0.41801	84	PRIN1(EQL)
85	LAM	Uruguay	0.38832	85	PRIN1(EQL)
86	SEA	Samoa, American	0.38753	86	PRIN1(EQL)
87	LAM	Turks & Caicos Is.	0.38092	87	PRIN1(EQL)
88	EEU	Serbia	0.36534	88	PRIN1(EQL)

TABLE 1.5 ECONOMIC QUALITY-OF-LIFE INDEX, PRINCIPAL COMPONENT OF THE ECONOMIC QUALITY-OF-LIFE INDICATORS, 2008

OBS	REGION	COUNTRY	EQLX	RANK	SOURCE
89	MEA	Libya	0.35621	89	PRIN1(EQL)
90	LAM	Mexico	0.34629	90	PRIN1(EQL)
91	LAM	St. Kitts & Nevis	0.33583	91	PRIN1(EQL)
92	LAM	Argentina	0.31272	92	PRIN1(EQL)
93	EEU	Romania	0.30839	93	PRIN1(EQL)
94	EEU	Bulgaria	0.28637	94	PRIN1(EQL)
95	LAM	Montserrat	0.26606	95	PRIN1(EQL)
96	LAM	Dominica	0.25255	96	PRIN1(EQL)
97	LAM	Venezuela	0.24874	97	PRIN1(EQL)
98	USR	Russia	0.20926	98	PRIN1(EQL)
99	LAM	Panama	0.20912	99	PRIN1(EQL)
100	LAM	Grenada	0.19836	100	PRIN1(EQL)
101	LAM	Trinidad & Tobago	0.19390	101	PRIN1(EQL)
102	EEU	Macedonia	0.18941	102	PRIN1(EQL)
103	MEA	Lebanon	0.18812	103	PRIN1(EQL)
104	LAM	St. Lucia	0.18535	104	PRIN1(EQL)
105	EEU	Albania	0.17641	105	PRIN1(EQL)
106	MEA	Turkey	0.16156	106	PRIN1(EQL)
107	AFR	Mauritius	0.15726	107	PRIN1(EQL)
108	EEU	Bosnia	0.15557	108	PRIN1(EQL)
109	USR	Belarus	0.14394	109	PRIN1(EQL)
110	SEA	Palau	0.11391	110	PRIN1(EQL)
111	LAM	Brazil	0.09883	111	PRIN1(EQL)
112	LAM	St. Vincent	0.09583	112	PRIN1(EQL)
113	LAM	Belize	0.07392	113	PRIN1(EQL)
114	LAM	Colombia	0.03863	114	PRIN1(EQL)
115	SEA	Cook Islands	0.02867	115	PRIN1(EQL)
116	LAM	Ecuador	-0.00520	116	PRIN1(EQL)
117	MEA	Tunisia	-0.01909	117	PRIN1(EQL)
118	LAM	Peru	-0.05251	118	PRIN1(EQL)
119	AFR	St. Helena	-0.07531	119	PRIN1(EQL)
120	LAM	El Salvador	-0.10029	120	PRIN1(EQL)
121	MEA	Iran	-0.10957	121	PRIN1(EQL)
122	LAM	Dominican Rep.	-0.11586	122	PRIN1(EQL)
123	SEA	Thailand	-0.11985	123	PRIN1(EQL)
124	LAM	Jamaica	-0.12267	124	PRIN1(EQL)
125	USR	Armenia	-0.12434	125	PRIN1(EQL)
126	CPA	China	-0.12708	126	PRIN1(EQL)
127	MEA	Jordan	-0.13333	127	PRIN1(EQL)
128	SEA	Wallis & Futuna	-0.13683	128	PRIN1(EQL)
129	USR	Ukraine	-0.14618	129	PRIN1(EQL)
130	MEA	Syria	-0.15305	130	PRIN1(EQL)
131	SAS	Sri Lanka	-0.15648	131	PRIN1(EQL)
132	USR	Kazakhstan	-0.16923	132	PRIN1(EQL)
133	SEA	Nauru	-0.18430	133	PRIN1(EQL)

TABLE 1.5 ECONOMIC QUALITY-OF-LIFE INDEX, PRINCIPAL COMPONENT OF THE ECONOMIC QUALITY-OF-LIFE INDICATORS, 2008

OBS	REGION	COUNTRY	EQLX	RANK	SOURCE
134	LAM	Suriname	-0.18610	134	PRIN1(EQL)
135	SEA	Niue	-0.19018	135	PRIN1(EQL)
136	MEA	Algeria	-0.19570	136	PRIN1(EQL)
137	SEA	Fiji	-0.22653	137	PRIN1(EQL)
138	SAS	Maldives	-0.22689	138	PRIN1(EQL)
139	USR	Azerbaijan	-0.23056	139	PRIN1(EQL)
140	SEA	Tonga	-0.25982	140	PRIN1(EQL)
141	AFR	Mayotte	-0.27233	141	PRIN1(EQL)
142	SEA	Samoa, Western	-0.28302	142	PRIN1(EQL)
143	AFR	Botswana	-0.30731	143	PRIN1(EQL)
144	AFR	Equatorial Guinea	-0.32841	144	PRIN1(EQL)
145	LAM	Paraguay	-0.32903	145	PRIN1(EQL)
146	CPA	Vietnam	-0.33269	146	PRIN1(EQL)
147	USR	Georgia	-0.33398	147	PRIN1(EQL)
148	MEA	Egypt	-0.33640	148	PRIN1(EQL)
149	AFR	Cape Verde	-0.35408	149	PRIN1(EQL)
150	AFR	Gabon	-0.36502	150	PRIN1(EQL)
151	MEA	West Bank	-0.36705	151	PRIN1(EQL)
152	LAM	Guatemala	-0.37794	152	PRIN1(EQL)
153	LAM	Honduras	-0.40045	153	PRIN1(EQL)
154	MEA	Morocco	-0.40199	154	PRIN1(EQL)
155	SEA	Vanuatu	-0.42435	155	PRIN1(EQL)
156	SEA	Philippines	-0.42740	156	PRIN1(EQL)
157	MEA	Gaza Strip	-0.44556	157	PRIN1(EQL)
158	SEA	Marshall Islands	-0.46292	158	PRIN1(EQL)
159	SEA	Indonesia	-0.46391	159	PRIN1(EQL)
160	AFR	Namibia	-0.46595	160	PRIN1(EQL)
161	SEA	Tuvalu	-0.46752	161	PRIN1(EQL)
162	USR	Moldova	-0.47112	162	PRIN1(EQL)
163	LAM	Nicaragua	-0.50345	163	PRIN1(EQL)
164	USR	Turkmenistan	-0.52469	164	PRIN1(EQL)
165	MEA	Iraq	-0.53736	165	PRIN1(EQL)
166	AFR	South Africa	-0.55709	166	PRIN1(EQL)
167	EEU	Kosovo	-0.56540	167	PRIN1(EQL)
168	SEA	Micronesia	-0.57287	168	PRIN1(EQL)
169	CPA	Mongolia	-0.63641	169	PRIN1(EQL)
170	SAS	Bhutan	-0.68031	170	PRIN1(EQL)
171	LAM	Bolivia	-0.71476	171	PRIN1(EQL)
172	SEA	Solomon Islands	-0.73316	172	PRIN1(EQL)
173	USR	Uzbekistan	-0.76817	173	PRIN1(EQL)
174	SEA	Kiribati	-0.78392	174	PRIN1(EQL)
175	LAM	Guyana	-0.79414	175	PRIN1(EQL)
176	SEA	Tokelau	-0.82816	176	PRIN1(EQL)
177	USR	Kyrgyzstan	-0.84576	177	PRIN1(EQL)
178	CPA	Korea, North	-0.89939	178	PRIN1(EQL)
179	SAS	India	-0.90614	179	PRIN1(EQL)

OBS	REGION	COUNTRY	EQLX	RANK	SOURCE
		TABLE 1.5 ECONOMIC QUALITY-OF-LIFE INDEX, PRINCIPAL COMPONENT OF THE ECONOMIC QUALITY-OF-LIFE INDICATORS, 2008			
180	AFR	Swaziland	-0.94571	180	PRIN1(EQL)
181	SAS	Pakistan	-0.96063	181	PRIN1(EQL)
182	MEA	Yemen	-0.98346	182	PRIN1(EQL)
183	CPA	Laos	-0.98384	183	PRIN1(EQL)
184	AFR	Congo, Rep.	-1.00829	184	PRIN1(EQL)
185	SEA	Papua New Guinea	-1.02130	185	PRIN1(EQL)
186	AFR	San Tome & Principe	-1.02820	186	PRIN1(EQL)
187	AFR	Angola	-1.03079	187	PRIN1(EQL)
188	USR	Tajikistan	-1.03341	188	PRIN1(EQL)
189	SAS	Bangladesh	-1.08488	189	PRIN1(EQL)
190	AFR	Sudan	-1.12063	190	PRIN1(EQL)
191	AFR	Western Sahara	-1.13186	191	PRIN1(EQL)
192	SAS	Nepal	-1.13993	192	PRIN1(EQL)
193	SEA	East Timor	-1.15486	193	PRIN1(EQL)
194	AFR	Senegal	-1.17347	194	PRIN1(EQL)
195	AFR	Djibouti	-1.18189	195	PRIN1(EQL)
196	AFR	Comoros	-1.19898	196	PRIN1(EQL)
197	CPA	Cambodia	-1.20114	197	PRIN1(EQL)
198	AFR	Mauritania	-1.20551	198	PRIN1(EQL)
199	LAM	Haiti	-1.21877	199	PRIN1(EQL)
200	AFR	Ghana	-1.23251	200	PRIN1(EQL)
201	AFR	Ivory Coast	-1.24084	201	PRIN1(EQL)
202	AFR	Benin	-1.24448	202	PRIN1(EQL)
203	AFR	Cameroon	-1.24701	203	PRIN1(EQL)
204	CPA	Burma	-1.29162	204	PRIN1(EQL)
205	AFR	Lesotho	-1.32834	205	PRIN1(EQL)
206	AFR	Nigeria	-1.32968	206	PRIN1(EQL)
207	AFR	Kenya	-1.33123	207	PRIN1(EQL)
208	AFR	Togo	-1.38269	208	PRIN1(EQL)
209	AFR	Madagascar	-1.38543	209	PRIN1(EQL)
210	AFR	Tanzania	-1.40442	210	PRIN1(EQL)
211	AFR	Eritrea	-1.43015	211	PRIN1(EQL)
212	AFR	Gambia	-1.44681	212	PRIN1(EQL)
213	AFR	Zambia	-1.46338	213	PRIN1(EQL)
214	AFR	Guinea	-1.46629	214	PRIN1(EQL)
215	AFR	Burkina Faso	-1.51686	215	PRIN1(EQL)
216	AFR	Uganda	-1.52200	216	PRIN1(EQL)
217	AFR	Rwanda	-1.54404	217	PRIN1(EQL)
218	AFR	Ethiopia	-1.56612	218	PRIN1(EQL)
219	AFR	Mali	-1.57152	219	PRIN1(EQL)
220	AFR	Chad	-1.57747	220	PRIN1(EQL)
221	AFR	Malawi	-1.57951	221	PRIN1(EQL)
222	AFR	Niger	-1.66422	222	PRIN1(EQL)
223	AFR	Mozambique	-1.67534	223	PRIN1(EQL)

TABLE 1.5 ECONOMIC QUALITY-OF-LIFE INDEX, PRINCIPAL COMPONENT OF THE ECONOMIC QUALITY-OF-LIFE INDICATORS, 2008					
OBS	REGION	COUNTRY	EQLX	RANK	SOURCE
224	AFR	CAR	-1.75326	224	PRIN1(EQL)
225	AFR	Sierra Leone	-1.79588	225	PRIN1(EQL)
226	AFR	Somalia	-1.82698	226	PRIN1(EQL)
227	AFR	Liberia	-1.84536	227	PRIN1(EQL)
228	SAS	Afghanistan	-1.86359	228	PRIN1(EQL)
229	AFR	Guinea-Bissau	-1.88911	229	PRIN1(EQL)
230	AFR	Zimbabwe	-1.93557	230	PRIN1(EQL)
231	AFR	Burundi	-1.98817	231	PRIN1(EQL)
232	AFR	Congo, Dem. Rep.	-2.09233	232	PRIN1(EQL)

TABLE 1.6 SOCIETAL INTEGRATION INDEX, OPENNESS OF POLITICAL PROCESS, 2008					
OBS	REGION	COUNTRY	SCINTX	RANK	SOURCE
1	LAM	Brazil	0.89174	1.0	08(CALC(CIA))
2	MEA	Morocco	0.88420	2.0	08(CALC(CIA))
3	LAM	Neth. Antilles	0.88017	3.0	08(CALC(CIA))
4	SEA	Vanuatu	0.87428	4.0	08(CALC(CIA))
5	DME	Belgium	0.87360	5.0	08(CALC(CIA))
6	DME	Israel	0.87250	6.0	08(CALC(CIA))
7	SEA	Hong Kong	0.86735	7.0	08(CALC(CIA))
8	MEA	Lebanon	0.86169	8.0	08(CALC(CIA))
9	SEA	Indonesia	0.85226	9.0	08(CALC(CIA))
10	EEU	Bosnia	0.84921	10.0	08(CALC(CIA))
11	LAM	Haiti	0.84912	11.0	08(CALC(CIA))
12	SAS	India	0.84382	12.0	08(CALC(CIA))
13	USR	Latvia	0.83340	13.0	08(CALC(CIA))
14	AFR	Liberia	0.82910	14.0	08(CALC(CIA))
15	USR	Lithuania	0.82833	15.0	08(CALC(CIA))
16	LAM	Ecuador	0.82640	16.0	08(CALC(CIA))
17	DME	Netherlands	0.81804	17.0	08(CALC(CIA))
18	DME	Denmark	0.81254	18.0	08(CALC(CIA))
19	LAM	Chile	0.80861	19.0	08(CALC(CIA))
20	LAM	Colombia	0.80766	20.0	08(CALC(CIA))
21	DME	Faeroe Islands	0.80624	21.0	08(CALC(CIA))
22	DME	Finland	0.80510	22.0	08(CALC(CIA))
23	AFR	Congo, Dem. Rep.	0.80491	23.0	08(CALC(CIA))
24	MEA	Algeria	0.80428	24.0	08(CALC(CIA))
25	LAM	Guatemala	0.80212	25.0	08(CALC(CIA))
26	SAS	Sri Lanka	0.80111	26.0	08(CALC(CIA))
27	SEA	Papua New Guinea	0.80094	27.0	08(CALC(CIA))
28	AFR	Mali	0.79837	28.0	08(CALC(CIA))
29	AFR	Mauritania	0.79579	29.0	08(CALC(CIA))
30	DME	Switzerland	0.79540	30.0	08(CALC(CIA))
31	EEU	Bulgaria	0.79253	31.0	08(CALC(CIA))
32	EEU	Slovakia	0.79227	32.0	08(CALC(CIA))
33	AFR	Reunion	0.78884	33.0	08(CALC(WIKI))
34	DME	Norway	0.78078	34.0	08(CALC(CIA))
35	SEA	Philippines	0.78062	35.0	08(CALC(CIA))
36	SEA	New Caledonia	0.77709	36.0	08(CALC(CIA))
37	EEU	Slovenia	0.77383	37.0	08(CALC(CIA))
38	SEA	East Timor	0.77112	38.0	08(CALC(CIA))
39	USR	Estonia	0.77110	39.0	08(CALC(CIA))
40	LAM	Argentina	0.76844	40.0	08(CALC(CIA))
41	DME	Austria	0.76568	41.0	08(CALC(CIA))
42	SAS	Nepal	0.76404	42.0	08(CALC(CIA))
43	AFR	CAR	0.76004	43.0	08(CALC(CIA))

OBS	REGION	COUNTRY	SCINTX	RANK	SOURCE
		TABLE 1.6 SOCIETAL INTEGRATION INDEX, OPENNESS OF POLITICAL PROCESS, 2008			
44	EEU	Kosovo	0.76000	44.0	08(CALC(CIA))
45	DME	Sweden	0.75899	45.0	08(CALC(CIA))
46	SAS	Pakistan	0.75868	46.0	08(CALC(CIA))
47	DME	Greenland	0.75546	47.0	08(CALC(CIA))
48	EEU	Serbia	0.74908	48.0	08(CALC(CIA))
49	DME	San Marino	0.74833	49.0	08(CALC(CIA))
50	MEA	Cyprus	0.74362	50.0	08(CALC(CIA))
51	DME	Luxembourg	0.73722	51.0	08(CALC(CIA))
52	LAM	Peru	0.73528	52.0	08(CALC(CIA))
53	AFR	Niger	0.73146	53.0	08(CALC(CIA))
54	MEA	Iraq	0.72937	54.0	08(CALC(CIA))
55	DME	Iceland	0.72411	55.0	08(CALC(CIA))
56	MEA	Kuwait	0.72400	56.0	08(CALC(CIA))
57	AFR	Malawi	0.72244	57.0	08(CALC(CIA))
58	EEU	Albania	0.72163	58.0	08(CALC(CIA))
59	LAM	Mexico	0.71998	59.0	08(CALC(CIA))
60	EEU	Romania	0.71984	60.0	08(CALC(CIA))
61	USR	Uzbekistan	0.71417	61.0	08(CALC(CIA))
62	LAM	Martinique	0.71210	62.0	08(CALC(WIKI))
63	DME	Germany	0.70954	63.0	08(CALC(CIA))
64	USR	Ukraine	0.70702	64.0	08(CALC(CIA))
65	LAM	Paraguay	0.70688	65.0	08(CALC(CIA))
66	EEU	Montenegro	0.70416	66.0	08(CALC(CIA))
67	USR	Armenia	0.70311	67.0	08(CALC(CIA))
68	AFR	Benin	0.70257	68.0	08(CALC(CIA))
69	MEA	Bahrain	0.69750	69.0	08(CALC(CIA))
70	LAM	Costa Rica	0.69498	70.0	08(CALC(CIA))
71	AFR	Kenya	0.69283	71.0	08(CALC(CIA))
72	LAM	Nicaragua	0.68998	72.0	08(CALC(CIA))
73	LAM	Suriname	0.68743	73.0	08(CALC(CIA))
74	DME	Canada	0.68216	74.0	08(CALC(CIA))
75	AFR	Lesotho	0.68111	75.0	08(CALC(CIA))
76	EEU	Czechia	0.67705	76.0	08(CALC(CIA))
77	DME	Italy	0.67477	77.0	08(CALC(CIA))
78	LAM	Panama	0.67193	78.0	08(CALC(CIA))
79	EEU	Croatia	0.67171	79.0	08(CALC(CIA))
80	LAM	El Salvador	0.67120	80.0	08(CALC(CIA))
81	DME	Ireland	0.66737	81.0	08(CALC(CIA))
82	LAM	Montserrat	0.66667	82.0	08(CALC(CIA))
83	DME	New Zealand	0.66403	83.0	08(CALC(CIA))
84	SEA	Kiribati	0.66100	84.0	08(CALC(CIA))
85	AFR	Mayotte	0.65928	85.0	08(CALC(CIA))
86	AFR	San Tome & Principe	0.65785	86.0	08(CALC(CIA))
87	LAM	Guadeloupe	0.65333	87.0	08(CALC(WIKI))
88	EEU	Poland	0.64552	88.0	08(CALC(CIA))

OBS	REGION	COUNTRY	SCINTX	RANK	SOURCE
		TABLE 1.6 SOCIETAL INTEGRATION INDEX, OPENNESS OF POLITICAL PROCESS, 2008			
89	EEU	Macedonia	0.64278	89.0	08(CALC(CIA))
90	SEA	Tonga	0.64198	90.0	08(CALC(CIA))
91	AFR	Zambia	0.64125	91.0	08(CALC(CIA))
92	SEA	Thailand	0.63913	92.0	08(CALC(CIA))
93	SEA	Macao	0.63020	93.0	08(CALC(CIA))
94	AFR	Ivory Coast	0.62635	94.0	08(CALC(CIA))
95	SEA	French Polynesia	0.62173	95.0	08(CALC(CIA))
96	DME	Greece	0.61902	96.0	08(CALC(CIA))
97	EEU	Hungary	0.61722	97.0	08(CALC(CIA))
98	SEA	Solomon Islands	0.61520	98.0	08(CALC(CIA))
99	DME	Portugal	0.60926	99.0	08(CALC(CIA))
100	LAM	Virgin Islands, US	0.60444	100.0	08(CALC(CIA))
101	AFR	Rwanda	0.60031	101.0	08(CALC(CIA))
102	DME	Liechtenstein	0.59520	102.0	08(CALC(CIA))
103	DME	United Kingdom	0.59180	103.0	08(CALC(CIA))
104	AFR	Congo, Rep.	0.59161	104.0	08(CALC(CIA))
105	AFR	Ethiopia	0.59115	105.0	08(CALC(CIA))
106	MEA	Iran	0.58459	106.0	08(CALC(CIA))
107	SEA	Korea, South	0.58286	107.0	08(CALC(CIA))
108	LAM	Uruguay	0.58157	108.0	08(CALC(CIA))
109	LAM	Dominican Rep.	0.58023	109.0	08(CALC(CIA))
110	LAM	Honduras	0.57800	110.0	08(CALC(CIA))
111	DME	France	0.57746	111.0	08(CALC(CIA))
112	LAM	Aruba	0.57596	112.0	08(CALC(CIA))
113	SEA	Northern Mariana Is.	0.57500	113.0	08(CALC(CIA))
114	LAM	Guyana	0.57183	114.0	08(CALC(CIA))
115	DME	Spain	0.57154	115.0	08(CALC(CIA))
116	LAM	Anguilla	0.57143	116.0	08(CALC(CIA))
117	LAM	Bolivia	0.56935	117.0	08(CALC(CIA))
118	DME	Gibraltar	0.56747	118.0	08(CALC(CIA))
119	USR	Moldova	0.56740	119.0	08(CALC(CIA))
120	AFR	Sierra Leone	0.56712	120.0	08(CALC(CIA))
121	DME	Andorra	0.56122	121.0	08(CALC(CIA))
122	DME	Japan	0.55707	122.0	08(CALC(CIA))
123	AFR	Burundi	0.55681	123.0	08(CALC(CIA))
124	MEA	Turkey	0.55523	124.0	08(CALC(CIA))
125	DME	Australia	0.55476	125.0	08(CALC(CIA))
126	SEA	Fiji	0.55068	126.0	08(CALC(CIA))
127	AFR	Burkina Faso	0.54590	127.0	08(CALC(CIA))

TABLE 1.6 SOCIETAL INTEGRATION INDEX, OPENNESS OF POLITICAL PROCESS, 2008

OBS	REGION	COUNTRY	SCINTX	RANK	SOURCE
128	LAM	St. Kitts & Nevis	0.54545	128.0	08(CALC(CIA))
129	AFR	Ghana	0.53743	129.0	08(CALC(CIA))
130	LAM	Dominica	0.52608	130.0	08(CALC(CIA))
131	LAM	Cayman Islands	0.52444	131.0	08(CALC(CIA))
132	CPA	Mongolia	0.52043	132.0	08(CALC(CIA))
133	AFR	Mauritius	0.51918	133.0	08(CALC(CIA))
134	AFR	Gabon	0.51875	134.0	08(CALC(CIA))
135	AFR	Zimbabwe	0.51687	135.0	08(CALC(CIA))
136	AFR	Cape Verde	0.51273	136.0	08(CALC(CIA))
137	AFR	Togo	0.50541	137.0	08(CALC(CIA))
138	AFR	Nigeria	0.50465	138.0	08(CALC(CIA))
139	DME	Malta	0.49989	139.0	08(CALC(CIA))
140	LAM	Venezuela	0.49905	140.0	08(CALC(CIA))
141	AFR	Uganda	0.49697	141.0	08(CALC(CIA))
142	SEA	Cook Islands	0.49653	142.0	08(CALC(CIA))
143	LAM	Jamaica	0.49500	143.0	08(CALC(CIA))
144	LAM	Bahamas	0.49256	144.0	08(CALC(CIA))
145	LAM	Guiana, French	0.49216	145.0	08(CALC(WIKI))
146	AFR	South Africa	0.48917	146.0	08(CALC(CIA))
147	DME	United States	0.48351	147.0	08(CALC(CIA))
148	AFR	Chad	0.47950	148.0	08(CALC(CIA))
149	USR	Russia	0.47892	149.0	08(CALC(CIA))
150	DME	Bermuda	0.47531	150.0	08(CALC(CIA))
151	AFR	Guinea-Bissau	0.47160	151.0	08(CALC(CIA))
152	SEA	Malaysia	0.46587	152.0	08(CALC(CIA))
153	LAM	Trinidad & Tobago	0.46401	153.0	08(CALC(CIA))
154	AFR	Mozambique	0.46080	154.0	08(CALC(CIA))
155	LAM	St. Lucia	0.45675	155.0	08(CALC(CIA))
156	SEA	Wallis & Futuna	0.45500	156.0	08(CALC(CIA))
157	LAM	Barbados	0.44444	158.0	08(CALC(CIA))
158	AFR	Comoros	0.44444	158.0	08(CALC(CIA))
159	SEA	Guam	0.44444	158.0	08(CALC(CIA))
160	SEA	Samoa, Western	0.44148	160.0	08(CALC(CIA))
161	AFR	Seychelles	0.43772	161.0	08(CALC(CIA))
162	SEA	Taiwan	0.42822	162.0	08(CALC(CIA))
163	CPA	Cambodia	0.41880	163.0	08(CALC(CIA))
164	AFR	Guinea	0.40705	164.0	08(CALC(CIA))
165	AFR	Namibia	0.40471	165.0	08(CALC(CIA))
166	MEA	Yemen	0.39900	166.0	08(CALC(CIA))
167	LAM	Puerto Rico	0.39831	167.0	08(CALC(CIA))

OBS	REGION	COUNTRY	SCINTX	RANK	SOURCE
		TABLE 1.6 SOCIETAL INTEGRATION INDEX, OPENNESS OF POLITICAL PROCESS, 2008			
168	SAS	Bangladesh	0.39273	168.0	08(CALC(CIA))
169	LAM	Grenada	0.39111	169.0	08(CALC(CIA))
170	LAM	Virgin Islands, Brit.	0.37870	170.0	08(CALC(CIA))
171	LAM	Antigua & Barbuda	0.35986	171.0	08(CALC(CIA))
172	AFR	Botswana	0.35950	172.0	08(CALC(CIA))
173	USR	Kyrgyzstan	0.35481	173.0	08(CALC(CIA))
174	USR	Georgia	0.34524	174.0	08(CALC(CIA))
175	MEA	Tunisia	0.34260	175.0	08(CALC(CIA))
176	USR	Tajikistan	0.33107	176.0	08(CALC(CIA))
177	LAM	St. Vincent	0.32000	177.0	08(CALC(CIA))
178	LAM	Belize	0.31217	178.0	08(CALC(CIA))
179	USR	Azerbaijan	0.31132	179.0	08(CALC(CIA))
180	DME	St. Pierre & Miquelon	0.27701	180.0	08(CALC(CIA))
181	AFR	Cameroon	0.25368	181.0	08(CALC(CIA))
182	AFR	Angola	0.23938	182.0	08(CALC(CIA))
183	LAM	Turks & Caicos Is.	0.23111	183.0	08(CALC(CIA))
184	DME	Isle of Man	0.22569	184.0	08(CALC(CIA))
185	AFR	Senegal	0.22124	185.0	08(CALC(CIA))
186	AFR	Tanzania	0.21933	186.0	08(CALC(CIA))
187	DME	Monaco	0.21875	187.0	08(CALC(CIA))
188	AFR	Gambia	0.20719	188.0	08(CALC(CIA))
189	AFR	Equatorial Guinea	0.19780	189.0	08(CALC(CIA))
190	MEA	Jordan	0.10314	190.0	08(CALC(CIA))
191	SAS	Bhutan	0.08148	191.0	08(CALC(CIA))
192	SEA	Singapore	0.04677	192.0	08(CALC(CIA))
193	MEA	Egypt	0.04101	193.0	08(CALC(CIA))
194	CPA	Laos	0.03418	194.0	08(CALC(CIA))
195	AFR	Sudan	0.02739	195.0	08(CALC(CIA))
196	AFR	Madagascar	0.01562	196.0	08(CALC(CIA))
197	SAS	Afghanistan	0.00000	214.5	08(CALC(CIA))
198	USR	Belarus	0.00000	214.5	08(CALC(CIA))
199	SEA	Brunei	0.00000	214.5	08(CALC(CIA))
200	CPA	Burma	0.00000	214.5	08(CALC(CIA))
201	CPA	China	0.00000	214.5	08(CALC(CIA))
202	LAM	Cuba	0.00000	214.5	08(CALC(CIA))
203	AFR	Djibouti	0.00000	214.5	08(CALC(CIA))
204	AFR	Eritrea	0.00000	214.5	08(CALC(CIA))
205	DME	Falkland Islands	0.00000	214.5	08(CALC(CIA))
206	MEA	Gaza Strip	0.00000	214.5	08(CALC(CIA))
207	DME	Guernsey	0.00000	214.5	08(CALC(CIA))

OBS	REGION	COUNTRY	SCINTX	RANK	SOURCE
\multicolumn{6}{c}{TABLE 1.6 SOCIETAL INTEGRATION INDEX, OPENNESS OF POLITICAL PROCESS, 2008}

OBS	REGION	COUNTRY	SCINTX	RANK	SOURCE
208	DME	Jersey	0.00000	214.5	08(CALC(CIA))
209	USR	Kazakhstan	0.00000	214.5	08(CALC(CIA))
210	CPA	Korea, North	0.00000	214.5	08(CALC(CIA))
211	MEA	Libya	0.00000	214.5	08(CALC(CIA))
212	SAS	Maldives	0.00000	214.5	08(CALC(CIA))
213	SEA	Marshall Islands	0.00000	214.5	08(CALC(CIA))
214	SEA	Micronesia	0.00000	214.5	08(CALC(CIA))
215	SEA	Nauru	0.00000	214.5	08(CALC(CIA))
216	SEA	Niue	0.00000	214.5	08(CALC(CIA))
217	MEA	Oman	0.00000	214.5	08(CALC(CIA))
218	SEA	Palau	0.00000	214.5	08(CALC(CIA))
219	MEA	Qatar	0.00000	214.5	08(CALC(CIA))
220	SEA	Samoa, American	0.00000	214.5	08(CALC(CIA))
221	MEA	Saudi Arabia	0.00000	214.5	08(CALC(CIA))
222	AFR	Somalia	0.00000	214.5	08(CALC(CIA))
223	AFR	St. Helena	0.00000	214.5	08(CALC(CIA))
224	AFR	Swaziland	0.00000	214.5	08(CALC(CIA))
225	MEA	Syria	0.00000	214.5	08(CALC(CIA))
226	SEA	Tokelau	0.00000	214.5	08(CALC(CIA))
227	USR	Turkmenistan	0.00000	214.5	08(CALC(CIA))
228	SEA	Tuvalu	0.00000	214.5	08(CALC(CIA))
229	MEA	UAE	0.00000	214.5	08(CALC(CIA))
230	CPA	Vietnam	0.00000	214.5	08(CALC(CIA))
231	MEA	West Bank	0.00000	214.5	08(CALC(CIA))
232	AFR	Western Sahara	0.00000	214.5	08(CALC(CIA))

OBS	REGION	COUNTRY	CPRX	RANK	SOURCE
		TABLE 1.7 CIVIL AND POLITICAL RIGHTS INDEX, 2008			
1	DME	Andorra	1.0	24.5	08(FH)
2	DME	Australia	1.0	24.5	08(FH)
3	DME	Austria	1.0	24.5	08(FH)
4	LAM	Bahamas	1.0	24.5	08(FH)
5	LAM	Barbados	1.0	24.5	08(FH)
6	DME	Belgium	1.0	24.5	08(FH)
7	DME	Canada	1.0	24.5	08(FH)
8	AFR	Cape Verde	1.0	24.5	08(FH)
9	LAM	Chile	1.0	24.5	08(FH)
10	LAM	Costa Rica	1.0	24.5	08(FH)
11	MEA	Cyprus	1.0	24.5	08(FH)
12	EEU	Czechia	1.0	24.5	08(FH)
13	DME	Denmark	1.0	24.5	08(FH)
14	LAM	Dominica	1.0	24.5	08(FH)
15	USR	Estonia	1.0	24.5	08(FH)
16	DME	Finland	1.0	24.5	08(FH)
17	DME	France	1.0	24.5	08(FH)
18	DME	Germany	1.0	24.5	08(FH)
19	EEU	Hungary	1.0	24.5	08(FH)
20	DME	Iceland	1.0	24.5	08(FH)
21	DME	Ireland	1.0	24.5	08(FH)
22	SEA	Kiribati	1.0	24.5	08(FH)
23	DME	Liechtenstein	1.0	24.5	08(FH)
24	USR	Lithuania	1.0	24.5	08(FH)
25	DME	Luxembourg	1.0	24.5	08(FH)
26	DME	Malta	1.0	24.5	08(FH)
27	SEA	Marshall Islands	1.0	24.5	08(FH)
28	SEA	Micronesia	1.0	24.5	08(FH)
29	SEA	Nauru	1.0	24.5	08(FH)
30	DME	Netherlands	1.0	24.5	08(FH)
31	DME	New Zealand	1.0	24.5	08(FH)
32	DME	Norway	1.0	24.5	08(FH)
33	SEA	Palau	1.0	24.5	08(FH)
34	EEU	Poland	1.0	24.5	08(FH)
35	DME	Portugal	1.0	24.5	08(FH)
36	LAM	Puerto Rico	1.0	24.5	08(FH)
37	DME	San Marino	1.0	24.5	08(FH)
38	EEU	Slovakia	1.0	24.5	08(FH)
39	EEU	Slovenia	1.0	24.5	08(FH)
40	DME	Spain	1.0	24.5	08(FH)
41	LAM	St. Kitts & Nevis	1.0	24.5	08(FH)
42	LAM	St. Lucia	1.0	24.5	08(FH)
43	DME	Sweden	1.0	24.5	08(FH)
44	DME	Switzerland	1.0	24.5	08(FH)
45	SEA	Tuvalu	1.0	24.5	08(FH)
46	DME	United Kingdom	1.0	24.5	08(FH)
47	DME	United States	1.0	24.5	08(FH)

		TABLE 1.7 CIVIL AND POLITICAL RIGHTS INDEX, 2008			
OBS	REGION	COUNTRY	CPRX	RANK	SOURCE
48	LAM	Uruguay	1.0	24.5	08(FH)
49	LAM	Belize	1.5	55.0	08(FH)
50	AFR	Ghana	1.5	55.0	08(FH)
51	DME	Greece	1.5	55.0	08(FH)
52	LAM	Grenada	1.5	55.0	08(FH)
53	DME	Israel	1.5	55.0	08(FH)
54	DME	Italy	1.5	55.0	08(FH)
55	DME	Japan	1.5	55.0	08(FH)
56	SEA	Korea, South	1.5	55.0	08(FH)
57	USR	Latvia	1.5	55.0	08(FH)
58	DME	Monaco	1.5	55.0	08(FH)
59	LAM	Panama	1.5	55.0	08(FH)
60	LAM	St. Vincent	1.5	55.0	08(FH)
61	SEA	Taiwan	1.5	55.0	08(FH)
62	DME	Faeroe Islands	1.5	62.0	(REG)
63	AFR	Reunion	2.0	63.0	(REG)
64	LAM	Anguilla	2.0	64.0	(REG)
65	LAM	Neth. Antilles	2.0	65.0	(REG)
66	SEA	New Caledonia	2.0	66.0	(REG)
67	LAM	Antigua & Barbuda	2.0	75.5	08(FH)
68	LAM	Argentina	2.0	75.5	08(FH)
69	AFR	Benin	2.0	75.5	08(FH)
70	AFR	Botswana	2.0	75.5	08(FH)
71	LAM	Brazil	2.0	75.5	08(FH)
72	EEU	Bulgaria	2.0	75.5	08(FH)
73	EEU	Croatia	2.0	75.5	08(FH)
74	LAM	Dominican Rep.	2.0	75.5	08(FH)
75	AFR	Mauritius	2.0	75.5	08(FH)
76	CPA	Mongolia	2.0	75.5	08(FH)
77	AFR	Namibia	2.0	75.5	08(FH)
78	EEU	Romania	2.0	75.5	08(FH)
79	SEA	Samoa, Western	2.0	75.5	08(FH)
80	AFR	San Tome & Principe	2.0	75.5	08(FH)
81	AFR	South Africa	2.0	75.5	08(FH)
82	LAM	Suriname	2.0	75.5	08(FH)
83	LAM	Trinidad & Tobago	2.0	75.5	08(FH)
84	SEA	Vanuatu	2.0	75.5	08(FH)
85	LAM	Martinique	2.0	85.0	(REG)
86	DME	Gibraltar	2.0	86.0	(REG)
87	LAM	Montserrat	2.0	87.0	(REG)
88	SEA	French Polynesia	2.5	88.0	(REG)
89	SEA	Northern Mariana Is.	2.5	89.0	(REG)
90	LAM	Guadeloupe	2.5	90.0	(REG)
91	LAM	Virgin Islands, US	2.5	91.0	(REG)
92	LAM	Cayman Islands	2.5	92.0	(REG)

	TABLE 1.7 CIVIL AND POLITICAL RIGHTS INDEX, 2008				
OBS	REGION	COUNTRY	CPRX	RANK	SOURCE
93	DME	Greenland	2.5	93.0	(REG)
94	LAM	El Salvador	2.5	99.0	08(FH)
95	LAM	Guyana	2.5	99.0	08(FH)
96	SAS	India	2.5	99.0	08(FH)
97	SEA	Indonesia	2.5	99.0	08(FH)
98	LAM	Jamaica	2.5	99.0	08(FH)
99	AFR	Lesotho	2.5	99.0	08(FH)
100	AFR	Mali	2.5	99.0	08(FH)
101	LAM	Mexico	2.5	99.0	08(FH)
102	LAM	Peru	2.5	99.0	08(FH)
103	EEU	Serbia	2.5	99.0	08(FH)
104	USR	Ukraine	2.5	99.0	08(FH)
105	SEA	Guam	2.5	105.0	(REG)
106	DME	Bermuda	2.5	106.0	(REG)
107	LAM	Aruba	3.0	107.0	(REG)
108	LAM	Guiana, French	3.0	108.0	(REG)
109	EEU	Albania	3.0	115.0	08(FH)
110	LAM	Bolivia	3.0	115.0	08(FH)
111	LAM	Ecuador	3.0	115.0	08(FH)
112	LAM	Honduras	3.0	115.0	08(FH)
113	EEU	Macedonia	3.0	115.0	08(FH)
114	EEU	Montenegro	3.0	115.0	08(FH)
115	AFR	Mozambique	3.0	115.0	08(FH)
116	LAM	Paraguay	3.0	115.0	08(FH)
117	AFR	Senegal	3.0	115.0	08(FH)
118	AFR	Seychelles	3.0	115.0	08(FH)
119	AFR	Sierra Leone	3.0	115.0	08(FH)
120	MEA	Turkey	3.0	115.0	08(FH)
121	AFR	Zambia	3.0	115.0	08(FH)
122	DME	Isle of Man	3.0	122.0	(REG)
123	DME	St. Pierre & Miquelon	3.0	123.0	(REG)
124	DME	Guernsey	3.5	124.0	(REG)
125	DME	Falkland Islands	3.5	125.0	(REG)
126	SEA	Wallis & Futuna	3.5	126.0	(REG)
127	LAM	Virgin Islands, Brit.	3.5	127.0	(REG)
128	EEU	Bosnia	3.5	135.5	08(FH)
129	LAM	Colombia	3.5	135.5	08(FH)
130	AFR	Comoros	3.5	135.5	08(FH)
131	SEA	East Timor	3.5	135.5	08(FH)
132	LAM	Guatemala	3.5	135.5	08(FH)
133	SEA	Hong Kong	3.5	135.5	08(FH)
134	AFR	Kenya	3.5	135.5	08(FH)
135	AFR	Liberia	3.5	135.5	08(FH)
136	SEA	Macao	3.5	135.5	08(EST)
137	AFR	Madagascar	3.5	135.5	08(FH)
138	LAM	Nicaragua	3.5	135.5	08(FH)

TABLE 1.7 CIVIL AND POLITICAL RIGHTS INDEX, 2008

OBS	REGION	COUNTRY	CPRX	RANK	SOURCE
139	AFR	Niger	3.5	135.5	08(FH)
140	SEA	Papua New Guinea	3.5	135.5	08(FH)
141	SEA	Philippines	3.5	135.5	08(FH)
142	SEA	Solomon Islands	3.5	135.5	08(FH)
143	AFR	Tanzania	3.5	135.5	08(FH)
144	DME	Jersey	3.5	144.0	(REG)
145	SEA	Cook Islands	3.5	145.0	(REG)
146	LAM	Turks & Caicos Is.	4.0	146.0	(REG)
147	AFR	Mayotte	4.0	147.0	(REG)
148	SEA	Samoa, American	4.0	148.0	(REG)
149	SAS	Bangladesh	4.0	155.0	08(FH)
150	AFR	Burkina Faso	4.0	155.0	08(FH)
151	USR	Georgia	4.0	155.0	08(FH)
152	AFR	Guinea-Bissau	4.0	155.0	08(FH)
153	MEA	Kuwait	4.0	155.0	08(FH)
154	AFR	Malawi	4.0	155.0	08(FH)
155	SEA	Malaysia	4.0	155.0	08(FH)
156	SAS	Maldives	4.0	155.0	08(FH)
157	USR	Moldova	4.0	155.0	08(FH)
158	SAS	Nepal	4.0	155.0	08(FH)
159	SAS	Sri Lanka	4.0	155.0	08(FH)
160	SEA	Tonga	4.0	155.0	08(FH)
161	LAM	Venezuela	4.0	155.0	08(FH)
162	SEA	Niue	4.5	162.0	(REG)
163	SAS	Bhutan	4.5	168.5	08(FH)
164	AFR	Burundi	4.5	168.5	08(FH)
165	AFR	Gambia	4.5	168.5	08(FH)
166	LAM	Haiti	4.5	168.5	08(FH)
167	USR	Kyrgyzstan	4.5	168.5	08(FH)
168	MEA	Lebanon	4.5	168.5	08(FH)
169	MEA	Morocco	4.5	168.5	08(FH)
170	AFR	Nigeria	4.5	168.5	08(FH)
171	SAS	Pakistan	4.5	168.5	08(FH)
172	SEA	Singapore	4.5	168.5	08(FH)
173	SEA	Thailand	4.5	168.5	08(FH)
174	AFR	Uganda	4.5	168.5	08(FH)
175	AFR	St. Helena	4.5	175.0	(REG)
176	USR	Armenia	5.0	180.5	08(FH)
177	MEA	Bahrain	5.0	180.5	08(FH)
178	AFR	CAR	5.0	180.5	08(FH)
179	AFR	Djibouti	5.0	180.5	08(FH)
180	AFR	Ethiopia	5.0	180.5	08(FH)
181	SEA	Fiji	5.0	180.5	08(FH)
182	AFR	Gabon	5.0	180.5	08(FH)
183	MEA	Jordan	5.0	180.5	08(FH)
184	AFR	Togo	5.0	180.5	08(FH)
185	MEA	Yemen	5.0	180.5	08(FH)

OBS	REGION	COUNTRY	CPRX	RANK	SOURCE
		TABLE 1.7 CIVIL AND POLITICAL RIGHTS INDEX, 2008			
186	SEA	Tokelau	5.0	186.0	(REG)
187	SAS	Afghanistan	5.5	196.0	08(FH)
188	MEA	Algeria	5.5	196.0	08(FH)
189	AFR	Angola	5.5	196.0	08(FH)
190	USR	Azerbaijan	5.5	196.0	08(FH)
191	SEA	Brunei	5.5	196.0	08(FH)
192	CPA	Cambodia	5.5	196.0	08(FH)
193	AFR	Congo, Rep.	5.5	196.0	08(FH)
194	MEA	Egypt	5.5	196.0	08(FH)
195	AFR	Ivory Coast	5.5	196.0	08(FH)
196	USR	Kazakhstan	5.5	196.0	08(FH)
197	EEU	Kosovo	5.5	196.0	08(FH)
198	AFR	Mauritania	5.5	196.0	08(FH)
199	MEA	Oman	5.5	196.0	08(FH)
200	MEA	Qatar	5.5	196.0	08(FH)
201	USR	Russia	5.5	196.0	08(FH)
202	AFR	Rwanda	5.5	196.0	08(FH)
203	USR	Tajikistan	5.5	196.0	08(FH)
204	MEA	UAE	5.5	196.0	08(FH)
205	MEA	West Bank	5.5	196.0	08(FH)
206	AFR	Cameroon	6.0	210.0	08(FH)
207	AFR	Congo, Dem. Rep.	6.0	210.0	08(FH)
208	MEA	Gaza Strip	6.0	210.0	08(FH)
209	AFR	Guinea	6.0	210.0	08(FH)
210	MEA	Iran	6.0	210.0	08(FH)
211	MEA	Iraq	6.0	210.0	08(FH)
212	AFR	Swaziland	6.0	210.0	08(FH)
213	MEA	Tunisia	6.0	210.0	08(FH)
214	CPA	Vietnam	6.0	210.0	08(FH)
215	USR	Belarus	6.5	219.5	08(FH)
216	AFR	Chad	6.5	219.5	08(FH)
217	CPA	China	6.5	219.5	08(FH)
218	LAM	Cuba	6.5	219.5	08(FH)
219	AFR	Eritrea	6.5	219.5	08(FH)
220	CPA	Laos	6.5	219.5	08(FH)
221	MEA	Saudi Arabia	6.5	219.5	08(FH)
222	MEA	Syria	6.5	219.5	08(FH)
223	AFR	Western Sahara	6.5	219.5	08(FH)
224	AFR	Zimbabwe	6.5	219.5	08(FH)
225	CPA	Burma	7.0	228.5	08(FH)
226	AFR	Equatorial Guinea	7.0	228.5	08(FH)
227	CPA	Korea, North	7.0	228.5	08(FH)
228	MEA	Libya	7.0	228.5	08(FH)
229	AFR	Somalia	7.0	228.5	08(FH)
230	AFR	Sudan	7.0	228.5	08(FH)
231	USR	Turkmenistan	7.0	228.5	08(FH)
232	USR	Uzbekistan	7.0	228.5	08(FH)

OBS	REGION	COUNTRY	HDX	RANK	SOURCE
\multicolumn{6}{c}{TABLE 1.8 HUMAN DEVELOPMENT INDEX, 2007}					
1	DME	Monaco	1.054	1.0	(REG)
2	DME	Bermuda	1.001	2.0	(REG)
3	SEA	Macao	0.991	3.0	(REG)
4	DME	Jersey	0.988	4.0	(REG)
5	DME	Guernsey	0.978	5.0	(REG)
6	LAM	Cayman Islands	0.978	6.0	(REG)
7	DME	San Marino	0.977	7.0	(REG)
8	DME	Norway	0.971	8.0	07(UN)
9	DME	Australia	0.970	9.0	07(UN)
10	DME	Iceland	0.969	10.0	07(UN)
11	DME	Canada	0.966	11.0	07(UN)
12	DME	Ireland	0.965	12.0	07(UN)
13	DME	Netherlands	0.964	13.0	07(UN)
14	DME	Sweden	0.963	14.0	07(UN)
15	DME	Gibraltar	0.962	15.0	(REG)
16	DME	France	0.961	16.0	07(UN)
17	DME	Falkland Islands	0.961	17.0	(REG)
18	DME	Japan	0.960	19.0	07(UN)
19	DME	Luxembourg	0.960	19.0	07(UN)
20	DME	Switzerland	0.960	19.0	07(UN)
21	DME	Finland	0.959	21.0	07(UN)
22	DME	United States	0.956	22.0	07(UN)
23	DME	Austria	0.955	24.0	07(UN)
24	DME	Denmark	0.955	24.0	07(UN)
25	DME	Spain	0.955	24.0	07(UN)
26	DME	Belgium	0.953	26.0	07(UN)
27	DME	Faeroe Islands	0.953	27.0	(REG)
28	DME	Italy	0.951	28.5	07(UN)
29	DME	Liechtenstein	0.951	28.5	07(UN)
30	DME	New Zealand	0.950	30.0	07(UN)
31	DME	Germany	0.947	31.5	07(UN)
32	DME	United Kingdom	0.947	31.5	07(UN)
33	DME	Isle of Man	0.946	33.0	(REG)
34	SEA	Hong Kong	0.944	34.5	07(UN)
35	SEA	Singapore	0.944	34.5	07(UN)
36	LAM	Virgin Islands, Brit.	0.942	36.0	(REG)
37	DME	Greece	0.942	37.0	07(UN)
38	SEA	Korea, South	0.937	38.0	07(UN)
39	LAM	Martinique	0.935	39.0	(REG)
40	DME	Israel	0.935	40.0	07(UN)
41	DME	Andorra	0.934	41.0	07(UN)
42	EEU	Slovenia	0.929	42.0	07(UN)
43	LAM	Guadeloupe	0.923	43.0	(REG)
44	SEA	Taiwan	0.922	44.0	(REG)
45	SEA	Brunei	0.920	45.0	07(UN)
46	MEA	Kuwait	0.916	46.0	07(UN)

| \multicolumn{6}{c}{TABLE 1.8 HUMAN DEVELOPMENT INDEX, 2007} |

OBS	REGION	COUNTRY	HDX	RANK	SOURCE
47	MEA	Cyprus	0.914	47.0	07(UN)
48	AFR	Reunion	0.911	48.0	(REG)
49	MEA	Qatar	0.910	49.0	07(UN)
50	DME	Portugal	0.909	50.0	07(UN)
51	LAM	Barbados	0.903	52.0	07(UN)
52	EEU	Czechia	0.903	52.0	07(UN)
53	MEA	UAE	0.903	52.0	07(UN)
54	DME	Malta	0.902	54.0	07(UN)
55	MEA	Bahrain	0.895	55.0	07(UN)
56	LAM	Puerto Rico	0.886	56.0	(REG)
57	LAM	Virgin Islands, US	0.886	57.0	(REG)
58	USR	Estonia	0.883	58.0	07(UN)
59	LAM	Guiana, French	0.881	59.0	(REG)
60	EEU	Poland	0.880	60.5	07(UN)
61	EEU	Slovakia	0.880	60.5	07(UN)
62	LAM	Aruba	0.880	62.0	(REG)
63	EEU	Hungary	0.879	63.0	07(UN)
64	LAM	Chile	0.878	64.0	07(UN)
65	EEU	Croatia	0.871	65.0	07(UN)
66	USR	Lithuania	0.870	66.0	07(UN)
67	LAM	Neth. Antilles	0.870	67.0	(REG)
68	SEA	New Caledonia	0.870	68.0	(REG)
69	LAM	Antigua & Barbuda	0.868	69.0	07(UN)
70	LAM	Argentina	0.866	70.5	07(UN)
71	USR	Latvia	0.866	70.5	07(UN)
72	SEA	Northern Mariana Is.	0.866	72.0	(REG)
73	LAM	Uruguay	0.865	73.0	07(UN)
74	LAM	Cuba	0.863	74.0	07(UN)
75	LAM	Anguilla	0.863	75.0	(REG)
76	SEA	Guam	0.858	76.0	(REG)
77	SEA	French Polynesia	0.856	77.0	(REG)
78	LAM	Bahamas	0.856	78.0	07(UN)
79	LAM	Costa Rica	0.854	79.5	07(UN)
80	LAM	Mexico	0.854	79.5	07(UN)
81	DME	Greenland	0.851	81.0	(REG)
82	MEA	Libya	0.847	82.0	07(UN)
83	MEA	Oman	0.846	83.0	07(UN)
84	LAM	Turks & Caicos Is.	0.846	84.0	(REG)
85	AFR	Seychelles	0.845	85.0	07(UN)
86	LAM	Venezuela	0.844	86.0	07(UN)
87	MEA	Saudi Arabia	0.843	87.0	07(UN)
88	DME	St. Pierre & Miquelon	0.842	88.0	(REG)
89	EEU	Bulgaria	0.840	89.5	07(UN)
90	LAM	Panama	0.840	89.5	07(UN)

OBS	REGION	COUNTRY	HDX	RANK	SOURCE
		TABLE 1.8 HUMAN DEVELOPMENT INDEX, 2007			
91	LAM	St. Kitts & Nevis	0.838	91.0	07(UN)
92	EEU	Romania	0.837	92.5	07(UN)
93	LAM	Trinidad & Tobago	0.837	92.5	07(UN)
94	EEU	Montenegro	0.834	94.0	07(UN)
95	SEA	Malaysia	0.829	95.0	07(UN)
96	USR	Belarus	0.826	96.5	07(UN)
97	EEU	Serbia	0.826	96.5	07(UN)
98	LAM	St. Lucia	0.821	98.0	07(UN)
99	EEU	Albania	0.818	99.0	07(UN)
100	EEU	Macedonia	0.817	100.5	07(UN)
101	USR	Russia	0.817	100.5	07(UN)
102	LAM	Dominica	0.814	102.0	07(UN)
103	LAM	Brazil	0.813	103.5	07(UN)
104	LAM	Grenada	0.813	103.5	07(UN)
105	SEA	Samoa, American	0.813	105.0	(REG)
106	EEU	Bosnia	0.812	106.0	07(UN)
107	LAM	Colombia	0.807	107.0	07(UN)
108	LAM	Ecuador	0.806	109.0	07(UN)
109	LAM	Peru	0.806	109.0	07(UN)
110	MEA	Turkey	0.806	109.0	07(UN)
111	USR	Kazakhstan	0.804	111.5	07(UN)
112	AFR	Mauritius	0.804	111.5	07(UN)
113	MEA	Lebanon	0.803	113.0	07(UN)
114	USR	Armenia	0.798	114.0	07(UN)
115	USR	Ukraine	0.796	115.0	07(UN)
116	SEA	Cook Islands	0.796	116.0	(REG)
117	LAM	Montserrat	0.789	117.0	(REG)
118	USR	Azerbaijan	0.787	118.0	07(UN)
119	SEA	Thailand	0.783	119.0	07(UN)
120	MEA	Iran	0.782	120.0	07(UN)
121	AFR	Mayotte	0.780	121.0	(REG)
122	USR	Georgia	0.778	122.0	07(UN)
123	LAM	Dominican Rep.	0.777	123.0	07(UN)
124	LAM	Belize	0.772	125.0	07(UN)
125	CPA	China	0.772	125.0	07(UN)
126	LAM	St. Vincent	0.772	125.0	07(UN)
127	SAS	Maldives	0.771	127.5	07(UN)
128	SEA	Samoa, Western	0.771	127.5	07(UN)
129	MEA	Jordan	0.770	129.0	07(UN)
130	AFR	St. Helena	0.770	130.0	(REG)
131	LAM	Suriname	0.769	131.5	07(UN)
132	MEA	Tunisia	0.769	131.5	07(UN)
133	SEA	Tonga	0.768	133.0	07(UN)
134	SEA	Palau	0.768	134.0	(REG)
135	LAM	Jamaica	0.766	135.0	07(UN)
136	SEA	Wallis & Futuna	0.762	136.0	(REG)

OBS	REGION	COUNTRY	HDX	RANK	SOURCE
TABLE 1.8 HUMAN DEVELOPMENT INDEX, 2007					
137	LAM	Paraguay	0.761	137.0	07(UN)
138	SAS	Sri Lanka	0.759	138.0	07(UN)
139	AFR	Gabon	0.755	139.0	07(UN)
140	MEA	Algeria	0.754	140.0	07(UN)
141	SEA	Philippines	0.751	141.0	07(UN)
142	LAM	El Salvador	0.747	142.0	07(UN)
143	MEA	Syria	0.742	143.0	07(UN)
144	SEA	Fiji	0.741	144.0	07(UN)
145	USR	Turkmenistan	0.739	145.0	07(UN)
146	MEA	Gaza Strip	0.737	146.5	07(UN)
147	MEA	West Bank	0.737	146.5	07(UN)
148	SEA	Indonesia	0.734	148.0	07(UN)
149	LAM	Honduras	0.732	149.0	07(UN)
150	LAM	Bolivia	0.729	150.5	07(UN)
151	LAM	Guyana	0.729	150.5	07(UN)
152	CPA	Mongolia	0.727	152.0	07(UN)
153	CPA	Vietnam	0.725	153.0	07(UN)
154	USR	Moldova	0.720	154.0	07(UN)
155	AFR	Equatorial Guinea	0.719	155.0	07(UN)
156	SEA	Niue	0.713	156.0	(REG)
157	USR	Kyrgyzstan	0.710	157.5	07(UN)
158	USR	Uzbekistan	0.710	157.5	07(UN)
159	AFR	Cape Verde	0.708	159.0	07(UN)
160	LAM	Guatemala	0.704	160.0	07(UN)
161	MEA	Egypt	0.703	161.0	07(UN)
162	LAM	Nicaragua	0.699	162.0	07(UN)
163	AFR	Botswana	0.694	163.0	07(UN)
164	SEA	Vanuatu	0.693	164.0	07(UN)
165	MEA	Iraq	0.691	165.0	(REG)
166	USR	Tajikistan	0.688	166.0	07(UN)
167	AFR	Namibia	0.686	167.0	07(UN)
168	AFR	South Africa	0.683	168.0	07(UN)
169	SEA	Nauru	0.682	169.0	(REG)
170	SEA	Marshall Islands	0.681	170.0	(REG)
171	SEA	Micronesia	0.671	171.0	(REG)
172	EEU	Kosovo	0.665	172.0	(REG)
173	MEA	Morocco	0.654	173.0	07(UN)
174	SEA	Tuvalu	0.652	174.0	(REG)
175	AFR	San Tome & Principe	0.651	175.0	07(UN)
176	SEA	Tokelau	0.645	176.0	(REG)
177	CPA	Korea, North	0.623	177.0	(REG)
178	SAS	Bhutan	0.619	178.5	07(UN)
179	CPA	Laos	0.619	178.5	07(UN)
180	SEA	Kiribati	0.615	180.0	(REG)
181	SAS	India	0.612	181.0	07(UN)
182	SEA	Solomon Islands	0.610	182.0	07(UN)

TABLE 1.8 HUMAN DEVELOPMENT INDEX, 2007

OBS	REGION	COUNTRY	HDX	RANK	SOURCE
183	AFR	Congo, Rep.	0.601	183.0	07(UN)
184	CPA	Cambodia	0.593	184.0	07(UN)
185	CPA	Burma	0.586	185.0	07(UN)
186	AFR	Comoros	0.576	186.0	07(UN)
187	MEA	Yemen	0.575	187.0	07(UN)
188	SAS	Pakistan	0.572	188.5	07(UN)
189	AFR	Swaziland	0.572	188.5	07(UN)
190	AFR	Angola	0.564	190.0	07(UN)
191	SAS	Nepal	0.553	191.0	07(UN)
192	SAS	Bangladesh	0.543	192.5	07(UN)
193	AFR	Madagascar	0.543	192.5	07(UN)
194	AFR	Western Sahara	0.543	194.0	(REG)
195	AFR	Kenya	0.541	195.5	07(UN)
196	SEA	Papua New Guinea	0.541	195.5	07(UN)
197	LAM	Haiti	0.532	197.0	07(UN)
198	AFR	Sudan	0.531	198.0	07(UN)
199	AFR	Tanzania	0.530	199.0	07(UN)
200	AFR	Ghana	0.526	200.0	07(UN)
201	AFR	Cameroon	0.523	201.0	07(UN)
202	AFR	Djibouti	0.520	202.5	07(UN)
203	AFR	Mauritania	0.520	202.5	07(UN)
204	AFR	Lesotho	0.514	204.5	07(UN)
205	AFR	Uganda	0.514	204.5	07(UN)
206	AFR	Nigeria	0.511	206.0	07(UN)
207	AFR	Togo	0.499	207.0	07(UN)
208	AFR	Malawi	0.493	208.0	07(UN)
209	AFR	Benin	0.492	209.0	07(UN)
210	SEA	East Timor	0.489	210.0	07(UN)
211	AFR	Ivory Coast	0.484	211.0	07(UN)
212	AFR	Zambia	0.481	212.0	07(UN)
213	AFR	Eritrea	0.472	213.0	07(UN)
214	AFR	Senegal	0.464	214.0	07(UN)
215	AFR	Rwanda	0.460	215.0	07(UN)
216	AFR	Gambia	0.456	216.0	07(UN)
217	AFR	Liberia	0.442	217.0	07(UN)
218	AFR	Guinea	0.435	218.0	07(UN)
219	AFR	Ethiopia	0.414	219.0	07(UN)
220	AFR	Somalia	0.406	220.0	(REG)
221	AFR	Mozambique	0.402	221.0	07(UN)
222	AFR	Guinea-Bissau	0.396	222.0	07(UN)
223	AFR	Burundi	0.394	223.0	07(UN)
224	AFR	Chad	0.392	224.0	07(UN)
225	AFR	Burkina Faso	0.389	225.5	07(UN)
226	AFR	Congo, Dem. Rep.	0.389	225.5	07(UN)
227	AFR	Mali	0.371	227.0	07(UN)
228	AFR	CAR	0.369	228.0	07(UN)

TABLE 1.8 HUMAN DEVELOPMENT INDEX, 2007					
OBS	REGION	COUNTRY	HDX	RANK	SOURCE
229	AFR	Sierra Leone	0.365	229.0	07(UN)
230	SAS	Afghanistan	0.352	230.0	07(UN)
231	AFR	Niger	0.340	231.0	07(UN)
232	AFR	Zimbabwe	0.280	232.0	(REG)

OBS	REGION	COUNTRY	GINI	RANK	SOURCE
	TABLE 1.9 GINI COEFFICIENT OF INCOME INEQUALITY, 2008

OBS	REGION	COUNTRY	GINI	RANK	SOURCE
1	DME	Denmark	24.70	1.0	08(WB)
2	DME	Japan	24.85	2.0	08(WB)
3	DME	Iceland	25.00	3.5	08(GPI)
4	DME	Sweden	25.00	3.5	08(WB)
5	DME	San Marino	25.28	5.0	(REG)
6	DME	Norway	25.79	6.0	08(WB)
7	EEU	Slovakia	25.81	7.0	08(WB)
8	EEU	Czechia	25.82	8.0	08(WB)
9	DME	Malta	26.00	9.0	07(CIA)
10	DME	Finland	26.88	10.0	08(WB)
11	USR	Ukraine	27.56	11.0	08(WB)
12	DME	Liechtenstein	27.94	12.0	(REG)
13	EEU	Serbia	28.18	13.0	08(WB)
14	DME	Germany	28.31	14.0	08(WB)
15	USR	Belarus	28.80	15.0	08(WB)
16	MEA	Cyprus	29.00	16.0	05(CIA)
17	EEU	Croatia	29.03	17.0	08(WB)
18	DME	Austria	29.15	18.0	08(WB)
19	EEU	Bulgaria	29.24	19.0	08(WB)
20	AFR	Ethiopia	29.76	20.0	08(WB)
21	LAM	Cuba	30.00	23.0	08(GPI)
22	EEU	Kosovo	30.00	23.0	06(CIA)
23	MEA	Kuwait	30.00	23.0	08(GPI)
24	EEU	Montenegro	30.00	23.0	03(CIA)
25	AFR	Somalia	30.00	23.0	08(GPI)
26	EEU	Hungary	30.04	26.0	08(WB)
27	USR	Armenia	30.25	27.0	08(WB)
28	LAM	Anguilla	30.74	28.0	(REG)
29	DME	Luxembourg	30.76	29.0	07(WB)
30	DME	Netherlands	30.90	30.0	08(WB)
31	USR	Kazakhstan	30.92	31.0	08(WB)
32	CPA	Korea, North	31.00	32.5	08(GPI)
33	MEA	UAE	31.00	32.5	08(GPI)
34	SAS	Bangladesh	31.02	34.0	08(WB)
35	EEU	Slovenia	31.15	35.0	08(WB)
36	SAS	Pakistan	31.18	36.0	08(WB)
37	SEA	Korea, South	31.59	37.0	08(WB)
38	SEA	Brunei	31.79	38.0	(REG)
39	SEA	East Timor	31.92	39.0	08(WB)
40	MEA	Oman	32.00	40.5	08(GPI)
41	MEA	Saudi Arabia	32.00	40.5	08(GPI)
42	MEA	Egypt	32.14	42.5	08(WB)
43	EEU	Romania	32.14	42.5	08(WB)
44	DME	Andorra	32.20	44.0	(REG)
45	DME	Canada	32.56	45.0	08(WB)
46	SEA	Taiwan	32.60	46.0	02(CIA)
47	CPA	Laos	32.63	47.0	08(WB)

TABLE 1.9 GINI COEFFICIENT OF INCOME INEQUALITY, 2008					
OBS	REGION	COUNTRY	GINI	RANK	SOURCE
48	DME	France	32.74	48.0	08(WB)
49	DME	Belgium	32.97	49.0	08(WB)
50	EEU	Albania	33.03	50.0	08(WB)
51	AFR	Burundi	33.27	51.0	08(WB)
52	USR	Kyrgyzstan	33.47	52.0	08(WB)
53	USR	Tajikistan	33.60	53.0	08(WB)
54	DME	Switzerland	33.68	54.0	08(WB)
55	DME	Falkland Islands	34.16	55.0	(REG)
56	LAM	Montserrat	34.18	56.0	(REG)
57	DME	Guernsey	34.20	57.0	(REG)
58	DME	Greece	34.27	58.0	08(WB)
59	DME	Ireland	34.28	59.0	08(WB)
60	AFR	Togo	34.41	60.0	08(WB)
61	AFR	Tanzania	34.62	61.0	08(WB)
62	DME	Spain	34.66	62.0	08(WB)
63	DME	St. Pierre & Miquelon	34.68	63.0	(REG)
64	SEA	Samoa, American	34.69	64.0	(REG)
65	EEU	Poland	34.92	65.0	08(WB)
66	SEA	Guam	35.08	66.0	(REG)
67	DME	Australia	35.19	67.0	08(WB)
68	DME	Jersey	35.27	68.0	(REG)
69	SEA	Nauru	35.28	69.0	(REG)
70	MEA	Algeria	35.33	70.0	08(WB)
71	AFR	Guinea-Bissau	35.52	71.0	08(WB)
72	DME	Isle of Man	35.67	72.0	(REG)
73	AFR	Eritrea	35.79	73.0	(REG)
74	USR	Lithuania	35.81	74.0	08(WB)
75	SEA	Northern Mariana Is.	35.90	75.0	(REG)
76	DME	United Kingdom	35.97	76.0	08(WB)
77	MEA	Bahrain	36.00	78.0	08(GPI)
78	USR	Estonia	36.00	78.0	08(WB)
79	MEA	Libya	36.00	78.0	08(GPI)
80	DME	Italy	36.03	80.0	08(WB)
81	DME	Monaco	36.09	81.0	(REG)
82	DME	Gibraltar	36.11	82.0	(REG)
83	DME	New Zealand	36.17	83.0	08(WB)
84	EEU	Bosnia	36.26	84.0	08(WB)
85	USR	Latvia	36.29	85.0	08(WB)
86	USR	Azerbaijan	36.50	86.0	08(WB)
87	SEA	Fiji	36.56	87.0	(REG)
88	CPA	Mongolia	36.57	88.0	08(WB)
89	SEA	Niue	36.71	89.0	(REG)
90	USR	Uzbekistan	36.72	90.0	08(WB)
91	SAS	India	36.80	91.0	08(WB)
92	SEA	French Polynesia	36.85	92.0	(REG)

OBS	REGION	COUNTRY	GINI	RANK	SOURCE
		TABLE 1.9 GINI COEFFICIENT OF INCOME INEQUALITY, 2008			
93	SEA	New Caledonia	37.16	93.0	(REG)
94	MEA	West Bank	37.28	94.0	(REG)
95	USR	Moldova	37.35	95.0	08(WB)
96	SAS	Maldives	37.41	96.0	08(WB)
97	LAM	Virgin Islands, US	37.46	97.0	(REG)
98	SEA	Indonesia	37.58	98.0	08(WB)
99	MEA	Yemen	37.69	99.0	08(WB)
100	MEA	Jordan	37.72	100.0	08(WB)
101	CPA	Vietnam	37.77	101.0	08(WB)
102	AFR	Reunion	37.90	102.0	(REG)
103	SEA	Malaysia	37.91	103.0	08(WB)
104	MEA	Gaza Strip	38.10	104.0	(REG)
105	MEA	Iran	38.28	105.0	08(WB)
106	DME	Portugal	38.45	106.0	08(WB)
107	AFR	Seychelles	38.60	107.0	(REG)
108	AFR	Benin	38.62	108.0	08(WB)
109	DME	Faeroe Islands	38.74	109.0	(REG)
110	LAM	Dominica	38.88	110.0	(REG)
111	LAM	Martinique	38.93	111.0	(REG)
112	AFR	Mali	38.99	112.0	08(WB)
113	AFR	Mauritius	39.00	113.5	06(CIA)
114	MEA	Qatar	39.00	113.5	08(GPI)
115	AFR	Malawi	39.02	115.0	08(WB)
116	AFR	Mauritania	39.04	116.0	08(WB)
117	SEA	Tonga	39.19	117.0	(REG)
118	AFR	Senegal	39.19	118.0	08(WB)
119	DME	Israel	39.20	119.0	08(WB)
120	LAM	St. Vincent	39.29	120.0	(REG)
121	LAM	Cayman Islands	39.34	121.0	(REG)
122	AFR	St. Helena	39.37	122.0	(REG)
123	LAM	Neth. Antilles	39.55	123.0	(REG)
124	AFR	Burkina Faso	39.60	124.0	08(WB)
125	LAM	Bahamas	39.67	125.0	(REG)
126	LAM	Guadeloupe	39.69	126.0	(REG)
127	AFR	Chad	39.78	127.0	08(WB)
128	AFR	Djibouti	39.85	128.0	08(WB)
129	CPA	Burma	40.00	129.0	08(GPI)
130	LAM	Trinidad & Tobago	40.27	130.0	08(WB)
131	LAM	Puerto Rico	40.27	131.0	(REG)
132	LAM	Turks & Caicos Is.	40.28	132.0	(REG)
133	SEA	Solomon Islands	40.45	133.0	(REG)
134	SEA	Tuvalu	40.64	134.0	(REG)
135	DME	Bermuda	40.66	135.0	(REG)
136	SEA	Palau	40.69	136.0	(REG)
137	LAM	Antigua & Barbuda	40.71	137.0	(REG)

	TABLE 1.9 GINI COEFFICIENT OF INCOME INEQUALITY, 2008				
OBS	REGION	COUNTRY	GINI	RANK	SOURCE
138	LAM	Guiana, French	40.73	138.0	(REG)
139	USR	Turkmenistan	40.77	139.0	08(WB)
140	USR	Georgia	40.80	140.0	08(WB)
141	MEA	Tunisia	40.81	141.5	08(WB)
142	DME	United States	40.81	141.5	08(WB)
143	MEA	Morocco	40.88	143.0	08(WB)
144	SEA	Wallis & Futuna	41.01	144.0	(REG)
145	SAS	Sri Lanka	41.06	145.0	08(WB)
146	MEA	Turkey	41.15	146.0	08(WB)
147	LAM	Grenada	41.30	147.0	(REG)
148	AFR	Gabon	41.45	148.0	08(WB)
149	SEA	Tokelau	41.51	149.0	(REG)
150	CPA	China	41.53	150.0	08(WB)
151	MEA	Iraq	42.00	151.5	08(GPI)
152	MEA	Syria	42.00	151.5	08(GPI)
153	LAM	Barbados	42.12	153.0	(REG)
154	DME	Greenland	42.14	154.0	(REG)
155	LAM	Aruba	42.24	155.0	(REG)
156	SEA	Thailand	42.45	156.0	08(WB)
157	SEA	Singapore	42.48	157.0	08(WB)
158	AFR	Sierra Leone	42.52	158.0	08(WB)
159	LAM	St. Lucia	42.60	159.0	08(WB)
160	AFR	Uganda	42.62	160.0	08(WB)
161	AFR	Western Sahara	42.73	161.0	(REG)
162	AFR	Ghana	42.76	162.0	08(WB)
163	EEU	Macedonia	42.80	163.0	08(WB)
164	AFR	Nigeria	42.93	164.0	08(WB)
165	LAM	St. Kitts & Nevis	42.97	165.0	(REG)
166	LAM	Guyana	43.20	166.0	08(WB)
167	AFR	Guinea	43.34	167.0	08(WB)
168	SEA	Macao	43.40	168.0	03(WB)
169	SEA	Hong Kong	43.44	169.5	08(WB)
170	LAM	Venezuela	43.44	169.5	08(WB)
171	SEA	Cook Islands	43.51	171.0	(REG)
172	AFR	CAR	43.57	172.0	08(WB)
173	USR	Russia	43.68	173.0	08(WB)
174	SEA	Vanuatu	43.79	174.0	(REG)
175	AFR	Niger	43.89	175.0	08(WB)
176	SEA	Philippines	44.04	176.0	08(WB)
177	LAM	Virgin Islands, Brit.	44.07	177.0	(REG)
178	SEA	Samoa, Western	44.12	178.0	(REG)
179	CPA	Cambodia	44.20	179.0	08(WB)
180	AFR	Congo, Dem. Rep.	44.43	180.0	08(WB)
181	AFR	Cameroon	44.56	181.0	08(WB)
182	MEA	Lebanon	45.00	182.0	08(GPI)
183	SEA	Marshall Islands	45.41	183.0	(REG)

OBS	REGION	COUNTRY	GINI	RANK	SOURCE
\multicolumn{6}{c}{TABLE 1.9 GINI COEFFICIENT OF INCOME INEQUALITY, 2008}
184	LAM	Jamaica	45.51	184.0	08(WB)
185	SEA	Kiribati	45.90	185.0	(REG)
186	SEA	Micronesia	45.91	186.0	(REG)
187	AFR	Rwanda	46.68	187.0	08(WB)
188	SAS	Bhutan	46.74	188.0	08(WB)
189	LAM	El Salvador	46.85	189.0	08(WB)
190	LAM	Uruguay	47.06	190.0	08(WB)
191	AFR	Mozambique	47.11	191.0	08(WB)
192	AFR	Madagascar	47.24	192.0	08(WB)
193	AFR	Gambia	47.28	193.0	08(WB)
194	SAS	Nepal	47.30	194.0	08(WB)
195	AFR	Congo, Rep.	47.32	195.0	08(WB)
196	AFR	Kenya	47.68	196.0	08(WB)
197	LAM	Dominican Rep.	48.35	197.0	08(WB)
198	AFR	Ivory Coast	48.39	198.0	08(WB)
199	LAM	Argentina	48.81	199.0	08(WB)
200	LAM	Costa Rica	48.91	200.0	08(WB)
201	LAM	Belize	49.20	201.0	08(GPI)
202	AFR	Zimbabwe	50.10	202.0	08(WB)
203	AFR	Cape Verde	50.40	203.0	08(WB)
204	LAM	Peru	50.52	204.0	08(WB)
205	AFR	San Tome & Principe	50.60	205.0	08(WB)
206	AFR	Swaziland	50.68	206.0	08(WB)
207	AFR	Zambia	50.74	207.0	08(WB)
208	AFR	Mayotte	50.75	208.0	(REG)
209	SEA	Papua New Guinea	50.88	209.0	08(WB)
210	AFR	Sudan	51.00	210.0	08(GPI)
211	LAM	Mexico	51.61	211.0	08(WB)
212	LAM	Chile	52.00	212.0	08(WB)
213	LAM	Nicaragua	52.33	213.0	08(WB)
214	AFR	Lesotho	52.50	214.0	08(WB)
215	AFR	Liberia	52.56	215.0	08(WB)
216	LAM	Suriname	52.81	216.0	08(WB)
217	LAM	Paraguay	53.24	217.0	08(WB)
218	LAM	Guatemala	53.69	218.0	08(WB)
219	LAM	Ecuador	54.37	219.0	08(WB)
220	LAM	Panama	54.93	220.0	08(WB)
221	LAM	Brazil	55.02	221.0	08(WB)
222	LAM	Honduras	55.31	222.0	08(WB)
223	LAM	Bolivia	57.19	223.0	08(WB)
224	AFR	South Africa	57.77	224.0	08(WB)
225	LAM	Colombia	58.49	225.0	08(WB)
226	AFR	Angola	58.64	226.0	08(WB)
227	LAM	Haiti	59.50	227.0	08(WB)
228	SAS	Afghanistan	60.00	228.0	08(GPI)

TABLE 1.9 GINI COEFFICIENT OF INCOME INEQUALITY, 2008					
OBS	REGION	COUNTRY	GINI	RANK	SOURCE
229	AFR	Botswana	60.96	229.0	08(WB)
230	AFR	Comoros	64.34	230.0	08(WB)
231	AFR	Equatorial Guinea	65.00	231.0	08(GPI)
232	AFR	Namibia	74.33	232.0	08(WB)

TABLE 1.10 HUMAN RIGHTS INDEX, PRINCIPAL COMPONENT 1 OF THE POLITICAL QUALITY-OF-LIFE INDICATORS, 2008

OBS	REGION	COUNTRY	PQLX	RANK	SOURCE
1	DME	Denmark	1.83075	1	PRIN1(PQL)
2	DME	Norway	1.80219	2	PRIN1(PQL)
3	DME	San Marino	1.79655	3	PRIN1(PQL)
4	DME	Sweden	1.78167	4	PRIN1(PQL)
5	DME	Finland	1.76819	5	PRIN1(PQL)
6	DME	Iceland	1.75734	6	PRIN1(PQL)
7	DME	Netherlands	1.67679	7	PRIN1(PQL)
8	DME	Belgium	1.65128	8	PRIN1(PQL)
9	DME	Austria	1.64794	9	PRIN1(PQL)
10	EEU	Slovakia	1.59362	10	PRIN1(PQL)
11	DME	Germany	1.59059	11	PRIN1(PQL)
12	DME	Luxembourg	1.58109	12	PRIN1(PQL)
13	DME	Switzerland	1.56026	13	PRIN1(PQL)
14	EEU	Slovenia	1.53524	14	PRIN1(PQL)
15	MEA	Cyprus	1.52827	15	PRIN1(PQL)
16	EEU	Czechia	1.52069	16	PRIN1(PQL)
17	DME	Liechtenstein	1.48369	17	PRIN1(PQL)
18	DME	Canada	1.48144	18	PRIN1(PQL)
19	DME	Japan	1.43156	19	PRIN1(PQL)
20	DME	Ireland	1.41206	20	PRIN1(PQL)
21	DME	France	1.34732	21	PRIN1(PQL)
22	DME	New Zealand	1.31648	22	PRIN1(PQL)
23	USR	Lithuania	1.31611	23	PRIN1(PQL)
24	DME	Malta	1.31550	24	PRIN1(PQL)
25	DME	Israel	1.30144	25	PRIN1(PQL)
26	DME	Andorra	1.27951	26	PRIN1(PQL)
27	USR	Estonia	1.27828	27	PRIN1(PQL)
28	DME	Australia	1.27195	28	PRIN1(PQL)
29	EEU	Hungary	1.27194	29	PRIN1(PQL)
30	DME	Spain	1.26982	30	PRIN1(PQL)
31	DME	Faeroe Islands	1.24140	31	PRIN1(PQL)
32	DME	United Kingdom	1.23455	32	PRIN1(PQL)
33	DME	Italy	1.21286	33	PRIN1(PQL)
34	SEA	Korea, South	1.20672	34	PRIN1(PQL)
35	DME	Greece	1.18053	35	PRIN1(PQL)
36	USR	Latvia	1.17584	36	PRIN1(PQL)
37	EEU	Poland	1.16270	37	PRIN1(PQL)
38	EEU	Bulgaria	1.15196	38	PRIN1(PQL)
39	AFR	Reunion	1.12276	39	PRIN1(PQL)
40	EEU	Croatia	1.09864	40	PRIN1(PQL)
41	DME	Portugal	1.08905	41	PRIN1(PQL)
42	LAM	Neth. Antilles	1.06922	42	PRIN1(PQL)
43	SEA	New Caledonia	1.01412	43	PRIN1(PQL)
44	LAM	Martinique	1.00571	44	PRIN1(PQL)
45	DME	United States	0.99364	45	PRIN1(PQL)
46	DME	Gibraltar	0.98262	46	PRIN1(PQL)

OBS	REGION	COUNTRY	PQLX	RANK	SOURCE
		TABLE 1.10 HUMAN RIGHTS INDEX, PRINCIPAL COMPONENT 1 OF THE POLITICAL QUALITY-OF-LIFE INDICATORS, 2008			
47	EEU	Romania	0.97854	47	PRIN1(PQL)
48	EEU	Serbia	0.97853	48	PRIN1(PQL)
49	LAM	Anguilla	0.97224	49	PRIN1(PQL)
50	SEA	Taiwan	0.96913	50	PRIN1(PQL)
51	DME	Monaco	0.95226	51	PRIN1(PQL)
52	USR	Ukraine	0.87706	52	PRIN1(PQL)
53	LAM	Chile	0.83844	53	PRIN1(PQL)
54	LAM	Guadeloupe	0.81801	54	PRIN1(PQL)
55	LAM	Bahamas	0.79453	55	PRIN1(PQL)
56	LAM	Barbados	0.78309	56	PRIN1(PQL)
57	LAM	Cayman Islands	0.77761	57	PRIN1(PQL)
58	EEU	Montenegro	0.77233	58	PRIN1(PQL)
59	LAM	Dominica	0.75323	59	PRIN1(PQL)
60	MEA	Kuwait	0.74912	60	PRIN1(PQL)
61	LAM	Puerto Rico	0.74550	61	PRIN1(PQL)
62	LAM	Costa Rica	0.74422	62	PRIN1(PQL)
63	LAM	Virgin Islands, US	0.73677	63	PRIN1(PQL)
64	LAM	Montserrat	0.72415	64	PRIN1(PQL)
65	LAM	St. Kitts & Nevis	0.71294	65	PRIN1(PQL)
66	SEA	French Polynesia	0.70754	66	PRIN1(PQL)
67	SEA	Northern Mariana Is.	0.70480	67	PRIN1(PQL)
68	SEA	Hong Kong	0.70458	68	PRIN1(PQL)
69	LAM	Uruguay	0.69877	69	PRIN1(PQL)
70	DME	Bermuda	0.68956	70	PRIN1(PQL)
71	EEU	Albania	0.66407	71	PRIN1(PQL)
72	DME	Greenland	0.64326	72	PRIN1(PQL)
73	LAM	Argentina	0.61389	73	PRIN1(PQL)
74	SEA	Indonesia	0.59451	74	PRIN1(PQL)
75	LAM	St. Lucia	0.58376	75	PRIN1(PQL)
76	EEU	Bosnia	0.57481	76	PRIN1(PQL)
77	SEA	Macao	0.55612	77	PRIN1(PQL)
78	SEA	Guam	0.48904	78	PRIN1(PQL)
79	AFR	Mauritius	0.47350	79	PRIN1(PQL)
80	SEA	Vanuatu	0.45941	80	PRIN1(PQL)
81	LAM	Trinidad & Tobago	0.45478	81	PRIN1(PQL)
82	LAM	Brazil	0.44053	82	PRIN1(PQL)
83	LAM	Grenada	0.40729	83	PRIN1(PQL)
84	LAM	Aruba	0.40306	84	PRIN1(PQL)
85	LAM	Antigua & Barbuda	0.40103	85	PRIN1(PQL)
86	LAM	Panama	0.38577	86	PRIN1(PQL)
87	CPA	Mongolia	0.35938	87	PRIN1(PQL)
88	LAM	Guiana, French	0.33906	88	PRIN1(PQL)
89	DME	Isle of Man	0.33601	89	PRIN1(PQL)

TABLE 1.10 HUMAN RIGHTS INDEX, PRINCIPAL COMPONENT 1 OF THE
POLITICAL QUALITY-OF-LIFE INDICATORS, 2008

OBS	REGION	COUNTRY	PQLX	RANK	SOURCE
90	LAM	Mexico	0.32647	90	PRIN1(PQL)
91	SAS	India	0.31201	91	PRIN1(PQL)
92	LAM	St. Vincent	0.28749	92	PRIN1(PQL)
93	EEU	Macedonia	0.28704	93	PRIN1(PQL)
94	LAM	Peru	0.25905	94	PRIN1(PQL)
95	AFR	Seychelles	0.24966	95	PRIN1(PQL)
96	MEA	Bahrain	0.24830	96	PRIN1(PQL)
97	SEA	Kiribati	0.21544	97	PRIN1(PQL)
98	MEA	Turkey	0.21118	98	PRIN1(PQL)
99	LAM	Dominican Rep.	0.20166	99	PRIN1(PQL)
100	USR	Armenia	0.18795	100	PRIN1(PQL)
101	LAM	Suriname	0.17088	101	PRIN1(PQL)
102	SEA	Samoa, Western	0.15650	102	PRIN1(PQL)
103	DME	St. Pierre & Miquelon	0.15650	103	PRIN1(PQL)
104	LAM	El Salvador	0.15218	104	PRIN1(PQL)
105	AFR	Cape Verde	0.14312	105	PRIN1(PQL)
106	LAM	Virgin Islands, Brit.	0.14132	106	PRIN1(PQL)
107	SAS	Sri Lanka	0.12962	107	PRIN1(PQL)
108	LAM	Ecuador	0.12552	108	PRIN1(PQL)
109	SEA	Philippines	0.12206	109	PRIN1(PQL)
110	DME	Guernsey	0.11095	110	PRIN1(PQL)
111	LAM	Guyana	0.10485	111	PRIN1(PQL)
112	DME	Jersey	0.08285	112	PRIN1(PQL)
113	MEA	Lebanon	0.06616	113	PRIN1(PQL)
114	DME	Falkland Islands	0.05837	114	PRIN1(PQL)
115	LAM	Jamaica	0.04118	115	PRIN1(PQL)
116	SEA	Tonga	0.02902	116	PRIN1(PQL)
117	SEA	Malaysia	0.01818	117	PRIN1(PQL)
118	SEA	Palau	0.00114	118	PRIN1(PQL)
119	LAM	Belize	-0.01210	119	PRIN1(PQL)
120	SEA	Nauru	-0.04819	120	PRIN1(PQL)
121	AFR	Benin	-0.06786	121	PRIN1(PQL)
122	LAM	Venezuela	-0.07072	122	PRIN1(PQL)
123	SEA	Cook Islands	-0.07506	123	PRIN1(PQL)
124	MEA	Algeria	-0.07722	124	PRIN1(PQL)
125	AFR	San Tome & Principe	-0.08352	125	PRIN1(PQL)
126	LAM	Paraguay	-0.08373	126	PRIN1(PQL)
127	USR	Moldova	-0.11666	127	PRIN1(PQL)
128	SEA	Wallis & Futuna	-0.11975	128	PRIN1(PQL)
129	LAM	Colombia	-0.13597	129	PRIN1(PQL)
130	MEA	Morocco	-0.14933	130	PRIN1(PQL)
131	SEA	Thailand	-0.15563	131	PRIN1(PQL)
132	SEA	East Timor	-0.16850	132	PRIN1(PQL)

TABLE 1.10 HUMAN RIGHTS INDEX, PRINCIPAL COMPONENT 1 OF THE POLITICAL QUALITY-OF-LIFE INDICATORS, 2008

OBS	REGION	COUNTRY	PQLX	RANK	SOURCE
133	AFR	Ghana	-0.16883	133	PRIN1(PQL)
134	EEU	Kosovo	-0.18667	134	PRIN1(PQL)
135	SAS	Pakistan	-0.20355	135	PRIN1(PQL)
136	LAM	Turks & Caicos Is.	-0.22090	136	PRIN1(PQL)
137	AFR	Mayotte	-0.22643	137	PRIN1(PQL)
138	LAM	Guatemala	-0.25119	138	PRIN1(PQL)
139	SEA	Tuvalu	-0.27905	139	PRIN1(PQL)
140	SEA	Solomon Islands	-0.29908	140	PRIN1(PQL)
141	SEA	Fiji	-0.30553	141	PRIN1(PQL)
142	USR	Georgia	-0.32483	142	PRIN1(PQL)
143	SEA	Marshall Islands	-0.34705	143	PRIN1(PQL)
144	LAM	Nicaragua	-0.34841	144	PRIN1(PQL)
145	LAM	Honduras	-0.35850	145	PRIN1(PQL)
146	SEA	Micronesia	-0.38561	146	PRIN1(PQL)
147	USR	Kyrgyzstan	-0.38616	147	PRIN1(PQL)
148	AFR	Mali	-0.38761	148	PRIN1(PQL)
149	AFR	South Africa	-0.40432	149	PRIN1(PQL)
150	SEA	Singapore	-0.42625	150	PRIN1(PQL)
151	LAM	Bolivia	-0.43059	151	PRIN1(PQL)
152	SEA	Samoa, American	-0.43607	152	PRIN1(PQL)
153	AFR	Gabon	-0.45055	153	PRIN1(PQL)
154	MEA	Iran	-0.46288	154	PRIN1(PQL)
155	SEA	Brunei	-0.46731	155	PRIN1(PQL)
156	MEA	UAE	-0.48524	156	PRIN1(PQL)
157	USR	Russia	-0.53210	157	PRIN1(PQL)
158	AFR	Malawi	-0.54355	158	PRIN1(PQL)
159	SAS	Bangladesh	-0.55502	159	PRIN1(PQL)
160	SEA	Papua New Guinea	-0.56549	160	PRIN1(PQL)
161	AFR	Lesotho	-0.56785	161	PRIN1(PQL)
162	USR	Azerbaijan	-0.58102	162	PRIN1(PQL)
163	AFR	Kenya	-0.59210	163	PRIN1(PQL)
164	SAS	Nepal	-0.59459	164	PRIN1(PQL)
165	AFR	Botswana	-0.61581	165	PRIN1(PQL)
166	SAS	Maldives	-0.62719	166	PRIN1(PQL)
167	MEA	Iraq	-0.63087	167	PRIN1(PQL)
168	MEA	Oman	-0.65287	168	PRIN1(PQL)
169	USR	Uzbekistan	-0.69160	169	PRIN1(PQL)
170	MEA	Qatar	-0.70302	170	PRIN1(PQL)
171	USR	Tajikistan	-0.71409	171	PRIN1(PQL)
172	USR	Kazakhstan	-0.72307	172	PRIN1(PQL)
173	AFR	Zambia	-0.76283	173	PRIN1(PQL)
174	AFR	Mauritania	-0.76325	174	PRIN1(PQL)
175	AFR	Tanzania	-0.76337	175	PRIN1(PQL)
176	MEA	Jordan	-0.76800	176	PRIN1(PQL)
177	LAM	Cuba	-0.79720	177	PRIN1(PQL)

TABLE 1.10 HUMAN RIGHTS INDEX, PRINCIPAL COMPONENT 1 OF THE
POLITICAL QUALITY-OF-LIFE INDICATORS, 2008

OBS	REGION	COUNTRY	PQLX	RANK	SOURCE
178	AFR	Liberia	-0.82358	178	PRIN1(PQL)
179	AFR	St. Helena	-0.82758	179	PRIN1(PQL)
180	MEA	Tunisia	-0.83843	180	PRIN1(PQL)
181	USR	Belarus	-0.85175	181	PRIN1(PQL)
182	AFR	Ethiopia	-0.85409	182	PRIN1(PQL)
183	SEA	Niue	-0.85942	183	PRIN1(PQL)
184	AFR	Togo	-0.87991	184	PRIN1(PQL)
185	AFR	Sierra Leone	-0.88567	185	PRIN1(PQL)
186	MEA	Saudi Arabia	-0.90441	186	PRIN1(PQL)
187	MEA	Yemen	-0.91039	187	PRIN1(PQL)
188	AFR	Burundi	-0.92176	188	PRIN1(PQL)
189	AFR	Niger	-0.92547	189	PRIN1(PQL)
190	AFR	Senegal	-0.93334	190	PRIN1(PQL)
191	AFR	Guinea-Bissau	-0.95580	191	PRIN1(PQL)
192	MEA	Egypt	-0.95819	192	PRIN1(PQL)
193	AFR	Uganda	-0.97172	193	PRIN1(PQL)
194	AFR	Namibia	-0.97717	194	PRIN1(PQL)
195	AFR	Nigeria	-0.97953	195	PRIN1(PQL)
196	AFR	Burkina Faso	-1.00968	196	PRIN1(PQL)
197	LAM	Haiti	-1.03084	197	PRIN1(PQL)
198	AFR	Congo, Rep.	-1.03733	198	PRIN1(PQL)
199	AFR	Mozambique	-1.04913	199	PRIN1(PQL)
200	MEA	West Bank	-1.07236	200	PRIN1(PQL)
201	MEA	Libya	-1.13422	201	PRIN1(PQL)
202	CPA	Cambodia	-1.15783	202	PRIN1(PQL)
203	AFR	CAR	-1.18025	203	PRIN1(PQL)
204	MEA	Gaza Strip	-1.21838	204	PRIN1(PQL)
205	CPA	Vietnam	-1.23788	205	PRIN1(PQL)
206	AFR	Comoros	-1.27297	206	PRIN1(PQL)
207	SAS	Bhutan	-1.30105	207	PRIN1(PQL)
208	AFR	Ivory Coast	-1.31385	208	PRIN1(PQL)
209	AFR	Madagascar	-1.32926	209	PRIN1(PQL)
210	SEA	Tokelau	-1.33663	210	PRIN1(PQL)
211	AFR	Rwanda	-1.35093	211	PRIN1(PQL)
212	AFR	Congo, Dem. Rep.	-1.35120	212	PRIN1(PQL)
213	CPA	China	-1.35632	213	PRIN1(PQL)
214	CPA	Laos	-1.42824	214	PRIN1(PQL)
215	MEA	Syria	-1.44290	215	PRIN1(PQL)
216	CPA	Korea, North	-1.53175	216	PRIN1(PQL)
217	USR	Turkmenistan	-1.53621	217	PRIN1(PQL)
218	AFR	Djibouti	-1.55201	218	PRIN1(PQL)
219	AFR	Gambia	-1.57221	219	PRIN1(PQL)
220	AFR	Cameroon	-1.64441	220	PRIN1(PQL)
221	AFR	Guinea	-1.65114	221	PRIN1(PQL)
222	AFR	Chad	-1.69236	222	PRIN1(PQL)
223	AFR	Angola	-1.85193	223	PRIN1(PQL)

TABLE 1.10 HUMAN RIGHTS INDEX, PRINCIPAL COMPONENT 1 OF THE POLITICAL QUALITY-OF-LIFE INDICATORS, 2008					
OBS	REGION	COUNTRY	PQLX	RANK	SOURCE
224	CPA	Burma	-1.88481	224	PRIN1(PQL)
225	AFR	Eritrea	-1.91566	225	PRIN1(PQL)
226	AFR	Western Sahara	-1.94721	226	PRIN1(PQL)
227	AFR	Swaziland	-1.98792	227	PRIN1(PQL)
228	AFR	Somalia	-2.02833	228	PRIN1(PQL)
229	AFR	Equatorial Guinea	-2.07527	229	PRIN1(PQL)
230	AFR	Zimbabwe	-2.22481	230	PRIN1(PQL)
231	AFR	Sudan	-2.31051	231	PRIN1(PQL)
232	SAS	Afghanistan	-2.67303	232	PRIN1(PQL)

TABLE 1.11 ECONOMICO-POLITICAL QUALITY-OF-LIFE INDEX, PRINCIPAL COMPONENT 1 OF THE ECONOMIC AND POLITICAL QUALITY-OF-LIFE INDICATORS, 2008

OBS	REGION	COUNTRY	EPQLX	RANK	SOURCE
1	DME	Liechtenstein	1.99345	1	PRIN1(EPQL)
2	DME	San Marino	1.86675	2	PRIN1(EPQL)
3	DME	Luxembourg	1.75223	3	PRIN1(EPQL)
4	DME	Monaco	1.73627	4	PRIN1(EPQL)
5	DME	Norway	1.72980	5	PRIN1(EPQL)
6	DME	Iceland	1.69464	6	PRIN1(EPQL)
7	DME	Sweden	1.67191	7	PRIN1(EPQL)
8	DME	Andorra	1.65998	8	PRIN1(EPQL)
9	DME	Japan	1.63411	9	PRIN1(EPQL)
10	DME	Switzerland	1.59001	10	PRIN1(EPQL)
11	DME	Finland	1.54211	11	PRIN1(EPQL)
12	DME	Austria	1.50456	12	PRIN1(EPQL)
13	DME	Denmark	1.49376	13	PRIN1(EPQL)
14	DME	Netherlands	1.49250	14	PRIN1(EPQL)
15	DME	France	1.47811	15	PRIN1(EPQL)
16	DME	Ireland	1.46295	16	PRIN1(EPQL)
17	DME	Germany	1.44617	17	PRIN1(EPQL)
18	DME	Italy	1.42208	18	PRIN1(EPQL)
19	DME	Belgium	1.42059	19	PRIN1(EPQL)
20	DME	Canada	1.38885	20	PRIN1(EPQL)
21	DME	Australia	1.38564	21	PRIN1(EPQL)
22	DME	Spain	1.37526	22	PRIN1(EPQL)
23	MEA	Cyprus	1.30372	23	PRIN1(EPQL)
24	EEU	Slovenia	1.30000	24	PRIN1(EPQL)
25	SEA	Hong Kong	1.29814	25	PRIN1(EPQL)
26	DME	United Kingdom	1.29450	26	PRIN1(EPQL)
27	DME	Greece	1.27038	27	PRIN1(EPQL)
28	DME	Israel	1.26148	28	PRIN1(EPQL)
29	DME	Gibraltar	1.24394	29	PRIN1(EPQL)
30	DME	Bermuda	1.24070	30	PRIN1(EPQL)
31	DME	New Zealand	1.22776	31	PRIN1(EPQL)
32	SEA	Macao	1.22259	32	PRIN1(EPQL)
33	DME	Faeroe Islands	1.21528	33	PRIN1(EPQL)
34	DME	Guernsey	1.20866	34	PRIN1(EPQL)
35	LAM	Cayman Islands	1.19507	35	PRIN1(EPQL)
36	DME	Jersey	1.18660	36	PRIN1(EPQL)
37	EEU	Czechia	1.18510	37	PRIN1(EPQL)
38	SEA	Korea, South	1.18491	38	PRIN1(EPQL)
39	DME	United States	1.16395	39	PRIN1(EPQL)
40	DME	Malta	1.14775	40	PRIN1(EPQL)
41	DME	Portugal	1.14086	41	PRIN1(EPQL)
42	SEA	Singapore	1.08026	42	PRIN1(EPQL)
43	DME	Falkland Islands	1.06647	43	PRIN1(EPQL)
44	LAM	Martinique	1.04929	44	PRIN1(EPQL)

TABLE 1.11 ECONOMICO-POLITICAL QUALITY-OF-LIFE INDEX, PRINCIPAL COMPONENT 1 OF THE ECONOMIC AND POLITICAL QUALITY-OF-LIFE INDICATORS, 2008

OBS	REGION	COUNTRY	EPQLX	RANK	SOURCE
45	DME	Isle of Man	1.04684	45	PRIN1(EPQL)
46	SEA	Taiwan	1.02343	46	PRIN1(EPQL)
47	MEA	Kuwait	1.01607	47	PRIN1(EPQL)
48	AFR	Reunion	0.96678	48	PRIN1(EPQL)
49	EEU	Slovakia	0.95588	49	PRIN1(EPQL)
50	LAM	Guadeloupe	0.92288	50	PRIN1(EPQL)
51	LAM	Anguilla	0.91600	51	PRIN1(EPQL)
52	LAM	Virgin Islands, US	0.89906	52	PRIN1(EPQL)
53	USR	Estonia	0.87785	53	PRIN1(EPQL)
54	EEU	Croatia	0.87029	54	PRIN1(EPQL)
55	SEA	New Caledonia	0.86758	55	PRIN1(EPQL)
56	EEU	Hungary	0.86061	56	PRIN1(EPQL)
57	SEA	Brunei	0.81979	57	PRIN1(EPQL)
58	EEU	Poland	0.81882	58	PRIN1(EPQL)
59	MEA	UAE	0.80850	59	PRIN1(EPQL)
60	MEA	Qatar	0.80458	60	PRIN1(EPQL)
61	LAM	Puerto Rico	0.78786	61	PRIN1(EPQL)
62	LAM	Neth. Antilles	0.74259	62	PRIN1(EPQL)
63	USR	Lithuania	0.74062	63	PRIN1(EPQL)
64	LAM	Bahamas	0.72639	64	PRIN1(EPQL)
65	LAM	Virgin Islands, Brit.	0.72225	65	PRIN1(EPQL)
66	SEA	Northern Mariana Is.	0.71704	66	PRIN1(EPQL)
67	SEA	Guam	0.71368	67	PRIN1(EPQL)
68	LAM	Barbados	0.70182	68	PRIN1(EPQL)
69	SEA	French Polynesia	0.68853	69	PRIN1(EPQL)
70	LAM	Chile	0.66476	70	PRIN1(EPQL)
71	USR	Latvia	0.65215	71	PRIN1(EPQL)
72	MEA	Bahrain	0.60964	72	PRIN1(EPQL)
73	LAM	Guiana, French	0.57199	73	PRIN1(EPQL)
74	LAM	Aruba	0.55940	74	PRIN1(EPQL)
75	EEU	Serbia	0.55203	75	PRIN1(EPQL)
76	EEU	Bulgaria	0.53907	76	PRIN1(EPQL)
77	DME	Greenland	0.53810	77	PRIN1(EPQL)
78	LAM	Costa Rica	0.53694	78	PRIN1(EPQL)
79	EEU	Montenegro	0.53650	79	PRIN1(EPQL)
80	EEU	Romania	0.50609	80	PRIN1(EPQL)
81	DME	St. Pierre & Miquelon	0.50103	81	PRIN1(EPQL)
82	LAM	Antigua & Barbuda	0.49583	82	PRIN1(EPQL)
83	LAM	Uruguay	0.47072	83	PRIN1(EPQL)

TABLE 1.11 ECONOMICO-POLITICAL QUALITY-OF-LIFE INDEX, PRINCIPAL COMPONENT 1 OF THE ECONOMIC AND POLITICAL QUALITY-OF-LIFE INDICATORS, 2008

OBS	REGION	COUNTRY	EPQLX	RANK	SOURCE
84	LAM	St. Kitts & Nevis	0.44278	84	PRIN1(EPQL)
85	AFR	Seychelles	0.42667	85	PRIN1(EPQL)
86	LAM	Dominica	0.40452	86	PRIN1(EPQL)
87	LAM	Montserrat	0.39508	87	PRIN1(EPQL)
88	MEA	Oman	0.39487	88	PRIN1(EPQL)
89	SEA	Malaysia	0.38289	89	PRIN1(EPQL)
90	LAM	Argentina	0.36359	90	PRIN1(EPQL)
91	LAM	Cuba	0.33602	91	PRIN1(EPQL)
92	EEU	Albania	0.32080	92	PRIN1(EPQL)
93	LAM	St. Lucia	0.31128	93	PRIN1(EPQL)
94	LAM	Mexico	0.30197	94	PRIN1(EPQL)
95	LAM	Trinidad & Tobago	0.28989	95	PRIN1(EPQL)
96	LAM	Grenada	0.28318	96	PRIN1(EPQL)
97	LAM	Turks & Caicos Is.	0.27873	97	PRIN1(EPQL)
98	SEA	Samoa, American	0.26408	98	PRIN1(EPQL)
99	AFR	Mauritius	0.25658	99	PRIN1(EPQL)
100	EEU	Bosnia	0.25128	100	PRIN1(EPQL)
101	LAM	Panama	0.21275	101	PRIN1(EPQL)
102	EEU	Macedonia	0.20730	102	PRIN1(EPQL)
103	MEA	Saudi Arabia	0.18782	103	PRIN1(EPQL)
104	LAM	Venezuela	0.17913	104	PRIN1(EPQL)
105	LAM	St. Vincent	0.17793	105	PRIN1(EPQL)
106	MEA	Turkey	0.17668	106	PRIN1(EPQL)
107	USR	Ukraine	0.16160	107	PRIN1(EPQL)
108	SEA	Palau	0.15056	108	PRIN1(EPQL)
109	LAM	Brazil	0.10833	109	PRIN1(EPQL)
110	MEA	Lebanon	0.10270	110	PRIN1(EPQL)
111	MEA	Libya	0.06137	111	PRIN1(EPQL)
112	LAM	Belize	0.05267	112	PRIN1(EPQL)
113	USR	Russia	0.01757	113	PRIN1(EPQL)
114	USR	Belarus	0.00449	114	PRIN1(EPQL)
115	SEA	Cook Islands	0.00388	115	PRIN1(EPQL)
116	LAM	Peru	-0.01251	116	PRIN1(EPQL)
117	USR	Armenia	-0.01540	117	PRIN1(EPQL)
118	LAM	Ecuador	-0.03943	118	PRIN1(EPQL)
119	LAM	Dominican Rep.	-0.05678	119	PRIN1(EPQL)
120	LAM	El Salvador	-0.07779	120	PRIN1(EPQL)
121	SEA	Nauru	-0.08808	121	PRIN1(EPQL)
122	LAM	Jamaica	-0.08856	122	PRIN1(EPQL)
123	LAM	Colombia	-0.08950	123	PRIN1(EPQL)
124	SAS	Sri Lanka	-0.11515	124	PRIN1(EPQL)

TABLE 1.11 ECONOMICO-POLITICAL QUALITY-OF-LIFE INDEX, PRINCIPAL COMPONENT 1 OF THE ECONOMIC AND POLITICAL QUALITY-OF-LIFE INDICATORS, 2008

OBS	REGION	COUNTRY	EPQLX	RANK	SOURCE
125	SEA	Wallis & Futuna	-0.12060	125	PRIN1(EPQL)
126	SEA	Thailand	-0.14062	126	PRIN1(EPQL)
127	LAM	Suriname	-0.14661	127	PRIN1(EPQL)
128	SEA	Samoa, Western	-0.15370	128	PRIN1(EPQL)
129	SEA	Tonga	-0.18385	129	PRIN1(EPQL)
130	MEA	Algeria	-0.18719	130	PRIN1(EPQL)
131	AFR	St. Helena	-0.19541	131	PRIN1(EPQL)
132	MEA	Iran	-0.19819	132	PRIN1(EPQL)
133	USR	Kazakhstan	-0.19830	133	PRIN1(EPQL)
134	SEA	Indonesia	-0.21377	134	PRIN1(EPQL)
135	MEA	Tunisia	-0.21392	135	PRIN1(EPQL)
136	MEA	Jordan	-0.23101	136	PRIN1(EPQL)
137	SEA	Fiji	-0.24196	137	PRIN1(EPQL)
138	SAS	Maldives	-0.24413	138	PRIN1(EPQL)
139	SEA	Vanuatu	-0.26227	139	PRIN1(EPQL)
140	AFR	Cape Verde	-0.26296	140	PRIN1(EPQL)
141	USR	Azerbaijan	-0.26926	141	PRIN1(EPQL)
142	USR	Georgia	-0.29246	142	PRIN1(EPQL)
143	AFR	Mayotte	-0.29838	143	PRIN1(EPQL)
144	SEA	Niue	-0.30339	144	PRIN1(EPQL)
145	SEA	Philippines	-0.31793	145	PRIN1(EPQL)
146	LAM	Paraguay	-0.31996	146	PRIN1(EPQL)
147	CPA	Mongolia	-0.35193	147	PRIN1(EPQL)
148	USR	Moldova	-0.37371	148	PRIN1(EPQL)
149	SEA	Tuvalu	-0.37650	149	PRIN1(EPQL)
150	CPA	China	-0.38199	150	PRIN1(EPQL)
151	AFR	Gabon	-0.38980	151	PRIN1(EPQL)
152	SEA	Marshall Islands	-0.39554	152	PRIN1(EPQL)
153	MEA	Morocco	-0.41925	153	PRIN1(EPQL)
154	MEA	Egypt	-0.42582	154	PRIN1(EPQL)
155	MEA	Syria	-0.43578	155	PRIN1(EPQL)
156	LAM	Guatemala	-0.43836	156	PRIN1(EPQL)
157	LAM	Honduras	-0.44423	157	PRIN1(EPQL)
158	AFR	Botswana	-0.45782	158	PRIN1(EPQL)
159	MEA	West Bank	-0.47225	159	PRIN1(EPQL)
160	EEU	Kosovo	-0.48592	160	PRIN1(EPQL)
161	SEA	Micronesia	-0.48878	161	PRIN1(EPQL)
162	CPA	Vietnam	-0.49750	162	PRIN1(EPQL)
163	LAM	Nicaragua	-0.53144	163	PRIN1(EPQL)
164	LAM	Guyana	-0.55763	164	PRIN1(EPQL)
165	MEA	Gaza Strip	-0.56951	165	PRIN1(EPQL)
166	AFR	South Africa	-0.58869	166	PRIN1(EPQL)
167	SEA	Kiribati	-0.58950	167	PRIN1(EPQL)
168	MEA	Iraq	-0.61042	168	PRIN1(EPQL)

TABLE 1.11 ECONOMICO-POLITICAL QUALITY-OF-LIFE INDEX, PRINCIPAL COMPONENT 1 OF THE ECONOMIC AND POLITICAL QUALITY-OF-LIFE INDICATORS, 2008

OBS	REGION	COUNTRY	EPQLX	RANK	SOURCE
169	SAS	India	-0.64675	169	PRIN1(EPQL)
170	SEA	Solomon Islands	-0.66948	170	PRIN1(EPQL)
171	USR	Kyrgyzstan	-0.67109	171	PRIN1(EPQL)
172	LAM	Bolivia	-0.69129	172	PRIN1(EPQL)
173	AFR	Namibia	-0.71571	173	PRIN1(EPQL)
174	USR	Turkmenistan	-0.72277	174	PRIN1(EPQL)
175	USR	Uzbekistan	-0.75925	175	PRIN1(EPQL)
176	SAS	Pakistan	-0.81067	176	PRIN1(EPQL)
177	AFR	San Tome & Principe	-0.83945	177	PRIN1(EPQL)
178	SAS	Bhutan	-0.84781	178	PRIN1(EPQL)
179	AFR	Equatorial Guinea	-0.85083	179	PRIN1(EPQL)
180	USR	Tajikistan	-0.89733	180	PRIN1(EPQL)
181	SEA	Tokelau	-0.91801	181	PRIN1(EPQL)
182	SAS	Bangladesh	-0.95011	182	PRIN1(EPQL)
183	SEA	East Timor	-0.97512	183	PRIN1(EPQL)
184	MEA	Yemen	-0.98605	184	PRIN1(EPQL)
185	CPA	Korea, North	-0.99685	185	PRIN1(EPQL)
186	AFR	Ghana	-1.01540	186	PRIN1(EPQL)
187	AFR	Benin	-1.02095	187	PRIN1(EPQL)
188	SEA	Papua New Guinea	-1.03113	188	PRIN1(EPQL)
189	CPA	Laos	-1.03999	189	PRIN1(EPQL)
190	AFR	Congo, Rep.	-1.08718	190	PRIN1(EPQL)
191	SAS	Nepal	-1.09685	191	PRIN1(EPQL)
192	AFR	Senegal	-1.15192	192	PRIN1(EPQL)
193	AFR	Mauritania	-1.18437	193	PRIN1(EPQL)
194	CPA	Cambodia	-1.22031	194	PRIN1(EPQL)
195	AFR	Tanzania	-1.22403	195	PRIN1(EPQL)
196	AFR	Kenya	-1.23037	196	PRIN1(EPQL)
197	AFR	Swaziland	-1.24097	197	PRIN1(EPQL)
198	AFR	Lesotho	-1.24722	198	PRIN1(EPQL)
199	AFR	Djibouti	-1.27360	199	PRIN1(EPQL)
200	AFR	Togo	-1.29017	200	PRIN1(EPQL)
201	AFR	Nigeria	-1.30684	201	PRIN1(EPQL)
202	AFR	Comoros	-1.32337	202	PRIN1(EPQL)
203	AFR	Angola	-1.32779	203	PRIN1(EPQL)
204	LAM	Haiti	-1.33026	204	PRIN1(EPQL)
205	AFR	Western Sahara	-1.34484	205	PRIN1(EPQL)

		TABLE 1.11 ECONOMICO-POLITICAL QUALITY-OF-LIFE INDEX, PRINCIPAL COMPONENT 1 OF THE ECONOMIC AND POLITICAL QUALITY-OF-LIFE INDICATORS, 2008			
OBS	REGION	COUNTRY	EPQLX	RANK	SOURCE
206	AFR	Madagascar	-1.36871	206	PRIN1(EPQL)
207	AFR	Ivory Coast	-1.37829	207	PRIN1(EPQL)
208	AFR	Malawi	-1.38464	208	PRIN1(EPQL)
209	AFR	Cameroon	-1.39304	209	PRIN1(EPQL)
210	AFR	Zambia	-1.39708	210	PRIN1(EPQL)
211	AFR	Mali	-1.40118	211	PRIN1(EPQL)
212	CPA	Burma	-1.41005	212	PRIN1(EPQL)
213	AFR	Uganda	-1.43292	213	PRIN1(EPQL)
214	AFR	Ethiopia	-1.44439	214	PRIN1(EPQL)
215	AFR	Sudan	-1.46883	215	PRIN1(EPQL)
216	AFR	Burkina Faso	-1.48922	216	PRIN1(EPQL)
217	AFR	Gambia	-1.54085	217	PRIN1(EPQL)
218	AFR	Eritrea	-1.54634	218	PRIN1(EPQL)
219	AFR	Guinea	-1.59934	219	PRIN1(EPQL)
220	AFR	Rwanda	-1.59940	220	PRIN1(EPQL)
221	AFR	Mozambique	-1.61664	221	PRIN1(EPQL)
222	AFR	Niger	-1.62742	222	PRIN1(EPQL)
223	AFR	Sierra Leone	-1.67276	223	PRIN1(EPQL)
224	AFR	Chad	-1.70675	224	PRIN1(EPQL)
225	AFR	Guinea-Bissau	-1.70736	225	PRIN1(EPQL)
226	AFR	Liberia	-1.72308	226	PRIN1(EPQL)
227	AFR	CAR	-1.75042	227	PRIN1(EPQL)
228	AFR	Burundi	-1.77103	228	PRIN1(EPQL)
229	AFR	Somalia	-1.86611	229	PRIN1(EPQL)
230	AFR	Congo, Dem. Rep.	-2.03120	230	PRIN1(EPQL)
231	AFR	Zimbabwe	-2.17891	231	PRIN1(EPQL)
232	SAS	Afghanistan	-2.18462	232	PRIN1(EPQL)

2. BALANCE OF POWER

TABLE 2.1 POPULATION, THOUSANDS, 2008					
OBS	REGION	COUNTRY	POP	RANK	SOURCE
1	CPA	China	1,324,681	1	08(E)
2	SAS	India	1,147,996	2	08(E)
3	DME	United States	305,146	3	08(E)
4	SEA	Indonesia	234,342	4	08(E)
5	LAM	Brazil	187,163	5	08(E)
6	SAS	Pakistan	161,910	6	08(E)
7	AFR	Nigeria	146,255	7	08(E)
8	SAS	Bangladesh	142,547	8	08(E)
9	USR	Russia	141,841	9	08(E)
10	DME	Japan	127,674	10	08(E)
11	LAM	Mexico	106,683	11	08(E)
12	SEA	Philippines	90,227	12	08(E)
13	CPA	Vietnam	88,537	13	08(E)
14	DME	Germany	82,143	14	08(E)
15	AFR	Ethiopia	78,254	15	08(E)
16	MEA	Egypt	74,805	16	08(E)
17	MEA	Iran	72,269	17	08(E)
18	MEA	Turkey	71,002	18	08(E)
19	AFR	Congo, Dem. Rep.	66,515	19	08(E)
20	SEA	Thailand	64,316	20	08(E)
21	DME	France	62,028	21	08(E)
22	DME	United Kingdom	61,446	22	08(E)
23	DME	Italy	59,760	23	08(E)
24	SEA	Korea, South	50,187	24	08(E)
25	AFR	South Africa	48,783	25	08(E)
26	CPA	Burma	47,758	26	08(E)
27	USR	Ukraine	46,222	27	08(E)
28	DME	Spain	45,661	28	08(E)
29	LAM	Colombia	44,442	29	08(E)
30	AFR	Tanzania	40,213	30	08(E)
31	LAM	Argentina	39,737	31	08(E)
32	AFR	Sudan	39,445	32	08(E)
33	EEU	Poland	38,111	33	08(E)
34	AFR	Kenya	37,954	34	08(E)
35	MEA	Algeria	34,574	35	08(E)
36	DME	Canada	33,213	36	08(E)
37	MEA	Morocco	31,606	37	08(E)
38	MEA	Iraq	29,492	38	08(E)
39	AFR	Uganda	29,166	39	08(E)
40	SAS	Nepal	28,757	40	08(E)
41	LAM	Peru	28,534	41	08(E)
42	SAS	Afghanistan	28,266	42	08(E)
43	LAM	Venezuela	27,884	43	08(E)
44	USR	Uzbekistan	27,345	44	08(E)
45	SEA	Malaysia	27,027	45	08(E)

TABLE 2.1 POPULATION, THOUSANDS, 2008					
OBS	REGION	COUNTRY	POP	RANK	SOURCE
46	MEA	Saudi Arabia	24,780	46	08(E)
47	CPA	Korea, North	23,867	47	08(E)
48	AFR	Ghana	23,383	48	08(E)
49	MEA	Yemen	23,013	49	08(E)
50	SEA	Taiwan	22,996	50	08(E)
51	EEU	Romania	21,508	51	08(E)
52	DME	Australia	21,338	52	08(E)
53	AFR	Mozambique	21,285	53	08(E)
54	AFR	Madagascar	20,215	54	08(E)
55	AFR	Ivory Coast	19,624	55	08(E)
56	MEA	Syria	19,514	56	08(E)
57	SAS	Sri Lanka	19,394	57	08(E)
58	AFR	Cameroon	18,468	58	08(E)
59	LAM	Chile	16,454	59	08(E)
60	DME	Netherlands	16,433	60	08(E)
61	USR	Kazakhstan	15,655	61	08(E)
62	AFR	Niger	14,731	62	08(E)
63	AFR	Burkina Faso	14,391	63	08(E)
64	CPA	Cambodia	14,242	64	08(E)
65	AFR	Malawi	13,932	65	08(E)
66	LAM	Ecuador	13,481	66	08(E)
67	LAM	Guatemala	13,002	67	08(E)
68	AFR	Senegal	12,688	68	08(E)
69	AFR	Angola	12,531	69	08(E)
70	AFR	Mali	12,324	70	08(E)
71	AFR	Zambia	11,670	71	08(E)
72	AFR	Zimbabwe	11,350	72	08(E)
73	DME	Greece	11,239	73	08(E)
74	LAM	Cuba	11,236	74	08(E)
75	DME	Belgium	10,697	75	08(E)
76	DME	Portugal	10,649	76	08(E)
77	EEU	Czechia	10,408	77	08(E)
78	MEA	Tunisia	10,325	78	08(E)
79	AFR	Chad	10,111	79	08(E)
80	EEU	Hungary	10,032	80	08(E)
81	AFR	Rwanda	10,009	81	08(E)
82	LAM	Haiti	9,751	82	08(E)
83	LAM	Bolivia	9,694	83	08(E)
84	USR	Belarus	9,675	84	08(E)
85	AFR	Guinea	9,572	85	08(E)
86	LAM	Dominican Rep.	9,507	86	08(E)
87	DME	Sweden	9,214	87	08(E)
88	AFR	Somalia	8,956	88	08(E)
89	AFR	Burundi	8,691	89	08(E)
90	DME	Austria	8,338	90	08(E)
91	AFR	Benin	8,295	91	08(E)
92	USR	Azerbaijan	8,178	92	08(E)

		TABLE 2.1 POPULATION, THOUSANDS, 2008			
OBS	REGION	COUNTRY	POP	RANK	SOURCE
93	LAM	Honduras	7,639	93	08(E)
94	DME	Switzerland	7,617	94	08(E)
95	EEU	Bulgaria	7,569	95	08(E)
96	EEU	Serbia	7,352	96	08(E)
97	DME	Israel	7,018	97	08(E)
98	SEA	Hong Kong	6,992	98	08(E)
99	USR	Tajikistan	6,839	99	08(E)
100	AFR	Togo	6,762	100	08(E)
101	SEA	Papua New Guinea	6,474	101	08(E)
102	LAM	Paraguay	6,238	102	08(E)
103	AFR	Sierra Leone	5,969	103	08(E)
104	CPA	Laos	5,963	104	08(E)
105	MEA	Libya	5,871	105	08(E)
106	MEA	Jordan	5,844	106	08(E)
107	LAM	El Salvador	5,794	107	08(E)
108	LAM	Nicaragua	5,667	108	08(E)
109	DME	Denmark	5,494	109	08(E)
110	EEU	Slovakia	5,401	110	08(E)
111	DME	Finland	5,310	111	08(E)
112	USR	Kyrgyzstan	5,281	112	08(E)
113	USR	Turkmenistan	5,180	113	08(E)
114	AFR	Eritrea	5,028	114	08(E)
115	SEA	Singapore	4,839	115	08(E)
116	DME	Norway	4,762	116	08(E)
117	MEA	UAE	4,660	117	08(E)
118	DME	Ireland	4,467	118	08(E)
119	EEU	Croatia	4,433	119	08(E)
120	AFR	CAR	4,424	120	08(E)
121	LAM	Costa Rica	4,389	121	08(E)
122	USR	Georgia	4,360	122	08(E)
123	DME	New Zealand	4,268	123	08(E)
124	MEA	Lebanon	4,142	124	08(E)
125	LAM	Puerto Rico	3,958	125	08(E)
126	EEU	Bosnia	3,858	126	08(E)
127	AFR	Congo, Rep.	3,847	127	08(E)
128	USR	Moldova	3,760	128	08(E)
129	AFR	Liberia	3,543	129	08(E)
130	MEA	Kuwait	3,530	130	08(E)
131	USR	Lithuania	3,358	131	08(E)
132	LAM	Uruguay	3,350	132	08(E)
133	LAM	Panama	3,310	133	08(E)
134	AFR	Mauritania	3,204	134	08(E)
135	EEU	Albania	3,194	135	08(E)
136	USR	Armenia	2,996	136	08(E)
137	LAM	Jamaica	2,688	137	08(E)
138	MEA	West Bank	2,656	138	08(E)
139	CPA	Mongolia	2,652	139	08(E)

TABLE 2.1 POPULATION, THOUSANDS, 2008					
OBS	REGION	COUNTRY	POP	RANK	SOURCE
140	MEA	Oman	2,651	140	08(E)
141	USR	Latvia	2,266	141	08(E)
142	EEU	Kosovo	2,143	142	08(WB)
143	AFR	Namibia	2,089	143	08(E)
144	EEU	Macedonia	2,039	144	08(E)
145	EEU	Slovenia	2,029	145	08(E)
146	AFR	Lesotho	2,020	146	08(E)
147	AFR	Botswana	1,842	147	08(E)
148	AFR	Gambia	1,754	148	08(E)
149	AFR	Guinea-Bissau	1,503	149	08(E)
150	AFR	Gabon	1,486	150	08(E)
151	MEA	Qatar	1,448	151	08(E)
152	MEA	Gaza Strip	1,444	152	08(E)
153	USR	Estonia	1,340	153	08(E)
154	LAM	Trinidad & Tobago	1,305	154	08(E)
155	AFR	Mauritius	1,269	155	08(E)
156	MEA	Bahrain	1,084	156	08(E)
157	SEA	East Timor	1,078	157	08(E)
158	MEA	Cyprus	1,076	158	08(E)
159	AFR	Swaziland	1,018	159	08(E)
160	SEA	Fiji	839	160	08(E)
161	AFR	Reunion	807	161	08(E)
162	LAM	Guyana	736	162	08(E)
163	SAS	Bhutan	682	163	08(E)
164	AFR	Comoros	645	164	08(E)
165	EEU	Montenegro	626	165	08(E)
166	AFR	Equatorial Guinea	616	166	08(E)
167	SEA	Macao	549	167	08(E)
168	SEA	Solomon Islands	517	168	08(E)
169	LAM	Suriname	516	169	08(E)
170	AFR	Djibouti	506	170	08(E)
171	AFR	Cape Verde	500	171	08(E)
172	AFR	Western Sahara	497	172	08(E)
173	DME	Luxembourg	488	173	08(E)
174	LAM	Guadeloupe	419	174	08(E)
175	DME	Malta	412	175	08(E)
176	LAM	Martinique	403	176	08(E)
177	SEA	Brunei	400	177	08(E)
178	SAS	Maldives	386	178	08(E)
179	LAM	Bahamas	335	179	08(E)
180	LAM	Belize	323	180	08(E)
181	DME	Iceland	315	181	08(E)
182	LAM	Barbados	282	182	08(E)
183	SEA	French Polynesia	263	183	08(E)
184	SEA	New Caledonia	247	184	08(E)
185	SEA	Vanuatu	233	185	08(E)
186	LAM	Guiana, French	217	186	08(E)

		TABLE 2.1 POPULATION, THOUSANDS, 2008			
OBS	REGION	COUNTRY	POP	RANK	SOURCE
187	LAM	Neth. Antilles	196	187	08(E)
188	AFR	Mayotte	192	188	08(E)
189	SEA	Samoa, Western	180	189	08(E)
190	SEA	Guam	179	190	08(E)
191	LAM	St. Lucia	171	191	08(E)
192	AFR	San Tome & Principe	160	192	08(E)
193	LAM	Virgin Islands, US	113	193	08(E)
194	SEA	Micronesia	110	194	08(E)
195	LAM	Grenada	108	195	08(E)
196	LAM	St. Vincent	106	196	08(E)
197	LAM	Aruba	105	197	08(E)
198	SEA	Tonga	103	198	08(E)
199	SEA	Kiribati	95	199	08(E)
200	DME	Jersey	91	200	08(E)
201	LAM	Antigua & Barbuda	88	201	08(E)
202	AFR	Seychelles	86	202	08(E)
203	DME	Andorra	84	203	08(E)
204	DME	Isle of Man	82	204	08(E)
205	LAM	Dominica	73	205	08(E)
206	SEA	Samoa, American	69	206	08(E)
207	DME	Bermuda	65	207	08(E)
208	DME	Guernsey	64	208	08(E)
209	SEA	Northern Mariana Is.	63	209	08(E)
210	DME	Greenland	57	210	08(E)
211	LAM	Cayman Islands	56	211	08(E)
212	SEA	Marshall Islands	53	212	08(E)
213	LAM	St. Kitts & Nevis	51	213	08(E)
214	DME	Faeroe Islands	48	214	08(E)
215	DME	Liechtenstein	36	215	08(E)
216	DME	Monaco	34	216	08(E)
217	DME	San Marino	31	217	08(E)
218	DME	Gibraltar	28	218	08(CIA)
219	LAM	Virgin Islands, Brit.	24	219	08(CIA)
220	LAM	Turks & Caicos Is.	22	220	08(CIA)
221	SEA	Cook Islands	22	221	08(CIA)
222	SEA	Palau	20	222	08(E)
223	SEA	Wallis & Futuna	16	223	08(CIA)
224	LAM	Anguilla	14	224	08(CIA)
225	SEA	Nauru	10	225	08(E)
226	SEA	Tuvalu	10	226	08(E)
227	LAM	Montserrat	10	227	08(CIA)
228	AFR	St. Helena	8	228	08(CIA)
229	DME	St. Pierre & Miquelon	7	229	08(CIA)
230	DME	Falkland Islands	3	230	08(CIA)
231	SEA	Niue	1	231	08(CIA)
232	SEA	Tokelau	1	232	08(CIA)

	TABLE 2.2 GDP AT PURCHASING POWER PARITIES, MILLIONS OF DOLLARS, 2008				
OBS	REGION	COUNTRY	GDPPPP	RANK	SOURCE
1	DME	United States	14,255,201	1	POP*GPCPPP
2	CPA	China	7,897,748	2	POP*GPCPPP
3	DME	Japan	4,353,556	3	POP*GPCPPP
4	SAS	India	3,411,844	4	POP*GPCPPP
5	DME	Germany	2,925,359	5	POP*GPCPPP
6	USR	Russia	2,289,172	6	POP*GPCPPP
7	DME	United Kingdom	2,177,953	7	POP*GPCPPP
8	DME	France	2,111,743	8	POP*GPCPPP
9	LAM	Brazil	1,927,030	9	POP*GPCPPP
10	DME	Italy	1,837,979	10	POP*GPCPPP
11	LAM	Mexico	1,546,370	11	POP*GPCPPP
12	DME	Spain	1,459,052	12	POP*GPCPPP
13	SEA	Korea, South	1,402,175	13	POP*GPCPPP
14	DME	Canada	1,210,415	14	POP*GPCPPP
15	MEA	Turkey	988,348	15	POP*GPCPPP
16	SEA	Indonesia	931,509	16	POP*GPCPPP
17	MEA	Iran	843,090	17	POP*GPCPPP
18	DME	Australia	761,276	18	POP*GPCPPP
19	SEA	Taiwan	733,572	19	POP*GPCPPP
20	EEU	Poland	671,706	20	POP*GPCPPP
21	DME	Netherlands	671,272	21	POP*GPCPPP
22	MEA	Saudi Arabia	592,738	22	POP*GPCPPP
23	LAM	Argentina	569,550	23	POP*GPCPPP
24	SEA	Thailand	495,426	24	POP*GPCPPP
25	AFR	South Africa	493,147	25	POP*GPCPPP
26	SAS	Pakistan	428,090	26	POP*GPCPPP
27	MEA	Egypt	405,144	27	POP*GPCPPP
28	LAM	Colombia	394,867	28	POP*GPCPPP
29	SEA	Malaysia	384,189	29	POP*GPCPPP
30	DME	Belgium	368,972	30	POP*GPCPPP
31	LAM	Venezuela	357,027	31	POP*GPCPPP
32	DME	Sweden	344,447	32	POP*GPCPPP
33	USR	Ukraine	336,080	33	POP*GPCPPP
34	DME	Greece	329,988	34	POP*GPCPPP
35	DME	Switzerland	323,997	35	POP*GPCPPP
36	DME	Austria	318,111	36	POP*GPCPPP
37	SEA	Philippines	316,697	37	POP*GPCPPP
38	SEA	Hong Kong	307,117	38	POP*GPCPPP
39	AFR	Nigeria	304,503	39	POP*GPCPPP
40	EEU	Romania	302,510	40	POP*GPCPPP
41	MEA	Algeria	277,733	41	POP*GPCPPP
42	DME	Norway	276,853	42	POP*GPCPPP
43	EEU	Czechia	257,202	43	POP*GPCPPP
44	CPA	Vietnam	246,576	44	POP*GPCPPP
45	DME	Portugal	245,715	45	POP*GPCPPP
46	LAM	Peru	242,739	46	POP*GPCPPP

		TABLE 2.2 GDP AT PURCHASING POWER PARITIES, MILLIONS OF DOLLARS, 2008			
OBS	REGION	COUNTRY	GDPPPP	RANK	SOURCE
47	SEA	Singapore	238,485	47	POP*GPCPPP
48	LAM	Chile	238,007	48	POP*GPCPPP
49	MEA	Kuwait	202,622	49	POP*GPCPPP
50	DME	Denmark	201,119	50	POP*GPCPPP
51	DME	Ireland	197,441	51	POP*GPCPPP
52	EEU	Hungary	193,919	52	POP*GPCPPP
53	DME	Israel	193,332	53	POP*GPCPPP
54	SAS	Bangladesh	190,158	54	POP*GPCPPP
55	DME	Finland	188,117	55	POP*GPCPPP
56	MEA	UAE	186,400	56	POP*GPCPPP
57	USR	Kazakhstan	177,136	57	POP*GPCPPP
58	MEA	Qatar	149,868	58	POP*GPCPPP
59	MEA	Morocco	138,687	59	POP*GPCPPP
60	EEU	Slovakia	119,259	60	POP*GPCPPP
61	USR	Belarus	118,625	61	POP*GPCPPP
62	MEA	Iraq	117,968	62	POP*GPCPPP
63	DME	New Zealand	115,360	63	POP*GPCPPP
64	LAM	Ecuador	107,969	64	POP*GPCPPP
65	LAM	Cuba	106,742	65	POP*GPCPPP
66	EEU	Bulgaria	93,803	66	POP*GPCPPP
67	MEA	Libya	90,425	67	POP*GPCPPP
68	SAS	Sri Lanka	88,437	68	POP*GPCPPP
69	MEA	Syria	86,642	69	POP*GPCPPP
70	AFR	Sudan	84,925	70	POP*GPCPPP
71	EEU	Croatia	84,599	71	POP*GPCPPP
72	EEU	Serbia	84,225	72	POP*GPCPPP
73	MEA	Tunisia	82,559	73	POP*GPCPPP
74	LAM	Dominican Rep.	78,119	74	POP*GPCPPP
75	AFR	Angola	73,920	75	POP*GPCPPP
76	USR	Uzbekistan	72,628	76	POP*GPCPPP
77	USR	Azerbaijan	71,680	77	POP*GPCPPP
78	LAM	Puerto Rico	70,452	78	POP*GPCPPP
79	AFR	Ethiopia	67,924	79	POP*GPCPPP
80	USR	Lithuania	63,211	80	POP*GPCPPP
81	LAM	Guatemala	61,890	81	POP*GPCPPP
82	AFR	Kenya	60,347	82	POP*GPCPPP
83	CPA	Burma	57,310	83	POP*GPCPPP
84	EEU	Slovenia	56,011	84	POP*GPCPPP
85	MEA	Yemen	55,231	85	POP*GPCPPP
86	MEA	Oman	53,550	86	POP*GPCPPP
87	AFR	Tanzania	50,789	87	POP*GPCPPP
88	LAM	Costa Rica	49,337	88	POP*GPCPPP
89	MEA	Lebanon	47,923	89	POP*GPCPPP
90	LAM	Uruguay	42,659	90	POP*GPCPPP
91	LAM	Bolivia	41,471	91	POP*GPCPPP
92	LAM	Panama	41,388	92	POP*GPCPPP

		TABLE 2.2 GDP AT PURCHASING POWER PARITIES, MILLIONS OF DOLLARS, 2008			
OBS	REGION	COUNTRY	GDPPPP	RANK	SOURCE
93	AFR	Cameroon	40,907	93	POP*GPCPPP
94	CPA	Korea, North	40,574	94	POP*GPCPPP
95	MEA	Bahrain	40,325	95	POP*GPCPPP
96	LAM	El Salvador	39,364	96	POP*GPCPPP
97	USR	Latvia	38,749	97	POP*GPCPPP
98	DME	Luxembourg	38,356	98	POP*GPCPPP
99	USR	Turkmenistan	34,400	99	POP*GPCPPP
100	AFR	Uganda	33,978	100	POP*GPCPPP
101	AFR	Ghana	33,952	101	POP*GPCPPP
102	SEA	Macao	32,627	102	POP*GPCPPP
103	AFR	Ivory Coast	32,399	103	POP*GPCPPP
104	EEU	Bosnia	32,369	104	POP*GPCPPP
105	LAM	Trinidad & Tobago	32,296	105	POP*GPCPPP
106	SAS	Nepal	31,978	106	POP*GPCPPP
107	MEA	Jordan	30,874	107	POP*GPCPPP
108	MEA	Cyprus	30,774	108	POP*GPCPPP
109	LAM	Honduras	30,289	109	POP*GPCPPP
110	LAM	Paraguay	29,375	110	POP*GPCPPP
111	USR	Estonia	27,687	111	POP*GPCPPP
112	CPA	Cambodia	27,131	112	POP*GPCPPP
113	AFR	Botswana	24,668	113	POP*GPCPPP
114	EEU	Albania	24,642	114	POP*GPCPPP
115	SAS	Afghanistan	22,613	115	POP*GPCPPP
116	AFR	Reunion	22,559	116	POP*GPCPPP
117	AFR	Senegal	22,483	117	POP*GPCPPP
118	AFR	Gabon	21,587	118	POP*GPCPPP
119	AFR	Congo, Dem. Rep.	21,351	119	POP*GPCPPP
120	USR	Georgia	21,347	120	POP*GPCPPP
121	SEA	Brunei	21,240	121	POP*GPCPPP
122	AFR	Madagascar	21,206	122	POP*GPCPPP
123	AFR	Equatorial Guinea	20,866	123	POP*GPCPPP
124	LAM	Jamaica	20,711	124	POP*GPCPPP
125	EEU	Macedonia	20,474	125	POP*GPCPPP
126	AFR	Mozambique	18,199	126	POP*GPCPPP
127	USR	Armenia	18,186	127	POP*GPCPPP
128	AFR	Burkina Faso	16,708	128	POP*GPCPPP
129	AFR	Zambia	15,825	129	POP*GPCPPP
130	AFR	Mauritius	15,328	130	POP*GPCPPP
131	LAM	Nicaragua	15,199	131	POP*GPCPPP
132	AFR	Congo, Rep.	15,180	132	POP*GPCPPP
133	AFR	Chad	14,712	133	POP*GPCPPP
134	SEA	Papua New Guinea	14,295	134	POP*GPCPPP
135	AFR	Mali	13,901	135	POP*GPCPPP
136	AFR	Namibia	13,251	136	POP*GPCPPP

	TABLE 2.2 GDP AT PURCHASING POWER PARITIES, MILLIONS OF DOLLARS, 2008				
OBS	REGION	COUNTRY	GDPPPP	RANK	SOURCE
137	USR	Tajikistan	13,035	137	POP*GPCPPP
138	CPA	Laos	12,725	138	POP*GPCPPP
139	LAM	Martinique	12,603	139	POP*GPCPPP
140	AFR	Benin	12,177	140	POP*GPCPPP
141	AFR	Malawi	11,661	141	POP*GPCPPP
142	DME	Iceland	11,584	142	POP*GPCPPP
143	USR	Kyrgyzstan	11,555	143	POP*GPCPPP
144	AFR	Guinea	11,525	144	POP*GPCPPP
145	LAM	Haiti	11,477	145	POP*GPCPPP
146	LAM	Guadeloupe	11,251	146	POP*GPCPPP
147	USR	Moldova	10,998	147	POP*GPCPPP
148	AFR	Rwanda	10,229	148	POP*GPCPPP
149	AFR	Niger	10,076	149	POP*GPCPPP
150	DME	Malta	9,733	150	POP*GPCPPP
151	LAM	Bahamas	9,581	151	POP*GPCPPP
152	CPA	Mongolia	9,457	152	POP*GPCPPP
153	EEU	Montenegro	8,733	153	POP*GPCPPP
154	MEA	West Bank	7,702	154	POP*GPCPPP
155	AFR	Mauritania	6,728	155	POP*GPCPPP
156	DME	Jersey	5,800	156	POP*GPCPPP
157	AFR	Togo	5,606	157	POP*GPCPPP
158	LAM	Barbados	5,443	158	POP*GPCPPP
159	AFR	Somalia	5,374	159	POP*GPCPPP
160	DME	Bermuda	5,353	160	POP*GPCPPP
161	DME	Monaco	5,211	161	POP*GPCPPP
162	EEU	Kosovo	5,045	162	POP*GPCPPP
163	AFR	Swaziland	5,017	163	POP*GPCPPP
164	SEA	French Polynesia	4,885	164	POP*GPCPPP
165	SEA	New Caledonia	4,605	165	POP*GPCPPP
166	AFR	Sierra Leone	4,572	166	POP*GPCPPP
167	DME	Liechtenstein	4,288	167	POP*GPCPPP
168	MEA	Gaza Strip	4,188	168	POP*GPCPPP
169	LAM	Guiana, French	4,015	169	POP*GPCPPP
170	LAM	Suriname	3,873	170	POP*GPCPPP
171	LAM	Neth. Antilles	3,689	171	POP*GPCPPP
172	SEA	Fiji	3,676	172	POP*GPCPPP
173	DME	Andorra	3,658	173	POP*GPCPPP
174	AFR	Burundi	3,329	174	POP*GPCPPP
175	AFR	CAR	3,256	175	POP*GPCPPP
176	SAS	Bhutan	3,243	176	POP*GPCPPP
177	AFR	Lesotho	3,208	177	POP*GPCPPP
178	DME	Guernsey	3,199	178	POP*GPCPPP
179	DME	Isle of Man	3,194	179	POP*GPCPPP
180	AFR	Eritrea	3,178	180	POP*GPCPPP
181	SEA	Guam	2,996	181	POP*GPCPPP
182	LAM	Cayman Islands	2,860	182	POP*GPCPPP

OBS	REGION	COUNTRY	GDPPPP	RANK	SOURCE
183	LAM	Aruba	2,636	183	POP*GPCPPP
184	AFR	Gambia	2,391	184	POP*GPCPPP
185	AFR	Zimbabwe	2,270	185	POP*GPCPPP
186	LAM	Belize	2,242	186	POP*GPCPPP
187	SAS	Maldives	2,125	187	POP*GPCPPP
188	DME	Faeroe Islands	1,983	188	POP*GPCPPP
189	LAM	Virgin Islands, US	1,928	189	POP*GPCPPP
190	LAM	Guyana	1,871	190	POP*GPCPPP
191	LAM	Antigua & Barbuda	1,866	191	POP*GPCPPP
192	AFR	Seychelles	1,841	192	POP*GPCPPP
193	AFR	Cape Verde	1,752	193	POP*GPCPPP
194	LAM	St. Lucia	1,694	194	POP*GPCPPP
195	DME	Greenland	1,531	195	POP*GPCPPP
196	AFR	Liberia	1,375	196	POP*GPCPPP
197	SEA	Solomon Islands	1,349	197	POP*GPCPPP
198	DME	San Marino	1,329	198	POP*GPCPPP
199	AFR	Western Sahara	1,243	199	POP*GPCPPP
200	DME	Gibraltar	1,193	200	POP*GPCPPP
201	LAM	Virgin Islands, Brit.	1,087	201	POP*GPCPPP
202	AFR	Djibouti	1,083	202	POP*GPCPPP
203	SEA	Northern Mariana Is.	1,063	203	POP*GPCPPP
204	AFR	Mayotte	1,050	204	POP*GPCPPP
205	LAM	St. Vincent	970	205	POP*GPCPPP
206	SEA	Vanuatu	927	206	POP*GPCPPP
207	LAM	Grenada	922	207	POP*GPCPPP
208	SEA	East Timor	863	208	POP*GPCPPP
209	LAM	St. Kitts & Nevis	829	209	POP*GPCPPP
210	AFR	Guinea-Bissau	809	210	POP*GPCPPP
211	SEA	Samoa, Western	807	211	POP*GPCPPP
212	AFR	Comoros	754	212	POP*GPCPPP
213	LAM	Dominica	630	213	POP*GPCPPP
214	SEA	Samoa, American	568	214	POP*GPCPPP
215	SEA	Tonga	394	215	POP*GPCPPP
216	LAM	Turks & Caicos Is.	332	216	POP*GPCPPP
217	SEA	Micronesia	311	217	POP*GPCPPP
218	AFR	San Tome & Principe	278	218	POP*GPCPPP
219	SEA	Kiribati	236	219	POP*GPCPPP
220	SEA	Cook Islands	223	220	POP*GPCPPP
221	SEA	Palau	164	221	POP*GPCPPP
222	LAM	Anguilla	146	222	POP*GPCPPP
223	DME	Falkland Islands	143	223	POP*GPCPPP
224	SEA	Marshall Islands	133	224	POP*GPCPPP

TABLE 2.2 GDP AT PURCHASING POWER PARITIES, MILLIONS OF DOLLARS, 2008					
OBS	REGION	COUNTRY	GDPPPP	RANK	SOURCE
225	SEA	Wallis & Futuna	73	225	POP*GPCPPP
226	DME	St. Pierre & Miquelon	65	226	POP*GPCPPP
227	SEA	Nauru	57	227	POP*GPCPPP
228	LAM	Montserrat	42	228	POP*GPCPPP
229	AFR	St. Helena	28	229	POP*GPCPPP
230	SEA	Tuvalu	20	230	POP*GPCPPP
231	SEA	Niue	10	231	POP*GPCPPP
232	SEA	Tokelau	3	232	POP*GPCPPP

		TABLE 2.3 GNI AT MARKET EXCHANGE RATES, MILLIONS OF DOLLARS, 2008			
OBS	REGION	COUNTRY	GDP	RANK	SOURCE
1	DME	United States	14,518,847	1	POP*GPC
2	DME	Japan	4,878,424	2	POP*GPC
3	CPA	China	3,894,562	3	POP*GPC
4	DME	Germany	3,486,149	4	POP*GPC
5	DME	United Kingdom	2,789,034	5	POP*GPC
6	DME	France	2,620,683	6	POP*GPC
7	DME	Italy	2,105,942	7	POP*GPC
8	DME	Spain	1,459,326	8	POP*GPC
9	DME	Canada	1,385,978	9	POP*GPC
10	LAM	Brazil	1,375,648	10	POP*GPC
11	USR	Russia	1,364,510	11	POP*GPC
12	SAS	India	1,228,356	12	POP*GPC
13	SEA	Korea, South	1,080,526	13	POP*GPC
14	LAM	Mexico	1,064,696	14	POP*GPC
15	DME	Australia	860,988	15	POP*GPC
16	DME	Netherlands	824,115	16	POP*GPC
17	MEA	Turkey	663,159	17	POP*GPC
18	DME	Switzerland	497,619	18	POP*GPC
19	DME	Belgium	474,198	19	POP*GPC
20	SEA	Indonesia	471,027	20	POP*GPC
21	DME	Sweden	469,361	21	POP*GPC
22	MEA	Saudi Arabia	463,832	22	POP*GPC
23	EEU	Poland	452,759	23	POP*GPC
24	DME	Norway	414,627	24	POP*GPC
25	SEA	Taiwan	403,396	25	POP*GPC
26	DME	Austria	385,716	26	POP*GPC
27	DME	Denmark	324,860	27	POP*GPC
28	DME	Greece	321,997	28	POP*GPC
29	LAM	Argentina	286,106	29	POP*GPC
30	AFR	South Africa	283,917	30	POP*GPC
31	MEA	UAE	266,058	31	POP*GPC
32	MEA	Iran	264,071	32	POP*GPC
33	LAM	Venezuela	257,369	33	POP*GPC
34	DME	Finland	255,517	34	POP*GPC
35	DME	Ireland	221,519	35	POP*GPC
36	SEA	Hong Kong	219,689	36	POP*GPC
37	DME	Portugal	218,943	37	POP*GPC
38	LAM	Colombia	207,100	38	POP*GPC
39	SEA	Malaysia	188,378	39	POP*GPC
40	SEA	Thailand	182,657	40	POP*GPC
41	DME	Israel	173,345	41	POP*GPC
42	EEU	Czechia	172,773	42	POP*GPC
43	EEU	Romania	170,558	43	POP*GPC
44	SEA	Philippines	170,529	44	POP*GPC
45	AFR	Nigeria	169,656	45	POP*GPC
46	SEA	Singapore	168,204	46	POP*GPC

OBS	REGION	COUNTRY	GDP	RANK	SOURCE
		TABLE 2.3 GNI AT MARKET EXCHANGE RATES, MILLIONS OF DOLLARS, 2008			
47	SAS	Pakistan	158,672	47	POP*GPC
48	LAM	Chile	154,668	48	POP*GPC
49	USR	Ukraine	148,373	49	POP*GPC
50	MEA	Algeria	147,285	50	POP*GPC
51	MEA	Kuwait	138,531	51	POP*GPC
52	MEA	Egypt	134,649	52	POP*GPC
53	MEA	Qatar	128,858	53	POP*GPC
54	EEU	Hungary	128,510	54	POP*GPC
55	DME	New Zealand	119,248	55	POP*GPC
56	LAM	Peru	113,851	56	POP*GPC
57	USR	Kazakhstan	96,122	57	POP*GPC
58	MEA	Morocco	81,543	58	POP*GPC
59	CPA	Vietnam	78,798	59	POP*GPC
60	EEU	Slovakia	78,531	60	POP*GPC
61	SAS	Bangladesh	74,124	61	POP*GPC
62	MEA	Iraq	72,078	62	POP*GPC
63	MEA	Libya	68,045	63	POP*GPC
64	LAM	Puerto Rico	60,949	64	POP*GPC
65	EEU	Croatia	60,156	65	POP*GPC
66	LAM	Cuba	52,674	66	POP*GPC
67	USR	Belarus	52,052	67	POP*GPC
68	LAM	Ecuador	49,071	68	POP*GPC
69	EEU	Slovenia	48,716	69	POP*GPC
70	MEA	Oman	47,410	70	POP*GPC
71	AFR	Sudan	44,573	71	POP*GPC
72	AFR	Angola	43,232	72	POP*GPC
73	EEU	Serbia	41,906	73	POP*GPC
74	LAM	Dominican Rep.	41,736	74	POP*GPC
75	EEU	Bulgaria	41,554	75	POP*GPC
76	DME	Luxembourg	41,426	76	POP*GPC
77	MEA	Syria	40,784	77	POP*GPC
78	USR	Lithuania	39,859	78	POP*GPC
79	LAM	Guatemala	34,845	79	POP*GPC
80	SAS	Sri Lanka	34,521	80	POP*GPC
81	MEA	Tunisia	33,969	81	POP*GPC
82	USR	Azerbaijan	31,322	82	POP*GPC
83	AFR	Kenya	29,225	83	POP*GPC
84	LAM	Uruguay	27,671	84	POP*GPC
85	CPA	Burma	27,604	85	POP*GPC
86	USR	Latvia	26,875	86	POP*GPC
87	LAM	Costa Rica	26,597	87	POP*GPC
88	MEA	Lebanon	26,302	88	POP*GPC
89	MEA	Cyprus	25,493	89	POP*GPC
90	USR	Uzbekistan	24,884	90	POP*GPC
91	CPA	Korea, North	24,655	91	POP*GPC
92	SEA	Macao	23,459	92	POP*GPC

	TABLE 2.3 GNI AT MARKET EXCHANGE RATES, MILLIONS OF DOLLARS, 2008				
OBS	REGION	COUNTRY	GDP	RANK	SOURCE
93	AFR	Ethiopia	21,911	93	POP*GPC
94	MEA	Yemen	21,862	94	POP*GPC
95	LAM	Trinidad & Tobago	21,585	95	POP*GPC
96	AFR	Cameroon	21,238	96	POP*GPC
97	LAM	Panama	20,456	97	POP*GPC
98	LAM	El Salvador	20,163	98	POP*GPC
99	AFR	Reunion	19,550	99	POP*GPC
100	MEA	Jordan	19,344	100	POP*GPC
101	AFR	Ivory Coast	19,232	101	POP*GPC
102	USR	Estonia	19,122	102	POP*GPC
103	AFR	Tanzania	17,694	103	POP*GPC
104	EEU	Bosnia	17,400	104	POP*GPC
105	AFR	Ghana	15,667	105	POP*GPC
106	USR	Turkmenistan	14,711	106	POP*GPC
107	MEA	Bahrain	14,475	107	POP*GPC
108	LAM	Bolivia	14,153	108	POP*GPC
109	LAM	Honduras	13,750	109	POP*GPC
110	LAM	Paraguay	13,599	110	POP*GPC
111	LAM	Jamaica	13,091	111	POP*GPC
112	SEA	Brunei	12,905	112	POP*GPC
113	DME	Iceland	12,622	113	POP*GPC
114	AFR	Senegal	12,307	114	POP*GPC
115	EEU	Albania	12,265	115	POP*GPC
116	AFR	Uganda	12,250	116	POP*GPC
117	AFR	Botswana	11,918	117	POP*GPC
118	SAS	Nepal	11,503	118	POP*GPC
119	LAM	Martinique	11,213	119	POP*GPC
120	AFR	Zambia	11,087	120	POP*GPC
121	SAS	Afghanistan	10,882	121	POP*GPC
122	USR	Georgia	10,769	122	POP*GPC
123	AFR	Gabon	10,759	123	POP*GPC
124	USR	Armenia	10,037	124	POP*GPC
125	AFR	Congo, Dem. Rep.	9,977	125	POP*GPC
126	LAM	Guadeloupe	9,659	126	POP*GPC
127	SEA	New Caledonia	9,295	127	POP*GPC
128	AFR	Equatorial Guinea	9,228	128	POP*GPC
129	AFR	Namibia	8,774	129	POP*GPC
130	CPA	Cambodia	8,545	130	POP*GPC
131	EEU	Macedonia	8,441	131	POP*GPC
132	AFR	Madagascar	8,288	132	POP*GPC
133	AFR	Mauritius	8,122	133	POP*GPC
134	AFR	Mozambique	7,875	134	POP*GPC
135	AFR	Congo, Rep.	7,579	135	POP*GPC
136	LAM	Bahamas	7,270	136	POP*GPC
137	AFR	Mali	7,148	137	POP*GPC

OBS	REGION	COUNTRY	GDP	RANK	SOURCE
		TABLE 2.3 GNI AT MARKET EXCHANGE RATES, MILLIONS OF DOLLARS, 2008			
138	DME	Malta	7,094	138	POP*GPC
139	AFR	Burkina Faso	6,908	139	POP*GPC
140	DME	Monaco	6,713	140	POP*GPC
141	SEA	Papua New Guinea	6,539	141	POP*GPC
142	LAM	Haiti	6,436	142	POP*GPC
143	LAM	Nicaragua	6,120	143	POP*GPC
144	SEA	French Polynesia	5,920	144	POP*GPC
145	DME	Jersey	5,782	145	POP*GPC
146	AFR	Benin	5,724	146	POP*GPC
147	DME	Bermuda	5,616	147	POP*GPC
148	USR	Moldova	5,527	148	POP*GPC
149	AFR	Chad	5,359	149	POP*GPC
150	AFR	Niger	4,861	150	POP*GPC
151	EEU	Kosovo	4,682	151	POP*GPC
152	CPA	Mongolia	4,455	152	POP*GPC
153	DME	Liechtenstein	4,441	153	POP*GPC
154	SEA	Guam	4,430	154	POP*GPC
155	CPA	Laos	4,413	155	POP*GPC
156	LAM	Virgin Islands, US	4,296	156	POP*GPC
157	AFR	Rwanda	4,104	157	POP*GPC
158	USR	Tajikistan	4,103	158	POP*GPC
159	AFR	Malawi	4,040	159	POP*GPC
160	EEU	Montenegro	4,031	160	POP*GPC
161	MEA	West Bank	3,942	161	POP*GPC
162	USR	Kyrgyzstan	3,908	162	POP*GPC
163	AFR	Guinea	3,858	163	POP*GPC
164	LAM	Neth. Antilles	3,833	164	POP*GPC
165	DME	Andorra	3,777	165	POP*GPC
166	DME	Isle of Man	3,680	166	POP*GPC
167	DME	Guernsey	3,550	167	POP*GPC
168	LAM	Barbados	3,545	168	POP*GPC
169	AFR	Zimbabwe	3,541	169	POP*GPC
170	SEA	Fiji	3,297	170	POP*GPC
171	LAM	Guiana, French	3,159	171	POP*GPC
172	AFR	Mauritania	2,778	172	POP*GPC
173	AFR	Togo	2,705	173	POP*GPC
174	SEA	East Timor	2,652	174	POP*GPC
175	LAM	Cayman Islands	2,593	175	POP*GPC
176	AFR	Somalia	2,579	176	POP*GPC
177	LAM	Aruba	2,575	177	POP*GPC
178	LAM	Suriname	2,575	178	POP*GPC
179	AFR	Swaziland	2,565	179	POP*GPC
180	DME	Faeroe Islands	2,344	180	POP*GPC
181	AFR	Lesotho	2,182	181	POP*GPC
182	MEA	Gaza Strip	2,143	182	POP*GPC

		TABLE 2.3 GNI AT MARKET EXCHANGE RATES, MILLIONS OF DOLLARS, 2008			
OBS	REGION	COUNTRY	GDP	RANK	SOURCE
183	AFR	Sierra Leone	1,910	183	POP*GPC
184	DME	Greenland	1,898	184	POP*GPC
185	DME	San Marino	1,889	185	POP*GPC
186	AFR	CAR	1,814	186	POP*GPC
187	AFR	Cape Verde	1,565	187	POP*GPC
188	AFR	Eritrea	1,508	188	POP*GPC
189	SAS	Maldives	1,401	189	POP*GPC
190	SAS	Bhutan	1,296	190	POP*GPC
191	LAM	Belize	1,234	191	POP*GPC
192	AFR	Burundi	1,217	192	POP*GPC
193	LAM	Antigua & Barbuda	1,192	193	POP*GPC
194	LAM	Guyana	1,045	194	POP*GPC
195	DME	Gibraltar	1,030	195	POP*GPC
196	LAM	Virgin Islands, Brit.	948	196	POP*GPC
197	LAM	St. Lucia	946	197	POP*GPC
198	SEA	Northern Mariana Is.	918	198	POP*GPC
199	AFR	Seychelles	880	199	POP*GPC
200	AFR	Mayotte	720	200	POP*GPC
201	AFR	Gambia	684	201	POP*GPC
202	AFR	Western Sahara	652	202	POP*GPC
203	LAM	Grenada	617	203	POP*GPC
204	SEA	Solomon Islands	610	204	POP*GPC
205	AFR	Liberia	602	205	POP*GPC
206	AFR	Djibouti	572	206	POP*GPC
207	LAM	St. Kitts & Nevis	562	207	POP*GPC
208	SEA	Samoa, American	561	208	POP*GPC
209	LAM	St. Vincent	545	209	POP*GPC
210	SEA	Vanuatu	543	210	POP*GPC
211	SEA	Samoa, Western	500	211	POP*GPC
212	AFR	Comoros	484	212	POP*GPC
213	AFR	Guinea-Bissau	376	213	POP*GPC
214	LAM	Dominica	346	214	POP*GPC
215	SEA	Tonga	264	215	POP*GPC
216	SEA	Micronesia	257	216	POP*GPC
217	LAM	Turks & Caicos Is.	238	217	POP*GPC
218	SEA	Kiribati	190	218	POP*GPC
219	SEA	Palau	176	219	POP*GPC
220	SEA	Marshall Islands	174	220	POP*GPC
221	AFR	San Tome & Principe	163	221	POP*GPC
222	SEA	Cook Islands	149	222	POP*GPC
223	DME	Falkland Islands	125	223	POP*GPC
224	LAM	Anguilla	98	224	POP*GPC

TABLE 2.3 GNI AT MARKET EXCHANGE RATES, MILLIONS OF DOLLARS, 2008					
OBS	REGION	COUNTRY	GDP	RANK	SOURCE
225	DME	St. Pierre & Miquelon	43	225	POP*GPC
226	SEA	Wallis & Futuna	43	226	POP*GPC
227	SEA	Nauru	37	227	POP*GPC
228	SEA	Tuvalu	28	228	POP*GPC
229	LAM	Montserrat	24	229	POP*GPC
230	AFR	St. Helena	16	230	POP*GPC
231	SEA	Niue	7	231	POP*GPC
232	SEA	Tokelau	1	232	POP*GPC

OBS	REGION	COUNTRY	ARMY	RANK	SOURCE
	TABLE 2.4 ARMED FORCES PERSONNEL, THOUSANDS, 2010				
1	CPA	China	2,945	1.0	10(IISS)
2	SAS	India	2,626	2.0	10(IISS)
3	DME	United States	1,580	3.0	10(IISS)
4	USR	Russia	1,476	4.0	10(IISS)
5	CPA	Korea, North	1,295	5.0	10(IISS)
6	SAS	Pakistan	921	6.0	10(IISS)
7	MEA	Egypt	866	7.0	10(IISS)
8	LAM	Brazil	723	8.0	10(IISS)
9	SEA	Korea, South	692	9.0	10(IISS)
10	MEA	Turkey	613	10.0	10(IISS)
11	SEA	Indonesia	582	11.0	10(IISS)
12	MEA	Iraq	578	12.0	10(IISS)
13	MEA	Iran	563	13.0	10(IISS)
14	CPA	Burma	513	14.0	10(IISS)
15	CPA	Vietnam	495	15.0	10(IISS)
16	DME	Italy	436	16.0	10(IISS)
17	MEA	Syria	433	17.0	10(IISS)
18	LAM	Colombia	429	18.0	10(IISS)
19	SEA	Thailand	420	19.0	10(IISS)
20	DME	France	353	20.0	10(IISS)
21	MEA	Algeria	334	21.0	10(IISS)
22	SEA	Taiwan	307	22.0	10(IISS)
23	LAM	Mexico	305	23.0	10(IISS)
24	DME	Germany	251	24.0	10(IISS)
25	MEA	Saudi Arabia	250	25.0	10(IISS)
26	MEA	Morocco	246	26.0	10(IISS)
27	DME	Japan	242	27.0	10(IISS)
28	SAS	Sri Lanka	223	28.0	10(IISS)
29	SAS	Bangladesh	221	29.0	10(IISS)
30	USR	Ukraine	215	30.0	10(IISS)
31	DME	Spain	208	31.0	10(IISS)
32	AFR	Eritrea	202	32.0	10(IISS)
33	CPA	Cambodia	191	33.5	10(IISS)
34	LAM	Peru	191	33.5	10(IISS)
35	USR	Belarus	183	35.0	10(IISS)
36	DME	Israel	177	36.0	10(IISS)
37	DME	United Kingdom	175	37.0	10(IISS)
38	SEA	Singapore	167	38.0	10(IISS)
39	AFR	Nigeria	162	39.0	10(IISS)
40	DME	Greece	161	40.5	10(IISS)
41	SEA	Philippines	161	40.5	10(IISS)
42	SAS	Nepal	158	42.0	10(IISS)
43	EEU	Romania	153	43.0	10(IISS)
44	AFR	Congo, Dem. Rep.	151	44.0	10(IISS)
45	AFR	Ethiopia	138	45.5	10(IISS)
46	MEA	Yemen	138	45.5	10(IISS)
47	SEA	Malaysia	134	47.0	10(IISS)

\multicolumn{6}{c}{TABLE 2.4 ARMED FORCES PERSONNEL, THOUSANDS, 2010}

OBS	REGION	COUNTRY	ARMY	RANK	SOURCE
48	CPA	Laos	129	48.0	10(IISS)
49	AFR	Sudan	127	49.0	10(IISS)
50	AFR	Angola	117	50.0	10(IISS)
51	LAM	Venezuela	115	51.0	10(IISS)
52	MEA	Jordan	111	52.0	10(IISS)
53	LAM	Argentina	104	53.0	10(IISS)
54	LAM	Chile	103	54.0	10(IISS)
55	EEU	Poland	100	55.0	10(IISS)
56	SAS	Afghanistan	94	56.0	10(IISS)
57	DME	Portugal	91	57.0	10(IISS)
58	USR	Uzbekistan	87	58.0	10(IISS)
59	LAM	Bolivia	83	59.0	10(IISS)
60	USR	Azerbaijan	82	60.0	10(IISS)
61	USR	Kazakhstan	81	61.0	10(IISS)
62	MEA	Lebanon	79	62.0	10(IISS)
63	LAM	Cuba	76	63.5	10(IISS)
64	MEA	Libya	76	63.5	10(IISS)
65	DME	Canada	66	65.0	10(IISS)
66	LAM	Dominican Rep.	65	66.0	10(IISS)
67	AFR	South Africa	62	67.0	10(IISS)
68	LAM	Ecuador	58	68.0	10(IISS)
69	DME	Australia	55	69.0	10(IISS)
70	USR	Armenia	52	70.0	10(IISS)
71	AFR	Burundi	51	72.0	10(IISS)
72	MEA	UAE	51	72.0	10(IISS)
73	AFR	Zimbabwe	51	72.0	10(IISS)
74	MEA	Tunisia	48	74.0	10(IISS)
75	DME	Netherlands	47	76.0	10(IISS)
76	MEA	Oman	47	76.0	10(IISS)
77	AFR	Uganda	47	76.0	10(IISS)
78	EEU	Hungary	41	78.0	10(IISS)
79	DME	Belgium	38	79.0	10(IISS)
80	MEA	West Bank	36	80.0	10(IISS)
81	EEU	Bulgaria	35	82.0	10(IISS)
82	AFR	Chad	35	82.0	10(IISS)
83	AFR	Rwanda	35	82.0	10(IISS)
84	LAM	Guatemala	34	84.0	10(IISS)
85	LAM	El Salvador	33	85.5	10(IISS)
86	USR	Georgia	33	85.5	10(IISS)
87	AFR	Kenya	29	87.5	10(IISS)
88	EEU	Serbia	29	87.5	10(IISS)
89	AFR	Tanzania	28	89.0	10(IISS)
90	DME	Austria	27	90.5	10(IISS)
91	DME	Denmark	27	90.5	10(IISS)
92	LAM	Paraguay	26	92.5	10(IISS)
93	LAM	Uruguay	26	92.5	10(IISS)
94	USR	Lithuania	24	94.5	10(IISS)
95	DME	Norway	24	94.5	10(IISS)

OBS	REGION	COUNTRY	ARMY	RANK	SOURCE
		TABLE 2.4 ARMED FORCES PERSONNEL, THOUSANDS, 2010			
96	AFR	Cameroon	23	97.0	10(IISS)
97	DME	Finland	23	97.0	10(IISS)
98	MEA	Kuwait	23	97.0	10(IISS)
99	AFR	Madagascar	22	100.0	10(IISS)
100	DME	Switzerland	22	100.0	10(IISS)
101	USR	Turkmenistan	22	100.0	10(IISS)
102	USR	Kyrgyzstan	21	102.0	10(IISS)
103	LAM	Honduras	20	103.0	10(IISS)
104	MEA	Gaza Strip	20	104.0	10(IISS)
105	MEA	Bahrain	19	107.0	10(IISS)
106	EEU	Croatia	19	107.0	10(IISS)
107	AFR	Guinea	19	107.0	10(IISS)
108	AFR	Ivory Coast	19	107.0	10(IISS)
109	AFR	Senegal	19	107.0	10(IISS)
110	EEU	Czechia	18	110.0	10(IISS)
111	CPA	Mongolia	17	112.0	10(IISS)
112	EEU	Slovakia	17	112.0	10(IISS)
113	USR	Tajikistan	17	112.0	10(IISS)
114	AFR	Ghana	16	115.0	10(IISS)
115	AFR	Mauritania	16	115.0	08(E)
116	AFR	Zambia	16	115.0	10(IISS)
117	AFR	Namibia	15	117.0	10(IISS)
118	EEU	Albania	14	118.5	10(IISS)
119	DME	Sweden	14	118.5	10(IISS)
120	AFR	Djibouti	13	120.0	10(IISS)
121	AFR	Congo, Rep.	12	123.5	10(IISS)
122	AFR	Mali	12	123.5	10(IISS)
123	LAM	Nicaragua	12	123.5	10(IISS)
124	LAM	Panama	12	123.5	10(IISS)
125	MEA	Qatar	12	123.5	10(IISS)
126	EEU	Slovenia	12	123.5	10(IISS)
127	EEU	Bosnia	11	129.5	10(IISS)
128	AFR	Botswana	11	129.5	10(IISS)
129	AFR	Burkina Faso	11	129.5	10(IISS)
130	MEA	Cyprus	11	129.5	10(IISS)
131	AFR	Mozambique	11	129.5	10(IISS)
132	AFR	Sierra Leone	11	129.5	10(IISS)
133	LAM	Costa Rica	10	135.0	10(IISS)
134	DME	Ireland	10	135.0	10(IISS)
135	DME	New Zealand	10	135.0	10(IISS)
136	AFR	Niger	10	135.0	10(IISS)
137	AFR	Togo	10	135.0	10(IISS)
138	SEA	Brunei	9	138.0	10(IISS)
139	AFR	Benin	8	140.5	10(IISS)
140	EEU	Macedonia	8	140.5	10(IISS)
141	USR	Moldova	8	140.5	10(IISS)
142	EEU	Montenegro	8	140.5	10(IISS)
143	AFR	Gabon	7	143.5	10(IISS)

OBS	REGION	COUNTRY	ARMY	RANK	SOURCE
		TABLE 2.4 ARMED FORCES PERSONNEL, THOUSANDS, 2010			
144	AFR	Malawi	7	143.5	10(IISS)
145	SAS	Bhutan	6	146.0	06(E)
146	AFR	Guinea-Bissau	6	146.0	10(IISS)
147	USR	Latvia	6	146.0	10(IISS)
148	USR	Estonia	5	148.0	10(IISS)
149	SEA	Fiji	4	149.5	10(IISS)
150	LAM	Trinidad & Tobago	4	149.5	10(IISS)
151	AFR	CAR	3	153.0	10(IISS)
152	LAM	Guyana	3	153.0	10(IISS)
153	LAM	Jamaica	3	153.0	10(IISS)
154	SEA	Papua New Guinea	3	153.0	10(IISS)
155	AFR	Swaziland	3	153.0	06(E)
156	AFR	Lesotho	2	159.5	10(IISS)
157	AFR	Liberia	2	159.5	10(IISS)
158	DME	Luxembourg	2	159.5	10(IISS)
159	SAS	Maldives	2	159.5	06(E)
160	DME	Malta	2	159.5	10(IISS)
161	AFR	Mauritius	2	159.5	10(IISS)
162	AFR	Somalia	2	159.5	10(IISS)
163	LAM	Suriname	2	159.5	10(IISS)
164	LAM	Bahamas	1	167.5	10(IISS)
165	LAM	Barbados	1	167.5	10(IISS)
166	LAM	Belize	1	167.5	10(IISS)
167	AFR	Cape Verde	1	167.5	10(IISS)
168	SEA	East Timor	1	167.5	10(IISS)
169	AFR	Equatorial Guinea	1	167.5	10(IISS)
170	AFR	Gambia	1	167.5	10(WB)
171	LAM	Haiti	1	167.5	06(IISS)
172	AFR	Comoros	1	172.0	00(IISS)
173	AFR	San Tome & Principe	1	173.5	05(E)
174	SEA	Tonga	1	173.5	07(E)
175	LAM	Antigua & Barbuda	0	175.5	08(E)
176	AFR	Seychelles	0	175.5	08(E)
177	DME	Iceland	0	177.0	08(E)
178	DME	Andorra	0	205.0	10(CIA)
179	LAM	Anguilla	0	205.0	10(CIA)
180	LAM	Aruba	0	205.0	10(CIA)
181	DME	Bermuda	0	205.0	10(CIA)
182	LAM	Cayman Islands	0	205.0	10(CIA)
183	SEA	Cook Islands	0	205.0	10(CIA)
184	LAM	Dominica	0	205.0	10(CIA)
185	DME	Faeroe Islands	0	205.0	10(CIA)
186	DME	Falkland Islands	0	205.0	10(CIA)
187	SEA	French Polynesia	0	205.0	10(CIA)

		TABLE 2.4 ARMED FORCES PERSONNEL, THOUSANDS, 2010			
OBS	REGION	COUNTRY	ARMY	RANK	SOURCE
188	DME	Gibraltar	0	205.0	10(CIA)
189	DME	Greenland	0	205.0	10(CIA)
190	LAM	Grenada	0	205.0	10(CIA)
191	LAM	Guadeloupe	0	205.0	10(CIA)
192	SEA	Guam	0	205.0	10(CIA)
193	DME	Guernsey	0	205.0	10(CIA)
194	LAM	Guiana, French	0	205.0	10(CIA)
195	SEA	Hong Kong	0	205.0	10(CIA)
196	DME	Isle of Man	0	205.0	10(CIA)
197	DME	Jersey	0	205.0	10(CIA)
198	SEA	Kiribati	0	205.0	10(CIA)
199	EEU	Kosovo	0	205.0	10(E)
200	DME	Liechtenstein	0	205.0	10(CIA)
201	SEA	Macao	0	205	10(CIA)
202	SEA	Marshall Islands	0	205	10(CIA)
203	LAM	Martinique	0	205	10(CIA)
204	AFR	Mayotte	0	205	10(CIA)
205	SEA	Micronesia	0	205	10(CIA)
206	DME	Monaco	0	205	10(CIA)
207	LAM	Montserrat	0	205	10(CIA)
208	SEA	Nauru	0	205	10(CIA)
209	LAM	Neth. Antilles	0	205	10(CIA)
210	SEA	New Caledonia	0	205	10(CIA)
211	SEA	Niue	0	205	10(CIA)
212	SEA	Northern Mariana Is.	0	205	10(CIA)
213	SEA	Palau	0	205	10(CIA)
214	LAM	Puerto Rico	0	205	10(CIA)
215	AFR	Reunion	0	205	10(CIA)
216	SEA	Samoa, American	0	205	10(CIA)
217	SEA	Samoa, Western	0	205	10(CIA)
218	DME	San Marino	0	205	10(CIA)
219	SEA	Solomon Islands	0	205	10(CIA)
220	AFR	St. Helena	0	205	10(CIA)
221	LAM	St. Kitts & Nevis	0	205	10(CIA)
222	LAM	St. Lucia	0	205	10(CIA)
223	DME	St. Pierre & Miquelon	0	205	10(CIA)
224	LAM	St. Vincent	0	205	10(CIA)
225	SEA	Tokelau	0	205	10(CIA)
226	LAM	Turks & Caicos Is.	0	205	10(CIA)
227	SEA	Tuvalu	0	205	10(CIA)
228	SEA	Vanuatu	0	205	10(CIA)
229	LAM	Virgin Islands, Brit.	0	205	10(CIA)

OBS	REGION	COUNTRY	ARMY	RANK	SOURCE
230	LAM	Virgin Islands, US	0	205	10(CIA)
231	SEA	Wallis & Futuna	0	205	10(CIA)
232	AFR	Western Sahara	0	205	10(CIA)

TABLE 2.4 ARMED FORCES PERSONNEL, THOUSANDS, 2010

OBS	REGION	COUNTRY	MILGDP	RANK	SOURCE
		TABLE 2.5 MILITARY EXPENDITURES AS SHARE OF GDP, PERCENT, 2008			
1	CPA	Korea, North	25.00	1.0	02(IISS)
2	AFR	Eritrea	23.55	2.0	03(WB)
3	MEA	Oman	10.39	3.0	07(WB)
4	MEA	Saudi Arabia	8.15	4.0	08(WB)
5	USR	Georgia	8.11	5.0	08(WB)
6	DME	Israel	8.01	6.0	08(WB)
7	MEA	Iraq	7.74	7.0	08(WB)
8	MEA	Gaza Strip	5.94	8.5	08(WB)
9	MEA	West Bank	5.94	8.5	08(WB)
10	MEA	Jordan	5.88	10.0	08(WB)
11	LAM	Guyana	5.80	11.0	08(IISS)
12	MEA	Yemen	4.50	12.0	08(WB)
13	MEA	Lebanon	4.45	13.0	08(WB)
14	DME	United States	4.31	14.0	08(WB)
15	AFR	Sudan	4.22	15.0	06(WB)
16	AFR	Djibouti	4.14	16.0	08(WB)
17	SEA	Singapore	4.13	17.0	08(WB)
18	AFR	Guinea-Bissau	4.01	18.0	05(WB)
19	LAM	Cuba	4.00	19.5	08(IISS)
20	AFR	Somalia	4.00	19.5	02(IISS)
21	AFR	Zimbabwe	3.85	21.0	05(WB)
22	AFR	Mauritania	3.83	22.0	08(WB)
23	AFR	Burundi	3.77	23.0	08(WB)
24	LAM	Colombia	3.72	24.0	08(WB)
25	MEA	Cyprus	3.68	25.0	08(WB)
26	DME	Greece	3.55	26.0	08(WB)
27	LAM	Chile	3.51	27.0	08(WB)
28	USR	Russia	3.50	28.0	08(WB)
29	SAS	Maldives	3.40	29.0	08(IISS)
30	AFR	Botswana	3.38	30.5	08(WB)
31	MEA	Syria	3.38	30.5	08(WB)
32	MEA	Morocco	3.31	32.0	08(WB)
33	SAS	Pakistan	3.27	33.0	08(WB)
34	USR	Armenia	3.18	34.0	08(WB)
35	MEA	Kuwait	3.15	35.0	08(WB)
36	MEA	Algeria	3.11	36.0	08(WB)
37	AFR	Namibia	3.02	37.5	08(WB)
38	SAS	Sri Lanka	3.02	37.5	08(WB)
39	MEA	Iran	2.87	39.0	07(WB)
40	AFR	Angola	2.86	40.0	08(WB)
41	LAM	Ecuador	2.83	41.0	08(WB)
42	SEA	Taiwan	2.76	42.0	08(IISS)
43	USR	Azerbaijan	2.68	43.0	08(WB)
44	MEA	Bahrain	2.67	44.5	08(WB)
45	USR	Ukraine	2.67	44.5	08(WB)
46	SEA	Korea, South	2.60	46.0	08(WB)
47	AFR	Lesotho	2.58	47.0	08(WB)

OBS	REGION	COUNTRY	MILGDP	RANK	SOURCE
\multicolumn{6}{}					

TABLE 2.5 MILITARY EXPENDITURES AS SHARE OF GDP, PERCENT, 2008

OBS	REGION	COUNTRY	MILGDP	RANK	SOURCE
48	SAS	India	2.45	48.5	08(WB)
49	DME	United Kingdom	2.45	48.5	08(WB)
50	USR	Kyrgyzstan	2.42	50.0	08(WB)
51	SEA	Brunei	2.41	51.0	07(WB)
52	MEA	Egypt	2.30	52.5	08(WB)
53	DME	France	2.30	52.5	08(WB)
54	EEU	Serbia	2.28	54.5	08(WB)
55	AFR	Sierra Leone	2.28	54.5	08(WB)
56	USR	Tajikistan	2.27	56.0	04(WB)
57	AFR	Uganda	2.26	57.0	07(WB)
58	USR	Estonia	2.24	58.0	08(WB)
59	AFR	Guinea	2.23	59.0	04(WB)
60	SAS	Afghanistan	2.22	60.0	08(WB)
61	EEU	Bulgaria	2.19	61.0	08(WB)
62	MEA	Turkey	2.17	62.0	08(WB)
63	AFR	Swaziland	2.10	63.0	07(WB)
64	EEU	Macedonia	2.05	64.0	08(WB)
65	EEU	Albania	2.03	65.5	08(WB)
66	EEU	Poland	2.03	65.5	08(WB)
67	CPA	Vietnam	2.02	67.0	08(WB)
68	DME	Portugal	1.98	68.0	08(WB)
69	AFR	Mali	1.97	69.5	08(WB)
70	AFR	Togo	1.97	69.5	08(WB)
71	CPA	China	1.96	72.0	08(WB)
72	AFR	Kenya	1.96	72.0	08(WB)
73	SEA	Malaysia	1.96	72.0	08(WB)
74	MEA	UAE	1.92	74.0	05(WB)
75	USR	Latvia	1.88	75.0	08(WB)
76	AFR	Zambia	1.83	76.0	08(WB)
77	EEU	Croatia	1.82	77.0	08(WB)
78	SEA	East Timor	1.80	78.0	05(CIA)
79	AFR	Burkina Faso	1.79	79.0	08(WB)
80	DME	Australia	1.78	80.0	08(WB)
81	DME	Italy	1.76	81.0	08(WB)
82	MEA	Qatar	1.75	82.0	08(IISS)
83	EEU	Slovenia	1.64	83.0	08(WB)
84	AFR	Senegal	1.63	84.0	08(WB)
85	AFR	CAR	1.58	85.0	08(WB)
86	USR	Lithuania	1.56	86.0	08(WB)
87	EEU	Slovakia	1.55	87.0	08(WB)
88	DME	Malta	1.54	88.0	07(WB)
89	AFR	Ethiopia	1.53	89.0	08(WB)
90	AFR	Rwanda	1.52	90.0	08(WB)
91	SEA	Thailand	1.51	91.0	08(WB)
92	LAM	Bolivia	1.50	92.5	08(WB)
93	EEU	Romania	1.50	92.5	08(WB)
94	LAM	Brazil	1.48	95.5	08(WB)

OBS	REGION	COUNTRY	MILGDP	RANK	SOURCE
\multicolumn{6}{TABLE 2.5 MILITARY EXPENDITURES AS SHARE OF GDP, PERCENT, 2008}					

OBS	REGION	COUNTRY	MILGDP	RANK	SOURCE
95	AFR	Cameroon	1.48	95.5	08(WB)
96	EEU	Czechia	1.48	95.5	08(WB)
97	SEA	Tonga	1.48	95.5	07(WB)
98	AFR	Ivory Coast	1.47	98.5	08(WB)
99	SAS	Nepal	1.47	98.5	08(WB)
100	EEU	Montenegro	1.46	100.0	08(WB)
101	CPA	Mongolia	1.44	101.0	07(WB)
102	EEU	Bosnia	1.40	102.5	08(WB)
103	DME	Netherlands	1.40	102.5	08(WB)
104	USR	Belarus	1.38	104.0	08(WB)
105	AFR	Congo, Dem. Rep.	1.37	105.0	08(WB)
106	AFR	South Africa	1.36	106.0	08(WB)
107	SEA	Fiji	1.34	107.0	08(WB)
108	LAM	Suriname	1.33	108.0	08(IISS)
109	DME	Sweden	1.32	109.0	08(WB)
110	AFR	Congo, Rep.	1.31	111.0	08(WB)
111	DME	Denmark	1.31	111.0	08(WB)
112	MEA	Tunisia	1.31	111.0	08(WB)
113	CPA	Burma	1.30	114.0	02(WB)
114	DME	Finland	1.30	114.0	08(WB)
115	DME	Norway	1.30	114.0	08(WB)
116	DME	Canada	1.28	116.5	08(WB)
117	DME	Germany	1.28	116.5	08(WB)
118	LAM	Peru	1.24	118.0	08(WB)
119	LAM	Uruguay	1.22	119.0	08(WB)
120	EEU	Hungary	1.21	120.0	08(WB)
121	AFR	San Tome & Principe	1.20	121.5	05(E)
122	DME	Spain	1.20	121.5	08(WB)
123	MEA	Libya	1.18	123.0	08(WB)
124	AFR	Malawi	1.16	124.0	07(WB)
125	SAS	Bangladesh	1.13	125.0	08(WB)
126	CPA	Cambodia	1.11	126.0	07(WB)
127	DME	Belgium	1.10	127.0	08(WB)
128	AFR	Madagascar	1.09	128.0	08(WB)
129	DME	New Zealand	1.08	129.5	08(WB)
130	AFR	Niger	1.08	129.5	08(IISS)
131	AFR	Gabon	1.06	131.5	07(WB)
132	LAM	Venezuela	1.06	131.5	08(WB)
133	AFR	Benin	1.01	133.0	08(WB)
134	LAM	Belize	1.00	135.0	06(WB)
135	SAS	Bhutan	1.00	135.0	05(E)
136	LAM	Haiti	1.00	135.0	02(IISS)
137	USR	Kazakhstan	0.99	137.0	08(WB)
138	SEA	Indonesia	0.98	138.5	08(WB)
139	AFR	Seychelles	0.98	138.5	08(WB)
140	LAM	Panama	0.97	140.0	08(IISS)

OBS	REGION	COUNTRY	MILGDP	RANK	SOURCE
		TABLE 2.5 MILITARY EXPENDITURES AS SHARE OF GDP, PERCENT, 2008			
141	AFR	Chad	0.96	141.0	08(WB)
142	DME	Japan	0.94	142.0	08(WB)
143	AFR	Tanzania	0.93	143.0	08(WB)
144	DME	Austria	0.86	144.0	08(WB)
145	AFR	Mozambique	0.85	145.0	08(WB)
146	LAM	Barbados	0.83	146.5	06(WB)
147	LAM	Paraguay	0.83	146.5	08(WB)
148	DME	Switzerland	0.82	148.0	08(WB)
149	LAM	Bahamas	0.81	149.5	07(WB)
150	SEA	Philippines	0.81	149.5	08(WB)
151	LAM	Argentina	0.76	151.0	08(WB)
152	DME	Luxembourg	0.74	152.0	07(WB)
153	USR	Turkmenistan	0.71	153.0	08(IISS)
154	AFR	Gambia	0.70	154.0	07(WB)
155	AFR	Ghana	0.68	155.0	08(WB)
156	LAM	Honduras	0.67	156.0	08(WB)
157	AFR	Nigeria	0.66	157.0	08(IISS)
158	LAM	Nicaragua	0.63	158.0	08(WB)
159	DME	Ireland	0.59	159.5	08(WB)
160	LAM	Trinidad & Tobago	0.59	159.5	08(IISS)
161	LAM	Dominican Rep.	0.58	161.0	08(WB)
162	LAM	Antigua & Barbuda	0.56	162.0	08(IISS)
163	AFR	Cape Verde	0.55	163.5	08(WB)
164	LAM	Jamaica	0.55	163.5	08(WB)
165	USR	Uzbekistan	0.54	165.0	03(WB)
166	LAM	Costa Rica	0.53	166.5	08(IISS)
167	LAM	El Salvador	0.53	166.5	08(WB)
168	AFR	Liberia	0.49	168.0	07(WB)
169	LAM	Guatemala	0.48	169.0	08(WB)
170	USR	Moldova	0.44	170.0	08(WB)
171	SEA	Papua New Guinea	0.43	171.0	08(WB)
172	LAM	Mexico	0.40	172.0	08(WB)
173	CPA	Laos	0.34	173.0	07(WB)
174	DME	Iceland	0.30	174.0	08(E)
175	AFR	Comoros	0.20	175.0	00(IISS)
176	AFR	Mauritius	0.16	176.0	07(WB)
177	AFR	Equatorial Guinea	0.06	177.0	08(IISS)
178	DME	Andorra	0.00	205.0	08(CIA)
179	LAM	Anguilla	0.00	205.0	08(CIA)
180	LAM	Aruba	0.00	205.0	08(CIA)
181	DME	Bermuda	0.00	205.0	08(CIA)
182	LAM	Cayman Islands	0.00	205.0	08(CIA)
183	SEA	Cook Islands	0.00	205.0	08(CIA)
184	LAM	Dominica	0.00	205.0	08(CIA)

OBS	REGION	COUNTRY	MILGDP	RANK	SOURCE

TABLE 2.5 MILITARY EXPENDITURES AS SHARE OF GDP, PERCENT, 2008

OBS	REGION	COUNTRY	MILGDP	RANK	SOURCE
185	DME	Faeroe Islands	0.00	205.0	08(CIA)
186	DME	Falkland Islands	0.00	205.0	08(CIA)
187	SEA	French Polynesia	0.00	205.0	08(CIA)
188	DME	Gibraltar	0.00	205.0	08(CIA)
189	DME	Greenland	0.00	205.0	08(CIA)
190	LAM	Grenada	0.00	205.0	08(CIA)
191	LAM	Guadeloupe	0.00	205.0	08(CIA)
192	SEA	Guam	0.00	205.0	08(CIA)
193	DME	Guernsey	0.00	205.0	08(CIA)
194	LAM	Guiana, French	0.00	205.0	08(CIA)
195	SEA	Hong Kong	0.00	205.0	08(CIA)
196	DME	Isle of Man	0.00	205.0	08(CIA)
197	DME	Jersey	0.00	205.0	08(CIA)
198	SEA	Kiribati	0.00	205.0	08(CIA)
199	EEU	Kosovo	0.00	205.0	08(E)
200	DME	Liechtenstein	0.00	205.0	08(CIA)
201	SEA	Macao	0.00	205.0	08(CIA)
202	SEA	Marshall Islands	0.00	205.0	08(CIA)
203	LAM	Martinique	0.00	205.0	08(CIA)
204	AFR	Mayotte	0.00	205.0	08(CIA)
205	SEA	Micronesia	0.00	205.0	08(CIA)
206	DME	Monaco	0.00	205.0	08(CIA)
207	LAM	Montserrat	0.00	205.0	08(CIA)
208	SEA	Nauru	0.00	205.0	08(CIA)
209	LAM	Neth. Antilles	0.00	205.0	08(CIA)
210	SEA	New Caledonia	0.00	205.0	08(CIA)
211	SEA	Niue	0.00	205.0	08(CIA)
212	SEA	Northern Mariana Is.	0.00	205.0	08(CIA)
213	SEA	Palau	0.00	205.0	08(CIA)
214	LAM	Puerto Rico	0.00	205.0	08(CIA)
215	AFR	Reunion	0.00	205.0	08(CIA)
216	SEA	Samoa, American	0.00	205.0	08(CIA)
217	SEA	Samoa, Western	0.00	205.0	08(CIA)
218	DME	San Marino	0.00	205.0	08(CIA)
219	SEA	Solomon Islands	0.00	205.0	08(CIA)
220	AFR	St. Helena	0.00	205.0	08(CIA)
221	LAM	St. Kitts & Nevis	0.00	205.0	08(CIA)
222	LAM	St. Lucia	0.00	205.0	08(CIA)
223	DME	St. Pierre & Miquelon	0.00	205.0	08(CIA)
224	LAM	St. Vincent	0.00	205.0	08(CIA)
225	SEA	Tokelau	0.00	205.0	08(CIA)
226	LAM	Turks & Caicos Is.	0.00	205.0	08(CIA)
227	SEA	Tuvalu	0.00	205.0	08(CIA)
228	SEA	Vanuatu	0.00	205.0	08(CIA)

TABLE 2.5 MILITARY EXPENDITURES AS SHARE OF GDP, PERCENT, 2008					
OBS	REGION	COUNTRY	MILGDP	RANK	SOURCE
229	LAM	Virgin Islands, Brit.	0.00	205.0	08(CIA)
230	LAM	Virgin Islands, US	0.00	205.0	08(CIA)
231	SEA	Wallis & Futuna	0.00	205.0	08(CIA)
232	AFR	Western Sahara	0.00	205.0	08(CIA)

OBS	REGION	COUNTRY	MILAID	RANK	SOURCE
		TABLE 2.6 FOREIGN MILITARY AID, MILLIONS OF DOLLARS, 2008			
1	SAS	Afghanistan	6011.6	1.0	08(USAID)
2	MEA	Iraq	4369.0	2.0	08(USAID)
3	DME	Israel	2380.6	3.0	08(USAID)
4	MEA	Egypt	1290.7	4.0	08(USAID)
5	SAS	Pakistan	358.1	5.0	08(USAID)
6	MEA	Jordan	301.3	6.0	08(USAID)
7	AFR	Sudan	198.8	7.0	08(USAID)
8	AFR	Liberia	87.6	8.0	08(USAID)
9	LAM	Colombia	54.0	9.0	08(USAID)
10	AFR	Somalia	48.3	10.0	08(USAID)
11	SEA	Philippines	29.3	11.0	08(USAID)
12	EEU	Poland	29.1	12.0	08(USAID)
13	SEA	Indonesia	13.9	13.0	08(USAID)
14	EEU	Romania	12.8	14.0	08(USAID)
15	MEA	Tunisia	10.1	15.0	08(USAID)
16	USR	Georgia	9.8	16.0	08(USAID)
17	MEA	Turkey	9.7	17.0	08(USAID)
18	MEA	Lebanon	8.4	18.0	08(USAID)
19	EEU	Bulgaria	8.2	19.0	08(USAID)
20	USR	Ukraine	7.9	20.0	08(USAID)
21	LAM	El Salvador	7.3	21.0	08(USAID)
22	AFR	Congo, Dem. Rep.	6.4	22.0	08(USAID)
23	MEA	Oman	6.1	23.0	08(USAID)
24	MEA	Morocco	5.3	24.0	08(USAID)
25	MEA	Yemen	4.9	25.0	08(USAID)
26	MEA	Bahrain	4.6	26.0	08(USAID)
27	EEU	Czechia	4.4	27.0	08(USAID)
28	EEU	Bosnia	4.3	28.0	08(USAID)
29	USR	Azerbaijan	3.9	29.0	08(USAID)
30	USR	Armenia	3.5	30.0	09(USAID)
31	EEU	Macedonia	3.4	31.0	08(USAID)
32	EEU	Albania	2.8	32.0	08(USAID)
33	USR	Estonia	2.6	33.5	08(USAID)
34	USR	Lithuania	2.6	33.5	08(USAID)
35	USR	Latvia	2.5	35.0	08(USAID)
36	AFR	Djibouti	2.3	36.5	08(USAID)
37	USR	Kazakhstan	2.3	36.5	08(USAID)
38	AFR	Nigeria	2.2	38.0	08(USAID)
39	EEU	Hungary	2.1	39.5	08(USAID)
40	EEU	Slovakia	2.1	39.5	08(USAID)
41	LAM	Honduras	2.0	41.5	08(USAID)
42	SEA	Thailand	2.0	41.5	08(USAID)
43	CPA	Mongolia	1.9	43.0	08(USAID)
44	USR	Kyrgyzstan	1.8	44.0	08(USAID)
45	LAM	Nicaragua	1.6	45.0	08(USAID)
46	LAM	Dominican Rep.	1.5	46.0	08(USAID)
47	SAS	Bangladesh	1.4	47.5	08(USAID)

OBS	REGION	COUNTRY	MILAID	RANK	SOURCE
		TABLE 2.6 FOREIGN MILITARY AID, MILLIONS OF DOLLARS, 2008			
48	AFR	Ethiopia	1.4	47.5	08(USAID)
49	SAS	India	1.3	50.0	08(USAID)
50	LAM	Jamaica	1.3	50.0	08(USAID)
51	AFR	Senegal	1.3	50.0	08(USAID)
52	LAM	Haiti	1.2	52.5	08(USAID)
53	EEU	Slovenia	1.2	52.5	08(USAID)
54	AFR	Comoros	1.1	54.5	08(USAID)
55	USR	Moldova	1.1	54.5	08(USAID)
56	AFR	Botswana	1.0	56.0	08(USAID)
57	LAM	Argentina	0.9	59.5	08(USAID)
58	LAM	Belize	0.9	59.5	08(USAID)
59	AFR	Ghana	0.9	59.5	08(USAID)
60	SAS	Nepal	0.9	59.5	08(USAID)
61	AFR	South Africa	0.9	59.5	08(USAID)
62	USR	Tajikistan	0.9	59.5	08(USAID)
63	AFR	Kenya	0.8	63.5	08(USAID)
64	SEA	Malaysia	0.8	63.5	08(USAID)
65	MEA	Algeria	0.7	66.5	08(USAID)
66	CPA	Cambodia	0.7	66.5	08(USAID)
67	LAM	Panama	0.7	66.5	08(USAID)
68	SEA	Tonga	0.7	66.5	08(USAID)
69	LAM	Bahamas	0.6	70.0	08(USAID)
70	SAS	Sri Lanka	0.6	70.0	08(USAID)
71	AFR	Uganda	0.6	70.0	08(USAID)
72	LAM	Chile	0.5	72.5	08(USAID)
73	LAM	Guatemala	0.5	72.5	08(USAID)
74	DME	Greece	0.4	78.0	08(USAID)
75	AFR	Guinea	0.4	78.0	08(USAID)
76	AFR	Madagascar	0.4	78.0	08(USAID)
77	AFR	Malawi	0.4	78.0	08(USAID)
78	LAM	Mexico	0.4	78.0	08(USAID)
79	DME	Portugal	0.4	78.0	08(USAID)
80	AFR	Rwanda	0.4	78.0	08(USAID)
81	AFR	Sierra Leone	0.4	78.0	08(USAID)
82	AFR	Zambia	0.4	78.0	08(USAID)
83	AFR	Angola	0.3	87.5	08(USAID)
84	AFR	Burundi	0.3	87.5	08(USAID)
85	AFR	Cameroon	0.3	87.5	08(USAID)
86	EEU	Croatia	0.3	87.5	08(USAID)
87	LAM	Guyana	0.3	87.5	08(USAID)
88	EEU	Kosovo	0.3	87.5	08(USAID)
89	AFR	Mozambique	0.3	87.5	08(USAID)
90	SEA	Papua New Guinea	0.3	87.5	08(USAID)
91	AFR	Tanzania	0.3	87.5	08(USAID)
92	USR	Turkmenistan	0.3	87.5	08(USAID)
93	LAM	Bolivia	0.2	101.5	08(USAID)

OBS	REGION	COUNTRY	MILAID	RANK	SOURCE
94	LAM	Brazil	0.2	101.5	08(USAID)
95	AFR	Burkina Faso	0.2	101.5	08(USAID)
96	AFR	Cape Verde	0.2	101.5	08(USAID)
97	AFR	Chad	0.2	101.5	08(USAID)
98	AFR	Congo, Rep.	0.2	101.5	08(USAID)
99	LAM	Costa Rica	0.2	101.5	08(USAID)
100	LAM	Ecuador	0.2	101.5	08(USAID)
101	AFR	Gabon	0.2	101.5	08(USAID)
102	AFR	Lesotho	0.2	101.5	08(USAID)
103	SAS	Maldives	0.2	101.5	08(USAID)
104	AFR	Mali	0.2	101.5	08(USAID)
105	LAM	Paraguay	0.2	101.5	08(USAID)
106	LAM	Peru	0.2	101.5	08(USAID)
107	LAM	Suriname	0.2	101.5	08(USAID)
108	AFR	Swaziland	0.2	101.5	08(USAID)
109	LAM	Uruguay	0.2	101.5	08(USAID)
110	CPA	Vietnam	0.2	101.5	08(USAID)
111	LAM	Antigua & Barbuda	0.1	123.5	08(USAID)
112	LAM	Barbados	0.1	123.5	08(USAID)
113	AFR	Benin	0.1	123.5	08(USAID)
114	AFR	CAR	0.1	123.5	08(USAID)
115	LAM	Dominica	0.1	123.5	08(USAID)
116	SEA	East Timor	0.1	123.5	08(USAID)
117	AFR	Gambia	0.1	123.5	08(USAID)
118	LAM	Grenada	0.1	123.5	08(USAID)
119	AFR	Guinea-Bissau	0.1	123.5	08(USAID)
120	CPA	Laos	0.1	123.5	08(USAID)
121	AFR	Mauritania	0.1	123.5	08(USAID)
122	AFR	Mauritius	0.1	123.5	08(USAID)
123	DME	Monaco	0.1	123.5	08(USAID)
124	EEU	Montenegro	0.1	123.5	08(USAID)
125	AFR	Namibia	0.1	123.5	08(USAID)
126	AFR	Niger	0.1	123.5	08(USAID)
127	USR	Russia	0.1	123.5	08(USAID)
128	AFR	San Tome & Principe	0.1	123.5	08(USAID)
129	AFR	Seychelles	0.1	123.5	08(USAID)
130	SEA	Solomon Islands	0.1	123.5	08(USAID)
131	LAM	St. Kitts & Nevis	0.1	123.5	08(USAID)
132	LAM	St. Lucia	0.1	123.5	08(USAID)
133	LAM	St. Vincent	0.1	123.5	08(USAID)
134	AFR	Togo	0.1	123.5	08(USAID)
135	LAM	Trinidad & Tobago	0.1	123.5	08(USAID)
136	SEA	Vanuatu	0.1	123.5	08(USAID)
137	DME	Andorra	0.0	184.5	08(USAID)

OBS	REGION	COUNTRY	MILAID	RANK	SOURCE
		TABLE 2.6 FOREIGN MILITARY AID, MILLIONS OF DOLLARS, 2008			
138	LAM	Anguilla	0.0	184.5	08(USAID)
139	LAM	Aruba	0.0	184.5	08(USAID)
140	DME	Australia	0.0	184.5	08(USAID)
141	DME	Austria	0.0	184.5	08(USAID)
142	USR	Belarus	0.0	184.5	08(USAID)
143	DME	Belgium	0.0	184.5	08(USAID)
144	DME	Bermuda	0.0	184.5	08(USAID)
145	SAS	Bhutan	0.0	184.5	08(USAID)
146	SEA	Brunei	0.0	184.5	08(USAID)
147	CPA	Burma	0.0	184.5	08(USAID)
148	DME	Canada	0.0	184.5	08(USAID)
149	LAM	Cayman Islands	0.0	184.5	08(USAID)
150	CPA	China	0.0	184.5	08(USAID)
151	SEA	Cook Islands	0.0	184.5	08(USAID)
152	LAM	Cuba	0.0	184.5	08(USAID)
153	MEA	Cyprus	0.0	184.5	08(USAID)
154	DME	Denmark	0.0	184.5	08(USAID)
155	AFR	Equatorial Guinea	0.0	184.5	08(USAID)
156	AFR	Eritrea	0.0	184.5	08(USAID)
157	DME	Faeroe Islands	0.0	184.5	08(USAID)
158	DME	Falkland Islands	0.0	184.5	08(USAID)
159	SEA	Fiji	0.0	184.5	08(USAID)
160	DME	Finland	0.0	184.5	08(USAID)
161	DME	France	0.0	184.5	08(USAID)
162	SEA	French Polynesia	0.0	184.5	08(USAID)
163	MEA	Gaza Strip	0.0	184.5	08(USAID)
164	DME	Germany	0.0	184.5	08(USAID)
165	DME	Gibraltar	0.0	184.5	08(USAID)
166	DME	Greenland	0.0	184.5	08(USAID)
167	LAM	Guadeloupe	0.0	184.5	08(USAID)
168	SEA	Guam	0.0	184.5	08(USAID)
169	DME	Guernsey	0.0	184.5	08(USAID)
170	LAM	Guiana, French	0.0	184.5	08(USAID)
171	SEA	Hong Kong	0.0	184.5	08(USAID)
172	DME	Iceland	0.0	184.5	08(USAID)
173	MEA	Iran	0.0	184.5	08(USAID)
174	DME	Ireland	0.0	184.5	08(USAID)
175	DME	Isle of Man	0.0	184.5	08(USAID)
176	DME	Italy	0.0	184.5	08(USAID)
177	AFR	Ivory Coast	0.0	184.5	08(USAID)
178	DME	Japan	0.0	184.5	08(USAID)
179	DME	Jersey	0.0	184.5	08(USAID)
180	SEA	Kiribati	0.0	184.5	08(USAID)
181	CPA	Korea, North	0.0	184.5	08(USAID)
182	SEA	Korea, South	0.0	184.5	08(USAID)
183	MEA	Kuwait	0.0	184.5	08(USAID)
184	MEA	Libya	0.0	184.5	08(USAID)

OBS	REGION	COUNTRY	MILAID	RANK	SOURCE
\multicolumn{6}{c}{TABLE 2.6 FOREIGN MILITARY AID, MILLIONS OF DOLLARS, 2008}
185	DME	Liechtenstein	0.0	184.5	08(USAID)
186	DME	Luxembourg	0.0	184.5	08(USAID)
187	SEA	Macao	0.0	184.5	08(USAID)
188	DME	Malta	0.0	184.5	08(USAID)
189	SEA	Marshall Islands	0.0	184.5	08(USAID)
190	LAM	Martinique	0.0	184.5	08(USAID)
191	AFR	Mayotte	0.0	184.5	08(USAID)
192	SEA	Micronesia	0.0	184.5	08(USAID)
193	LAM	Montserrat	0.0	184.5	08(USAID)
194	SEA	Nauru	0.0	184.5	08(USAID)
195	LAM	Neth. Antilles	0.0	184.5	08(USAID)
196	DME	Netherlands	0.0	184.5	08(USAID)
197	SEA	New Caledonia	0.0	184.5	08(USAID)
198	DME	New Zealand	0.0	184.5	08(USAID)
199	SEA	Niue	0.0	184.5	08(USAID)
200	SEA	Northern Mariana Is.	0.0	184.5	08(USAID)
201	DME	Norway	0.0	184.5	08(USAID)
202	SEA	Palau	0.0	184.5	08(USAID)
203	LAM	Puerto Rico	0.0	184.5	08(USAID)
204	MEA	Qatar	0.0	184.5	08(USAID)
205	AFR	Reunion	0.0	184.5	08(USAID)
206	SEA	Samoa, American	0.0	184.5	08(USAID)
207	SEA	Samoa, Western	0.0	184.5	08(USAID)
208	DME	San Marino	0.0	184.5	08(USAID)
209	MEA	Saudi Arabia	0.0	184.5	08(USAID)
210	EEU	Serbia	0.0	184.5	08(USAID)
211	SEA	Singapore	0.0	184.5	08(USAID)
212	DME	Spain	0.0	184.5	08(USAID)
213	AFR	St. Helena	0.0	184.5	08(USAID)
214	DME	St. Pierre & Miquelon	0.0	184.5	08(USAID)
215	DME	Sweden	0.0	184.5	08(USAID)
216	DME	Switzerland	0.0	184.5	08(USAID)
217	MEA	Syria	0.0	184.5	08(USAID)
218	SEA	Taiwan	0.0	184.5	08(USAID)
219	SEA	Tokelau	0.0	184.5	08(USAID)
220	LAM	Turks & Caicos Is.	0.0	184.5	08(USAID)
221	SEA	Tuvalu	0.0	184.5	08(USAID)
222	MEA	UAE	0.0	184.5	08(USAID)
223	DME	United Kingdom	0.0	184.5	08(USAID)
224	DME	United States	0.0	184.5	08(USAID)
225	USR	Uzbekistan	0.0	184.5	08(USAID)
226	LAM	Venezuela	0.0	184.5	08(USAID)
227	LAM	Virgin Islands, Brit.	0.0	184.5	08(USAID)
228	LAM	Virgin Islands, US	0.0	184.5	08(USAID)

TABLE 2.6 FOREIGN MILITARY AID, MILLIONS OF DOLLARS, 2008					
OBS	REGION	COUNTRY	MILAID	RANK	SOURCE
229	SEA	Wallis & Futuna	0.0	184.5	08(USAID)
230	MEA	West Bank	0.0	184.5	08(USAID)
231	AFR	Western Sahara	0.0	184.5	08(USAID)
232	AFR	Zimbabwe	0.0	184.5	08(USAID)

TABLE 2.7 MILITARY EXPENDITURES AT PURCHASING POWER PARITIES PLUS FOREIGN MILITARY AID, MILLIONS OF DOLLARS, 2008

OBS	REGION	COUNTRY	MILXPP	RANK	SOURCE
1	DME	United States	614,399	1.0	GDPPPP*MILGDP+MILAID
2	CPA	China	154,796	2.0	GDPPPP*MILGDP+MILAID
3	SAS	India	83,591	3.0	GDPPPP*MILGDP+MILAID
4	USR	Russia	80,121	4.0	GDPPPP*MILGDP+MILAID
5	DME	United Kingdom	53,360	5.0	GDPPPP*MILGDP+MILAID
6	DME	France	48,570	6.0	GDPPPP*MILGDP+MILAID
7	MEA	Saudi Arabia	48,308	7.0	GDPPPP*MILGDP+MILAID
8	DME	Japan	40,923	8.0	GDPPPP*MILGDP+MILAID
9	DME	Germany	37,445	9.0	GDPPPP*MILGDP+MILAID
10	SEA	Korea, South	36,457	10.0	GDPPPP*MILGDP+MILAID
11	DME	Italy	32,348	11.0	GDPPPP*MILGDP+MILAID
12	LAM	Brazil	28,520	12.0	GDPPPP*MILGDP+MILAID
13	MEA	Iran	24,197	13.0	GDPPPP*MILGDP+MILAID
14	MEA	Turkey	21,457	14.0	GDPPPP*MILGDP+MILAID
15	SEA	Taiwan	20,247	15.0	GDPPPP*MILGDP+MILAID
16	DME	Israel	17,866	16.0	GDPPPP*MILGDP+MILAID
17	DME	Spain	17,509	17.0	GDPPPP*MILGDP+MILAID
18	DME	Canada	15,493	18.0	GDPPPP*MILGDP+MILAID
19	LAM	Colombia	14,743	19.0	GDPPPP*MILGDP+MILAID
20	SAS	Pakistan	14,357	20.0	GDPPPP*MILGDP+MILAID
21	EEU	Poland	13,665	21.0	GDPPPP*MILGDP+MILAID
22	DME	Australia	13,551	22.0	GDPPPP*MILGDP+MILAID
23	MEA	Iraq	13,500	23.0	GDPPPP*MILGDP+MILAID
24	DME	Greece	11,715	24.0	GDPPPP*MILGDP+MILAID
25	MEA	Egypt	10,609	25.0	GDPPPP*MILGDP+MILAID
26	CPA	Korea, North	10,143	26.0	GDPPPP*MILGDP+MILAID
27	SEA	Singapore	9,849	27.0	GDPPPP*MILGDP+MILAID
28	DME	Netherlands	9,398	28.0	GDPPPP*MILGDP+MILAID
29	SEA	Indonesia	9,143	29.0	GDPPPP*MILGDP+MILAID
30	USR	Ukraine	8,981	30.0	GDPPPP*MILGDP+MILAID
31	MEA	Algeria	8,638	31.0	GDPPPP*MILGDP+MILAID
32	LAM	Chile	8,355	32.0	GDPPPP*MILGDP+MILAID
33	SEA	Malaysia	7,531	33.0	GDPPPP*MILGDP+MILAID
34	SEA	Thailand	7,483	34.0	GDPPPP*MILGDP+MILAID
35	AFR	South Africa	6,708	35.0	GDPPPP*MILGDP+MILAID
36	SAS	Afghanistan	6,514	36.0	GDPPPP*MILGDP+MILAID
37	MEA	Kuwait	6,383	37.0	GDPPPP*MILGDP+MILAID
38	LAM	Mexico	6,186	38.0	GDPPPP*MILGDP+MILAID
39	MEA	Oman	5,570	39.0	GDPPPP*MILGDP+MILAID
40	CPA	Vietnam	4,981	40.0	GDPPPP*MILGDP+MILAID
41	DME	Portugal	4,866	41.0	GDPPPP*MILGDP+MILAID

TABLE 2.7 MILITARY EXPENDITURES AT PURCHASING POWER PARITIES PLUS FOREIGN MILITARY AID, MILLIONS OF DOLLARS, 2008					
OBS	REGION	COUNTRY	MILXPP	RANK	SOURCE
42	MEA	Morocco	4,596	42.0	GDPPPP*MILGDP+MILAID
43	EEU	Romania	4,550	43.0	GDPPPP*MILGDP+MILAID
44	DME	Sweden	4,547	44.0	GDPPPP*MILGDP+MILAID
45	LAM	Argentina	4,329	45.0	GDPPPP*MILGDP+MILAID
46	LAM	Cuba	4,270	46.0	GDPPPP*MILGDP+MILAID
47	DME	Belgium	4,059	47.0	GDPPPP*MILGDP+MILAID
48	EEU	Czechia	3,811	48.0	GDPPPP*MILGDP+MILAID
49	LAM	Venezuela	3,784	49.0	GDPPPP*MILGDP+MILAID
50	AFR	Sudan	3,783	50.0	GDPPPP*MILGDP+MILAID
51	DME	Norway	3,599	51.0	GDPPPP*MILGDP+MILAID
52	MEA	UAE	3,579	52.0	GDPPPP*MILGDP+MILAID
53	LAM	Ecuador	3,056	53.0	GDPPPP*MILGDP+MILAID
54	LAM	Peru	3,010	54.0	GDPPPP*MILGDP+MILAID
55	MEA	Syria	2,929	55.0	GDPPPP*MILGDP+MILAID
56	DME	Austria	2,736	56.0	GDPPPP*MILGDP+MILAID
57	SAS	Sri Lanka	2,671	57.0	GDPPPP*MILGDP+MILAID
58	DME	Switzerland	2,657	58.0	GDPPPP*MILGDP+MILAID
59	DME	Denmark	2,635	59.0	GDPPPP*MILGDP+MILAID
60	MEA	Qatar	2,623	60.0	GDPPPP*MILGDP+MILAID
61	SEA	Philippines	2,595	61.0	GDPPPP*MILGDP+MILAID
62	MEA	Yemen	2,490	62.0	GDPPPP*MILGDP+MILAID
63	DME	Finland	2,446	63.0	GDPPPP*MILGDP+MILAID
64	EEU	Hungary	2,349	64.0	GDPPPP*MILGDP+MILAID
65	SAS	Bangladesh	2,150	65.0	GDPPPP*MILGDP+MILAID
66	MEA	Lebanon	2,141	66.0	GDPPPP*MILGDP+MILAID
67	MEA	Jordan	2,117	67.0	GDPPPP*MILGDP+MILAID
68	AFR	Angola	2,114	68.0	GDPPPP*MILGDP+MILAID
69	EEU	Bulgaria	2,062	69.0	GDPPPP*MILGDP+MILAID
70	AFR	Nigeria	2,012	70.0	GDPPPP*MILGDP+MILAID
71	USR	Azerbaijan	1,925	71.0	GDPPPP*MILGDP+MILAID
72	EEU	Serbia	1,920	72.0	GDPPPP*MILGDP+MILAID
73	EEU	Slovakia	1,851	73.0	GDPPPP*MILGDP+MILAID
74	USR	Kazakhstan	1,756	74.0	GDPPPP*MILGDP+MILAID
75	USR	Georgia	1,741	75.0	GDPPPP*MILGDP+MILAID
76	USR	Belarus	1,637	76.0	GDPPPP*MILGDP+MILAID
77	EEU	Croatia	1,540	77.0	GDPPPP*MILGDP+MILAID
78	DME	New Zealand	1,246	78.0	GDPPPP*MILGDP+MILAID
79	AFR	Kenya	1,184	79.0	GDPPPP*MILGDP+MILAID
80	DME	Ireland	1,165	80.0	GDPPPP*MILGDP+MILAID
81	MEA	Cyprus	1,132	81.0	GDPPPP*MILGDP+MILAID
82	MEA	Tunisia	1,092	82.0	GDPPPP*MILGDP+MILAID
83	MEA	Bahrain	1,081	83.0	GDPPPP*MILGDP+MILAID

TABLE 2.7 MILITARY EXPENDITURES AT PURCHASING POWER PARITIES
PLUS FOREIGN MILITARY AID, MILLIONS OF DOLLARS, 2008

OBS	REGION	COUNTRY	MILXPP	RANK	SOURCE
84	MEA	Libya	1,067	84.0	GDPPPP*MILGDP+MILAID
85	AFR	Ethiopia	1,041	85.0	GDPPPP*MILGDP+MILAID
86	USR	Lithuania	989	86.0	GDPPPP*MILGDP+MILAID
87	EEU	Slovenia	920	87.0	GDPPPP*MILGDP+MILAID
88	AFR	Botswana	835	88.0	GDPPPP*MILGDP+MILAID
89	AFR	Uganda	769	89.0	GDPPPP*MILGDP+MILAID
90	AFR	Eritrea	748	90.0	GDPPPP*MILGDP+MILAID
91	CPA	Burma	745	91.0	GDPPPP*MILGDP+MILAID
92	USR	Latvia	731	92.0	GDPPPP*MILGDP+MILAID
93	USR	Estonia	623	93.0	GDPPPP*MILGDP+MILAID
94	LAM	Bolivia	622	94.0	GDPPPP*MILGDP+MILAID
95	AFR	Cameroon	606	95.0	GDPPPP*MILGDP+MILAID
96	USR	Armenia	582	96.0	GDPPPP*MILGDP+MILAID
97	LAM	Uruguay	521	97.0	GDPPPP*MILGDP+MILAID
98	SEA	Brunei	512	98.0	GDPPPP*MILGDP+MILAID
99	EEU	Albania	503	99.0	GDPPPP*MILGDP+MILAID
100	AFR	Ivory Coast	476	100.0	GDPPPP*MILGDP+MILAID
101	AFR	Tanzania	473	101.0	GDPPPP*MILGDP+MILAID
102	SAS	Nepal	471	102.0	GDPPPP*MILGDP+MILAID
103	MEA	West Bank	458	103.0	GDPPPP*MILGDP+MILAID
104	EEU	Bosnia	457	104.0	GDPPPP*MILGDP+MILAID
105	LAM	Dominican Rep.	455	105.0	GDPPPP*MILGDP+MILAID
106	EEU	Macedonia	423	106.0	GDPPPP*MILGDP+MILAID
107	LAM	Panama	402	107.0	GDPPPP*MILGDP+MILAID
108	AFR	Namibia	400	108.0	GDPPPP*MILGDP+MILAID
109	USR	Uzbekistan	392	109.0	GDPPPP*MILGDP+MILAID
110	AFR	Senegal	368	110.0	GDPPPP*MILGDP+MILAID
111	CPA	Cambodia	302	111.0	GDPPPP*MILGDP+MILAID
112	AFR	Burkina Faso	299	112.0	GDPPPP*MILGDP+MILAID
113	AFR	Congo, Dem. Rep.	299	113.0	GDPPPP*MILGDP+MILAID
114	LAM	Guatemala	298	114.0	GDPPPP*MILGDP+MILAID
115	USR	Tajikistan	297	115.0	GDPPPP*MILGDP+MILAID
116	AFR	Zambia	290	116.0	GDPPPP*MILGDP+MILAID
117	DME	Luxembourg	284	117.0	GDPPPP*MILGDP+MILAID
118	USR	Kyrgyzstan	281	118.0	GDPPPP*MILGDP+MILAID
119	AFR	Mali	274	119.0	GDPPPP*MILGDP+MILAID
120	AFR	Somalia	263	120.0	GDPPPP*MILGDP+MILAID
121	LAM	Costa Rica	262	121.0	GDPPPP*MILGDP+MILAID
122	AFR	Mauritania	258	122.0	GDPPPP*MILGDP+MILAID
123	AFR	Guinea	257	123.0	GDPPPP*MILGDP+MILAID

OBS	REGION	COUNTRY	MILXPP	RANK	SOURCE
TABLE 2.7 MILITARY EXPENDITURES AT PURCHASING POWER PARITIES PLUS FOREIGN MILITARY AID, MILLIONS OF DOLLARS, 2008					
124	MEA	Gaza Strip	249	124.0	GDPPPP*MILGDP+MILAID
125	USR	Turkmenistan	245	125.0	GDPPPP*MILGDP+MILAID
126	LAM	Paraguay	244	126.0	GDPPPP*MILGDP+MILAID
127	AFR	Ghana	232	127.0	GDPPPP*MILGDP+MILAID
128	AFR	Madagascar	232	128.0	GDPPPP*MILGDP+MILAID
129	AFR	Gabon	229	129.0	GDPPPP*MILGDP+MILAID
130	LAM	El Salvador	216	130.0	GDPPPP*MILGDP+MILAID
131	LAM	Honduras	205	131.0	GDPPPP*MILGDP+MILAID
132	AFR	Congo, Rep.	199	132.0	GDPPPP*MILGDP+MILAID
133	LAM	Trinidad & Tobago	191	133.0	GDPPPP*MILGDP+MILAID
134	AFR	Rwanda	156	134.0	GDPPPP*MILGDP+MILAID
135	AFR	Mozambique	155	135.0	GDPPPP*MILGDP+MILAID
136	DME	Malta	150	136.0	GDPPPP*MILGDP+MILAID
137	AFR	Chad	141	137.0	GDPPPP*MILGDP+MILAID
138	CPA	Mongolia	138	138.0	GDPPPP*MILGDP+MILAID
139	AFR	Malawi	136	139.0	GDPPPP*MILGDP+MILAID
140	EEU	Montenegro	128	140.0	GDPPPP*MILGDP+MILAID
141	AFR	Burundi	126	141.0	GDPPPP*MILGDP+MILAID
142	AFR	Benin	123	142.0	GDPPPP*MILGDP+MILAID
143	LAM	Haiti	116	143.0	GDPPPP*MILGDP+MILAID
144	LAM	Jamaica	115	144.0	GDPPPP*MILGDP+MILAID
145	AFR	Togo	111	145.0	GDPPPP*MILGDP+MILAID
146	AFR	Niger	109	146.0	GDPPPP*MILGDP+MILAID
147	LAM	Guyana	109	147.0	GDPPPP*MILGDP+MILAID
148	AFR	Swaziland	106	148.0	GDPPPP*MILGDP+MILAID
149	AFR	Sierra Leone	105	149.0	GDPPPP*MILGDP+MILAID
150	LAM	Nicaragua	97	150.0	GDPPPP*MILGDP+MILAID
151	AFR	Liberia	94	151.0	GDPPPP*MILGDP+MILAID
152	AFR	Zimbabwe	87	152.0	GDPPPP*MILGDP+MILAID
153	AFR	Lesotho	83	153.0	GDPPPP*MILGDP+MILAID
154	LAM	Bahamas	78	154.0	GDPPPP*MILGDP+MILAID
155	SAS	Maldives	72	155.0	GDPPPP*MILGDP+MILAID
156	SEA	Papua New Guinea	62	156.0	GDPPPP*MILGDP+MILAID
157	LAM	Suriname	52	157.0	GDPPPP*MILGDP+MILAID
158	AFR	CAR	52	158.0	GDPPPP*MILGDP+MILAID
159	USR	Moldova	49	159.0	GDPPPP*MILGDP+MILAID
160	SEA	Fiji	49	160.0	GDPPPP*MILGDP+MILAID
161	AFR	Djibouti	47	161.0	GDPPPP*MILGDP+MILAID
162	LAM	Barbados	45	162.0	GDPPPP*MILGDP+MILAID
163	CPA	Laos	43	163.0	GDPPPP*MILGDP+MILAID

OBS	REGION	COUNTRY	MILXPP	RANK	SOURCE
		TABLE 2.7 MILITARY EXPENDITURES AT PURCHASING POWER PARITIES PLUS FOREIGN MILITARY AID, MILLIONS OF DOLLARS, 2008			
164	DME	Iceland	35	164.0	GDPPPP*MILGDP+MILAID
165	AFR	Guinea-Bissau	33	165.0	GDPPPP*MILGDP+MILAID
166	SAS	Bhutan	32	166.0	GDPPPP*MILGDP+MILAID
167	AFR	Mauritius	25	167.0	GDPPPP*MILGDP+MILAID
168	LAM	Belize	23	168.0	GDPPPP*MILGDP+MILAID
169	AFR	Seychelles	18	169.0	GDPPPP*MILGDP+MILAID
170	AFR	Gambia	17	170.0	GDPPPP*MILGDP+MILAID
171	SEA	East Timor	16	171.0	GDPPPP*MILGDP+MILAID
172	AFR	Equatorial Guinea	13	172.0	GDPPPP*MILGDP+MILAID
173	LAM	Antigua & Barbuda	11	173.0	GDPPPP*MILGDP+MILAID
174	AFR	Cape Verde	10	174.0	GDPPPP*MILGDP+MILAID
175	SEA	Tonga	7	175.0	GDPPPP*MILGDP+MILAID
176	AFR	San Tome & Principe	3	176.0	GDPPPP*MILGDP+MILAID
177	AFR	Comoros	3	177.0	GDPPPP*MILGDP+MILAID
178	EEU	Kosovo	0	178.0	GDPPPP*MILGDP+MILAID
179	LAM	Dominica	0	182.5	GDPPPP*MILGDP+MILAID
180	LAM	Grenada	0	182.5	GDPPPP*MILGDP+MILAID
181	DME	Monaco	0	182.5	GDPPPP*MILGDP+MILAID
182	SEA	Solomon Islands	0	182.5	GDPPPP*MILGDP+MILAID
183	LAM	St. Kitts & Nevis	0	182.5	GDPPPP*MILGDP+MILAID
184	LAM	St. Lucia	0	182.5	GDPPPP*MILGDP+MILAID
185	LAM	St. Vincent	0	182.5	GDPPPP*MILGDP+MILAID
186	SEA	Vanuatu	0	182.5	GDPPPP*MILGDP+MILAID
187	DME	Andorra	0	209.5	GDPPPP*MILGDP+MILAID
188	LAM	Anguilla	0	209.5	GDPPPP*MILGDP+MILAID
189	LAM	Aruba	0	209.5	GDPPPP*MILGDP+MILAID
190	DME	Bermuda	0	209.5	GDPPPP*MILGDP+MILAID
191	LAM	Cayman Islands	0	209.5	GDPPPP*MILGDP+MILAID
192	SEA	Cook Islands	0	209.5	GDPPPP*MILGDP+MILAID
193	DME	Faeroe Islands	0	209.5	GDPPPP*MILGDP+MILAID
194	DME	Falkland Islands	0	209.5	GDPPPP*MILGDP+MILAID
195	SEA	French Polynesia	0	209.5	GDPPPP*MILGDP+MILAID
196	DME	Gibraltar	0	209.5	GDPPPP*MILGDP+MILAID
197	DME	Greenland	0	209.5	GDPPPP*MILGDP+MILAID
198	LAM	Guadeloupe	0	209.5	GDPPPP*MILGDP+MILAID

TABLE 2.7 MILITARY EXPENDITURES AT PURCHASING POWER PARITIES PLUS FOREIGN MILITARY AID, MILLIONS OF DOLLARS, 2008

OBS	REGION	COUNTRY	MILXPP	RANK	SOURCE
199	SEA	Guam	0	209.5	GDPPPP*MILGDP+MILAID
200	DME	Guernsey	0	209.5	GDPPPP*MILGDP+MILAID
201	LAM	Guiana, French	0	209.5	GDPPPP*MILGDP+MILAID
202	SEA	Hong Kong	0	209.5	GDPPPP*MILGDP+MILAID
203	DME	Isle of Man	0	209.5	GDPPPP*MILGDP+MILAID
204	DME	Jersey	0	209.5	GDPPPP*MILGDP+MILAID
205	SEA	Kiribati	0	209.5	GDPPPP*MILGDP+MILAID
206	DME	Liechtenstein	0	209.5	GDPPPP*MILGDP+MILAID
207	SEA	Macao	0	209.5	GDPPPP*MILGDP+MILAID
208	SEA	Marshall Islands	0	209.5	GDPPPP*MILGDP+MILAID
209	LAM	Martinique	0	209.5	GDPPPP*MILGDP+MILAID
210	AFR	Mayotte	0	209.5	GDPPPP*MILGDP+MILAID
211	SEA	Micronesia	0	209.5	GDPPPP*MILGDP+MILAID
212	LAM	Montserrat	0	209.5	GDPPPP*MILGDP+MILAID
213	SEA	Nauru	0	209.5	GDPPPP*MILGDP+MILAID
214	LAM	Neth. Antilles	0	209.5	GDPPPP*MILGDP+MILAID
215	SEA	New Caledonia	0	209.5	GDPPPP*MILGDP+MILAID
216	SEA	Niue	0	209.5	GDPPPP*MILGDP+MILAID
217	SEA	Northern Mariana Is.	0	209.5	GDPPPP*MILGDP+MILAID
218	SEA	Palau	0	209.5	GDPPPP*MILGDP+MILAID
219	LAM	Puerto Rico	0	209.5	GDPPPP*MILGDP+MILAID
220	AFR	Reunion	0	209.5	GDPPPP*MILGDP+MILAID
221	SEA	Samoa, American	0	209.5	GDPPPP*MILGDP+MILAID
222	SEA	Samoa, Western	0	209.5	GDPPPP*MILGDP+MILAID
223	DME	San Marino	0	209.5	GDPPPP*MILGDP+MILAID
224	AFR	St. Helena	0	209.5	GDPPPP*MILGDP+MILAID
225	DME	St. Pierre & Miquelon	0	209.5	GDPPPP*MILGDP+MILAID
226	SEA	Tokelau	0	209.5	GDPPPP*MILGDP+MILAID
227	LAM	Turks & Caicos Is.	0	209.5	GDPPPP*MILGDP+MILAID
228	SEA	Tuvalu	0	209.5	GDPPPP*MILGDP+MILAID
229	LAM	Virgin Islands, Brit.	0	209.5	GDPPPP*MILGDP+MILAID
230	LAM	Virgin Islands, US	0	209.5	GDPPPP*MILGDP+MILAID

OBS	REGION	COUNTRY	MILXPP	RANK	SOURCE
231	SEA	Wallis & Futuna	0	209.5	GDPPPP*MILGDP+MILAID
232	AFR	Western Sahara	0	209.5	GDPPPP*MILGDP+MILAID

TABLE 2.7 MILITARY EXPENDITURES AT PURCHASING POWER PARITIES PLUS FOREIGN MILITARY AID, MILLIONS OF DOLLARS, 2008

TABLE 2.8 MILITARY EXPENDITURES AT MARKET EXCHANGE RATES PLUS FOREIGN MILITARY AID, MILLIONS OF DOLLARS, 2008

OBS	REGION	COUNTRY	MILEXP	RANK	SOURCE
1	DME	United States	625,762	1.0	GDP*MILGDP+MILAID
2	CPA	China	76,333	2.0	GDP*MILGDP+MILAID
3	DME	United Kingdom	68,331	3.0	GDP*MILGDP+MILAID
4	DME	France	60,276	4.0	GDP*MILGDP+MILAID
5	USR	Russia	47,758	5.0	GDP*MILGDP+MILAID
6	DME	Japan	45,857	6.0	GDP*MILGDP+MILAID
7	DME	Germany	44,623	7.0	GDP*MILGDP+MILAID
8	MEA	Saudi Arabia	37,802	8.0	GDP*MILGDP+MILAID
9	DME	Italy	37,065	9.0	GDP*MILGDP+MILAID
10	SAS	India	30,096	10.0	GDP*MILGDP+MILAID
11	SEA	Korea, South	28,094	11.0	GDP*MILGDP+MILAID
12	LAM	Brazil	20,360	12.0	GDP*MILGDP+MILAID
13	DME	Canada	17,741	13.0	GDP*MILGDP+MILAID
14	DME	Spain	17,512	14.0	GDP*MILGDP+MILAID
15	DME	Israel	16,266	15.0	GDP*MILGDP+MILAID
16	DME	Australia	15,326	16.0	GDP*MILGDP+MILAID
17	MEA	Turkey	14,400	17.0	GDP*MILGDP+MILAID
18	DME	Netherlands	11,538	18.0	GDP*MILGDP+MILAID
19	DME	Greece	11,431	19.0	GDP*MILGDP+MILAID
20	SEA	Taiwan	11,134	20.0	GDP*MILGDP+MILAID
21	MEA	Iraq	9,948	21.0	GDP*MILGDP+MILAID
22	EEU	Poland	9,220	22.0	GDP*MILGDP+MILAID
23	LAM	Colombia	7,758	23.0	GDP*MILGDP+MILAID
24	MEA	Iran	7,579	24.0	GDP*MILGDP+MILAID
25	SEA	Singapore	6,947	25.0	GDP*MILGDP+MILAID
26	SAS	Afghanistan	6,253	26.0	GDP*MILGDP+MILAID
27	DME	Sweden	6,196	27.0	GDP*MILGDP+MILAID
28	CPA	Korea, North	6,164	28.0	GDP*MILGDP+MILAID
29	SAS	Pakistan	5,547	29.0	GDP*MILGDP+MILAID
30	LAM	Chile	5,429	30.0	GDP*MILGDP+MILAID
31	DME	Norway	5,390	31.0	GDP*MILGDP+MILAID
32	DME	Belgium	5,216	32.0	GDP*MILGDP+MILAID
33	MEA	UAE	5,108	33.0	GDP*MILGDP+MILAID
34	MEA	Oman	4,932	34.0	GDP*MILGDP+MILAID
35	SEA	Indonesia	4,630	35.0	GDP*MILGDP+MILAID
36	MEA	Algeria	4,581	36.0	GDP*MILGDP+MILAID
37	MEA	Egypt	4,388	37.0	GDP*MILGDP+MILAID
38	MEA	Kuwait	4,364	38.0	GDP*MILGDP+MILAID
39	DME	Portugal	4,335	39.0	GDP*MILGDP+MILAID
40	LAM	Mexico	4,259	40.0	GDP*MILGDP+MILAID
41	DME	Denmark	4,256	41.0	GDP*MILGDP+MILAID
42	DME	Switzerland	4,080	42.0	GDP*MILGDP+MILAID
43	USR	Ukraine	3,969	43.0	GDP*MILGDP+MILAID
44	AFR	South Africa	3,862	44.0	GDP*MILGDP+MILAID
45	SEA	Malaysia	3,693	45.0	GDP*MILGDP+MILAID

TABLE 2.8 MILITARY EXPENDITURES AT MARKET EXCHANGE RATES
PLUS FOREIGN MILITARY AID, MILLIONS OF DOLLARS, 2008

OBS	REGION	COUNTRY	MILEXP	RANK	SOURCE
46	DME	Finland	3,322	46.0	GDP*MILGDP+MILAID
47	DME	Austria	3,317	47.0	GDP*MILGDP+MILAID
48	SEA	Thailand	2,760	48.0	GDP*MILGDP+MILAID
49	LAM	Venezuela	2,728	49.0	GDP*MILGDP+MILAID
50	MEA	Morocco	2,704	50.0	GDP*MILGDP+MILAID
51	EEU	Romania	2,571	51.0	GDP*MILGDP+MILAID
52	EEU	Czechia	2,561	52.0	GDP*MILGDP+MILAID
53	MEA	Qatar	2,255	53.0	GDP*MILGDP+MILAID
54	LAM	Argentina	2,175	54.0	GDP*MILGDP+MILAID
55	LAM	Cuba	2,107	55.0	GDP*MILGDP+MILAID
56	AFR	Sudan	2,080	56.0	GDP*MILGDP+MILAID
57	CPA	Vietnam	1,592	57.0	GDP*MILGDP+MILAID
58	EEU	Hungary	1,557	58.0	GDP*MILGDP+MILAID
59	MEA	Jordan	1,439	59.0	GDP*MILGDP+MILAID
60	LAM	Peru	1,412	60.0	GDP*MILGDP+MILAID
61	SEA	Philippines	1,411	61.0	GDP*MILGDP+MILAID
62	LAM	Ecuador	1,389	62.0	GDP*MILGDP+MILAID
63	MEA	Syria	1,379	63.0	GDP*MILGDP+MILAID
64	DME	Ireland	1,307	64.0	GDP*MILGDP+MILAID
65	DME	New Zealand	1,288	65.0	GDP*MILGDP+MILAID
66	AFR	Angola	1,237	66.0	GDP*MILGDP+MILAID
67	EEU	Slovakia	1,219	67.0	GDP*MILGDP+MILAID
68	MEA	Lebanon	1,179	68.0	GDP*MILGDP+MILAID
69	AFR	Nigeria	1,122	69.0	GDP*MILGDP+MILAID
70	EEU	Croatia	1,095	70.0	GDP*MILGDP+MILAID
71	SAS	Sri Lanka	1,043	71.0	GDP*MILGDP+MILAID
72	MEA	Yemen	989	72.0	GDP*MILGDP+MILAID
73	EEU	Serbia	955	73.0	GDP*MILGDP+MILAID
74	USR	Kazakhstan	954	74.0	GDP*MILGDP+MILAID
75	MEA	Cyprus	938	75.0	GDP*MILGDP+MILAID
76	EEU	Bulgaria	918	76.0	GDP*MILGDP+MILAID
77	USR	Georgia	883	77.0	GDP*MILGDP+MILAID
78	USR	Azerbaijan	843	78.0	GDP*MILGDP+MILAID
79	SAS	Bangladesh	839	79.0	GDP*MILGDP+MILAID
80	MEA	Libya	803	80.0	GDP*MILGDP+MILAID
81	EEU	Slovenia	800	81.0	GDP*MILGDP+MILAID
82	USR	Belarus	718	82.0	GDP*MILGDP+MILAID
83	USR	Lithuania	624	83.0	GDP*MILGDP+MILAID
84	AFR	Kenya	574	84.0	GDP*MILGDP+MILAID
85	USR	Latvia	508	85.0	GDP*MILGDP+MILAID
86	MEA	Tunisia	455	86.0	GDP*MILGDP+MILAID
87	USR	Estonia	431	87.0	GDP*MILGDP+MILAID
88	AFR	Botswana	404	88.0	GDP*MILGDP+MILAID
89	MEA	Bahrain	391	89.0	GDP*MILGDP+MILAID
90	CPA	Burma	359	90.0	GDP*MILGDP+MILAID
91	AFR	Eritrea	355	91.0	GDP*MILGDP+MILAID

OBS	REGION	COUNTRY	MILEXP	RANK	SOURCE
		TABLE 2.8 MILITARY EXPENDITURES AT MARKET EXCHANGE RATES PLUS FOREIGN MILITARY AID, MILLIONS OF DOLLARS, 2008			
92	LAM	Uruguay	338	92.0	GDP*MILGDP+MILAID
93	AFR	Ethiopia	337	93.0	GDP*MILGDP+MILAID
94	USR	Armenia	323	94.0	GDP*MILGDP+MILAID
95	AFR	Cameroon	315	95.0	GDP*MILGDP+MILAID
96	SEA	Brunei	311	96.0	GDP*MILGDP+MILAID
97	DME	Luxembourg	307	97.0	GDP*MILGDP+MILAID
98	AFR	Ivory Coast	283	98.0	GDP*MILGDP+MILAID
99	AFR	Uganda	277	99.0	GDP*MILGDP+MILAID
100	AFR	Namibia	265	100.0	GDP*MILGDP+MILAID
101	EEU	Albania	252	101.0	GDP*MILGDP+MILAID
102	EEU	Bosnia	248	102.0	GDP*MILGDP+MILAID
103	LAM	Dominican Rep.	244	103.0	GDP*MILGDP+MILAID
104	MEA	West Bank	234	104.0	GDP*MILGDP+MILAID
105	LAM	Bolivia	212	105.0	GDP*MILGDP+MILAID
106	AFR	Zambia	203	106.0	GDP*MILGDP+MILAID
107	AFR	Senegal	202	107.0	GDP*MILGDP+MILAID
108	LAM	Panama	199	108.0	GDP*MILGDP+MILAID
109	EEU	Macedonia	176	109.0	GDP*MILGDP+MILAID
110	SAS	Nepal	170	110.0	GDP*MILGDP+MILAID
111	LAM	Guatemala	168	111.0	GDP*MILGDP+MILAID
112	AFR	Tanzania	165	112.0	GDP*MILGDP+MILAID
113	AFR	Somalia	151	113.0	GDP*MILGDP+MILAID
114	AFR	Congo, Dem. Rep.	143	114.0	GDP*MILGDP+MILAID
115	LAM	Costa Rica	141	115.0	GDP*MILGDP+MILAID
116	AFR	Mali	141	116.0	GDP*MILGDP+MILAID
117	AFR	Zimbabwe	136	117.0	GDP*MILGDP+MILAID
118	USR	Uzbekistan	134	118.0	GDP*MILGDP+MILAID
119	LAM	Trinidad & Tobago	127	119.0	GDP*MILGDP+MILAID
120	MEA	Gaza Strip	127	120.0	GDP*MILGDP+MILAID
121	AFR	Burkina Faso	124	121.0	GDP*MILGDP+MILAID
122	AFR	Gabon	114	122.0	GDP*MILGDP+MILAID
123	LAM	El Salvador	114	123.0	GDP*MILGDP+MILAID
124	LAM	Paraguay	113	124.0	GDP*MILGDP+MILAID
125	DME	Malta	109	125.0	GDP*MILGDP+MILAID
126	AFR	Ghana	107	126.0	GDP*MILGDP+MILAID
127	AFR	Mauritania	106	127.0	GDP*MILGDP+MILAID
128	USR	Turkmenistan	105	128.0	GDP*MILGDP+MILAID
129	AFR	Congo, Rep.	99	129.0	GDP*MILGDP+MILAID
130	USR	Kyrgyzstan	96	130.0	GDP*MILGDP+MILAID
131	CPA	Cambodia	96	131.0	GDP*MILGDP+MILAID
132	LAM	Honduras	94	132.0	GDP*MILGDP+MILAID
133	USR	Tajikistan	94	133.0	GDP*MILGDP+MILAID
134	AFR	Madagascar	91	134.0	GDP*MILGDP+MILAID
135	AFR	Liberia	91	135.0	GDP*MILGDP+MILAID

OBS	REGION	COUNTRY	MILEXP	RANK	SOURCE
		TABLE 2.8 MILITARY EXPENDITURES AT MARKET EXCHANGE RATES PLUS FOREIGN MILITARY AID, MILLIONS OF DOLLARS, 2008			
136	AFR	Guinea	86	136.0	GDP*MILGDP+MILAID
137	LAM	Jamaica	73	137.0	GDP*MILGDP+MILAID
138	AFR	Mozambique	67	138.0	GDP*MILGDP+MILAID
139	CPA	Mongolia	66	139.0	GDP*MILGDP+MILAID
140	LAM	Haiti	66	140.0	GDP*MILGDP+MILAID
141	AFR	Rwanda	63	141.0	GDP*MILGDP+MILAID
142	LAM	Guyana	61	142.0	GDP*MILGDP+MILAID
143	LAM	Bahamas	59	143.0	GDP*MILGDP+MILAID
144	EEU	Montenegro	59	144.0	GDP*MILGDP+MILAID
145	AFR	Benin	58	145.0	GDP*MILGDP+MILAID
146	AFR	Lesotho	56	146.0	GDP*MILGDP+MILAID
147	AFR	Swaziland	54	147.0	GDP*MILGDP+MILAID
148	AFR	Togo	53	148.0	GDP*MILGDP+MILAID
149	AFR	Niger	53	149.0	GDP*MILGDP+MILAID
150	AFR	Chad	52	150.0	GDP*MILGDP+MILAID
151	SAS	Maldives	48	151.0	GDP*MILGDP+MILAID
152	SEA	East Timor	48	152.0	GDP*MILGDP+MILAID
153	AFR	Malawi	47	153.0	GDP*MILGDP+MILAID
154	AFR	Burundi	46	154.0	GDP*MILGDP+MILAID
155	SEA	Fiji	44	155.0	GDP*MILGDP+MILAID
156	AFR	Sierra Leone	44	156.0	GDP*MILGDP+MILAID
157	LAM	Nicaragua	40	157.0	GDP*MILGDP+MILAID
158	DME	Iceland	38	158.0	GDP*MILGDP+MILAID
159	LAM	Suriname	34	159.0	GDP*MILGDP+MILAID
160	LAM	Barbados	30	160.0	GDP*MILGDP+MILAID
161	AFR	CAR	29	161.0	GDP*MILGDP+MILAID
162	SEA	Papua New Guinea	28	162.0	GDP*MILGDP+MILAID
163	AFR	Djibouti	26	163.0	GDP*MILGDP+MILAID
164	USR	Moldova	25	164.0	GDP*MILGDP+MILAID
165	AFR	Guinea-Bissau	15	165.0	GDP*MILGDP+MILAID
166	CPA	Laos	15	166.0	GDP*MILGDP+MILAID
167	LAM	Belize	13	167.0	GDP*MILGDP+MILAID
168	AFR	Mauritius	13	168.0	GDP*MILGDP+MILAID
169	SAS	Bhutan	13	169.0	GDP*MILGDP+MILAID
170	AFR	Cape Verde	9	170.0	GDP*MILGDP+MILAID
171	AFR	Seychelles	9	171.0	GDP*MILGDP+MILAID
172	LAM	Antigua & Barbuda	7	172.0	GDP*MILGDP+MILAID
173	AFR	Equatorial Guinea	6	173.0	GDP*MILGDP+MILAID
174	AFR	Gambia	5	174.0	GDP*MILGDP+MILAID
175	SEA	Tonga	5	175.0	GDP*MILGDP+MILAID
176	AFR	Comoros	2	176.0	GDP*MILGDP+MILAID
177	AFR	San Tome & Principe	2	177.0	GDP*MILGDP+MILAID

TABLE 2.8 MILITARY EXPENDITURES AT MARKET EXCHANGE RATES PLUS FOREIGN MILITARY AID, MILLIONS OF DOLLARS, 2008

OBS	REGION	COUNTRY	MILEXP	RANK	SOURCE
178	EEU	Kosovo	0	178.0	GDP*MILGDP+MILAID
179	LAM	Dominica	0	182.5	GDP*MILGDP+MILAID
180	LAM	Grenada	0	182.5	GDP*MILGDP+MILAID
181	DME	Monaco	0	182.5	GDP*MILGDP+MILAID
182	SEA	Solomon Islands	0	182.5	GDP*MILGDP+MILAID
183	LAM	St. Kitts & Nevis	0	182.5	GDP*MILGDP+MILAID
184	LAM	St. Lucia	0	182.5	GDP*MILGDP+MILAID
185	LAM	St. Vincent	0	182.5	GDP*MILGDP+MILAID
186	SEA	Vanuatu	0	182.5	GDP*MILGDP+MILAID
187	DME	Andorra	0	209.5	GDP*MILGDP+MILAID
188	LAM	Anguilla	0	209.5	GDP*MILGDP+MILAID
189	LAM	Aruba	0	209.5	GDP*MILGDP+MILAID
190	DME	Bermuda	0	209.5	GDP*MILGDP+MILAID
191	LAM	Cayman Islands	0	209.5	GDP*MILGDP+MILAID
192	SEA	Cook Islands	0	209.5	GDP*MILGDP+MILAID
193	DME	Faeroe Islands	0	209.5	GDP*MILGDP+MILAID
194	DME	Falkland Islands	0	209.5	GDP*MILGDP+MILAID
195	SEA	French Polynesia	0	209.5	GDP*MILGDP+MILAID
196	DME	Gibraltar	0	209.5	GDP*MILGDP+MILAID
197	DME	Greenland	0	209.5	GDP*MILGDP+MILAID
198	LAM	Guadeloupe	0	209.5	GDP*MILGDP+MILAID
199	SEA	Guam	0	209.5	GDP*MILGDP+MILAID
200	DME	Guernsey	0	209.5	GDP*MILGDP+MILAID
201	LAM	Guiana, French	0	209.5	GDP*MILGDP+MILAID
202	SEA	Hong Kong	0	209.5	GDP*MILGDP+MILAID
203	DME	Isle of Man	0	209.5	GDP*MILGDP+MILAID
204	DME	Jersey	0	209.5	GDP*MILGDP+MILAID
205	SEA	Kiribati	0	209.5	GDP*MILGDP+MILAID
206	DME	Liechtenstein	0	209.5	GDP*MILGDP+MILAID
207	SEA	Macao	0	209.5	GDP*MILGDP+MILAID
208	SEA	Marshall Islands	0	209.5	GDP*MILGDP+MILAID
209	LAM	Martinique	0	209.5	GDP*MILGDP+MILAID
210	AFR	Mayotte	0	209.5	GDP*MILGDP+MILAID
211	SEA	Micronesia	0	209.5	GDP*MILGDP+MILAID
212	LAM	Montserrat	0	209.5	GDP*MILGDP+MILAID
213	SEA	Nauru	0	209.5	GDP*MILGDP+MILAID
214	LAM	Neth. Antilles	0	209.5	GDP*MILGDP+MILAID
215	SEA	New Caledonia	0	209.5	GDP*MILGDP+MILAID
216	SEA	Niue	0	209.5	GDP*MILGDP+MILAID

TABLE 2.8 MILITARY EXPENDITURES AT MARKET EXCHANGE RATES
PLUS FOREIGN MILITARY AID, MILLIONS OF DOLLARS, 2008

OBS	REGION	COUNTRY	MILEXP	RANK	SOURCE
217	SEA	Northern Mariana Is.	0	209.5	GDP*MILGDP+MILAID
218	SEA	Palau	0	209.5	GDP*MILGDP+MILAID
219	LAM	Puerto Rico	0	209.5	GDP*MILGDP+MILAID
220	AFR	Reunion	0	209.5	GDP*MILGDP+MILAID
221	SEA	Samoa, American	0	209.5	GDP*MILGDP+MILAID
222	SEA	Samoa, Western	0	209.5	GDP*MILGDP+MILAID
223	DME	San Marino	0	209.5	GDP*MILGDP+MILAID
224	AFR	St. Helena	0	209.5	GDP*MILGDP+MILAID
225	DME	St. Pierre & Miquelon	0	209.5	GDP*MILGDP+MILAID
226	SEA	Tokelau	0	209.5	GDP*MILGDP+MILAID
227	LAM	Turks & Caicos Is.	0	209.5	GDP*MILGDP+MILAID
228	SEA	Tuvalu	0	209.5	GDP*MILGDP+MILAID
229	LAM	Virgin Islands, Brit.	0	209.5	GDP*MILGDP+MILAID
230	LAM	Virgin Islands, US	0	209.5	GDP*MILGDP+MILAID
231	SEA	Wallis & Futuna	0	209.5	GDP*MILGDP+MILAID
232	AFR	Western Sahara	0	209.5	GDP*MILGDP+MILAID

TABLE 2.9 OPERATIONAL NUCLEAR DELIVERY SYSTEMS, 2009-2010

NAME/ DESIGNATION	AKA	NUMBER OF SYSTEMS Active+Spares	YEAR FIRST DEPLOYED	WARHEAD TYPE	NUMBER OF WARHEADS x YIELD (kilotons)	RANGE (km)	TOTAL NUMBER OF WARHEADS Active+Spares
LAND BALLISTIC MISSILES							
UNITED STATES							
ICBM							
LGM-30G	Minuteman III					13,000	
	MK-12	-0	1970	Single	1 x 170		-0
	MK-12A	250	1979	MIRV, Single	1-3 x 335		250
	MK-21 SERV	200	2006 (1986)	Single	1 x 300		250
TOTAL 09(BULL) 09(SIPRI)		450					500
SRBM							
ATACMS Block I		Some	1991	Single	1 x 560 kg payload	165	Some
ATACMS Block IA		Some	1998	Single	1 x 160 kg payload	300	Some
ATACMS Block II		Some	2002	Single	1 x 270 kg payload	140	Some
TOTAL 08(WIKI)		Some					Some
RUSSIA							
ICBM							
SS-18	Satan	50	1979	MIRV	10 x 500-800	11,000-15,000	500
SS-19	Stiletto	60	1980	MIRV	6 x 400	10,000	360
SS-25	Sickle	150	1985	Single	1 x 800	10,500	150
SS-27	Topol-M1 (SILO)	50	1997	Single	1 x 800	10,500	50
SS-27	Topol-M1 (MOBILE)	18	2006	Single	1 x 800?	10,500	18
SS-27	Topol-M2 (RS-24)	3	2009	MIRV	-4 x 400?	10,500	12

TABLE 2.9 OPERATIONAL NUCLEAR DELIVERY SYSTEMS, 2009-2010							
NAME/ DESIGNATION	AKA	NUMBER OF SYSTEMS Active+Spares	YEAR FIRST DEPLOYED	WARHEAD TYPE	NUMBER OF WARHEADS x YIELD (kilotons)	RANGE (km)	TOTAL NUMBER OF WARHEADS Active+Spares
TOTAL 10(BULL) 09(SIPRI)		331					1,090
SRBM							
SS-1c Mod 1	Scud-B	Some	1964	Single	1 x 1,000kg payload	300	Some
SS-1c Mod 2	Scud-B	Some	1964	Single	1 x 950kg payload	240	Some
SS-26	Iskander	Some	1995	Single	1 x 480kg payload	400	Some
	Iskander-E	Some	1999	Single	1 x 480kg payload	280	Some
TOTAL 08(WIKI)		Some					Some
CHINA							
ICBM							
CSS-4	DF-5A	20	1981	Single	1 x 4,000-5,000	13,000	20
CSS-X-10	DF-31	-10	2007			>7,200	-10
				Single	1 x 200-300		
				MIRV	3 x 50-100		
?	DF-31A	-10	2008-2010			>11,200	-10
				Single	1 x 200-300		
				MIRV	3-5 x 20-150		
TOTAL 09(SIPRI) 08(BULL)		-40					-40
IRBM							
CSS-2	DF-3A	17	1971	Single	1 x 3,300	3,100	17
CSS-3	DF-4	17	1980	Single	1 x 3,300	5,500	17
CSS-5	DF-21, DF-21A	-60	1991	Single	1 x 200-300	2,100	-60

NAME/ DESIGNATION	AKA	NUMBER OF SYSTEMS Active+Spares	YEAR FIRST DEPLOYED	WARHEAD TYPE	NUMBER OF WARHEADS x YIELD (kilotons)	RANGE (km)	TOTAL NUMBER OF WARHEADS Active+Spares
TABLE 2.9 OPERATIONAL NUCLEAR DELIVERY SYSTEMS, 2009-2010							
TOTAL 09(SIPRI) 08(BULL)		-94					-94
SRBM							
CSS-6	DF-15/M-9	24	1989	Single	1 x 50-350	600	Some
CSS-7	DF-11/M-11	32	1999	Single	1 x 0.5	300	Some
CSS-8	DF-7	30	?	Single	1 x 500kg payload	150	?
TOTAL 04(IISS), 08(SIPRI)		96					Some
INDIA							
IRBM							
Agni II		Some	2004	Single	1 x 15-250	>2,000	Some
Agni III		0	(2010-2011)	Single	1 x 15-250	>3,000	0
TOTAL 09(SIPRI) 08(BULL)		Some					Some
SRBM							
Agni I		Some	2007	Single	1 x 1,000kg payload	700	Some
Prithvi I		<50	1998	Single	1 x1,000kg payload	150	Some
Prithvi II		Some	2004	Single	1 x 500kg payload	250	Some
Prithvi III		30	2004	Single	1 x 10-20	350-600	Some
TOTAL 09(SIPRI) 08(BULL)		Some					Some
PAKISTAN							
IRBM							

				TABLE 2.9 OPERATIONAL NUCLEAR DELIVERY SYSTEMS, 2009-2010			
NAME/ DESIGNATION	AKA	NUMBER OF SYSTEMS Active+Spares	YEAR FIRST DEPLOYED	WARHEAD TYPE	NUMBER OF WARHEADS x YIELD (kilotons)	RANGE (km)	TOTAL NUMBER OF WARHEADS Active+Spares
Ghauri-1	Haft 5	<50	2003	Single	1 x 700- 1,000kg payload	1,500	Some
Ghauri-2	Haft 5A	Some	2003	Single	1 x 1,200kg payload	2,300	Some
Shaheen-2	Haft 6	Some	2007	Single	1 x 1,000+kg payload	2,000- 2,500	Some
TOTAL 09(SIPRI)		Some					Some
SRBM							
Abdali	Haft 2	Some	2006	Single	1 x 250- 450kg payload	180-200	Some
Ghaznavi	Haft 3	<50	2004	Single	1 x 500kg payload	-400	Some
Shaheen-1	Haft 4	<50	2008	Single	1 x 750- 1,000kg payload	600- 1,500	Some
TOTAL 09(SIPRI)		Some					Some
				ISRAEL			
ICBM Jericho 3		Some	2008				Some
				Single	1 x 350kg payload	7,800	
				MIRV	2-3 x 350kg payload	4,800	
				Single	1 x 1,000- 1,300kg payload	4,800	
TOTAL 09(SIPRI) 08(WIKI)		Some					Some
IRBM							

TABLE 2.9 OPERATIONAL NUCLEAR DELIVERY SYSTEMS, 2009-2010							
NAME/ DESIGNATION	AKA	NUMBER OF SYSTEMS Active+Spares	YEAR FIRST DEPLOYED	WARHEAD TYPE	NUMBER OF WARHEADS x YIELD (kilotons)	RANGE (km)	TOTAL NUMBER OF WARHEADS Active+Spares
Jericho 2		50	1990	Single	1 x 750-1,000kg payload	1,500-1,800	Some
TOTAL 09(SIPRI)		50					Some
NORTH KOREA							
IRBM							
No-Dong-1		Some	1997	Single	1 x 700-1,000kg payload	1,300	Some
TOTAL 09(SIPRI)		Some					Some
SRBM							
Scud-B		Some	1979-1980	Single	1 x 1,000kg payload	300	Some
Scud-C variant		Some	1989	Single	1 x 700kg payload	500	Some
Scud-D		Some	2006	Single	1 x 500kg payload	700	Some
TOTAL 09(SIPRI)		Some					Some
SLBM							
UNITED STATES							
UGM-133	Trident II D-5	288					
	MK-4		1992	MIRV	4-6 x 100	12,000	568
	MK-4A		2008	MIRV	4-6 x 100	?	200
	MK-5		1990	MIRV	4-6 x 455	12,000	384
TOTAL 09(BULL) 09(SIPRI)		288					1,152
UNITED KINGDOM							
UGM-135	Trident II D-5	48	1994	MIRV	1-3 x 100	12,000	160

NAME/ DESIGNATION	AKA	NUMBER OF SYSTEMS Active+Spares	YEAR FIRST DEPLOYED	WARHEAD TYPE	NUMBER OF WARHEADS x YIELD (kilotons)	RANGE (km)	TOTAL NUMBER OF WARHEADS Active+Spares
TABLE 2.9 OPERATIONAL NUCLEAR DELIVERY SYSTEMS, 2009-2010							
TOTAL 09(SIPRI)		48					160
RUSSIA							
SS-N-18 M1	Stingray	4/64	1978	MIRV	3 x 50	6,500	192
SS-N-23	Skiff	2/48	1986	MIRV	4 x 100	9,000	128
SS-N-23 M1	Sineva	4/48	2007	MIRV	4 x 100	9,000	256
SS-N-32	Bulava-30	(1/16)	-2010	MIRV	6 x 100	8,000-10,000	0
TOTAL 10(BULL) 08(SIPRI)		10/160					576
FRANCE							
M-45		48	1997, 1999, 2005	MIRV	4-6 x 100	6,000	240
M-51		0	(2010)	MIRV	4-6 x 100	8,000-10,000	0
TOTAL 09(SIPRI) 08(BULL)		48					240
CHINA							
CSS-N-3		12	1986				12
	JL-1			Single	1 x 200-300	1,000-1,700	
	JL-1			Single	1 x 25-50	2,150	
	JL-1A			Single	1 x 25-50	2,500	
CSS-NX-5	JL-2	(36)	(2009-2010)			>8,000	(36)
				Single	1 x 200-300		
				MIRV	3-4 x 90		
TOTAL 09(SIPRI) 08(BULL)		12					12
INDIA							

NAME/ DESIGNATION	AKA	NUMBER OF SYSTEMS Active+Spares	YEAR FIRST DEPLOYED	WARHEAD TYPE	NUMBER OF WARHEADS x YIELD (kilotons)	RANGE (km)	TOTAL NUMBER OF WARHEADS Active+Spares
Sagarika	K-15	0	(2010)	Single	1 x 500-600kg payload	700	0
Dhanush		Some	2007	Single	1 x 1,000kg payload	350	Some
TOTAL 09(SIPRI) 08(BULL)		Some					Some
AIRCRAFT							
UNITED STATES							
STRATEGIC							
B-52H	Strato-fortress	93+44	1961	ALCM	5-150	16,000	216
				ACM	5-150		
B-2	Spirit	20+16	1994	Bombs B61-7, B83-1	ACM 5-150	11,000	100
TOTAL 09(BULL) 09(SIPRI)		113+60					316
SUB-STRATEGIC							
F-15E	Strike Eagle	Some	1988	Bomb B61-3, B61-4	1 x 0.3-170, 1 x 0.3-45	2,500	Some
F-16A/B/C/D	Fighting Falcon	Some	1976	Bomb B61-3, B61-4	1 x 0.3-170, 1 x 0.3-45	2,500	Some
F-117A	Nighthawk	Some	1983	Bomb B61-3, B61-4	1 x 0.3-170, 1 x 0.3-45	2,100	Some
TOTAL 09(WIKI) 04(IISS) 08(SIPRI) 08(BULL)		Some					400
RUSSIA							
STRATEGIC							

TABLE 2.9 OPERATIONAL NUCLEAR DELIVERY SYSTEMS, 2009-2010

TABLE 2.9 OPERATIONAL NUCLEAR DELIVERY SYSTEMS, 2009-2010							
NAME/ DESIGNATION	AKA	NUMBER OF SYSTEMS Active+Spares	YEAR FIRST DEPLOYED	WARHEAD TYPE	NUMBER OF WARHEADS x YIELD (kilotons)	RANGE (km)	TOTAL NUMBER OF WARHEADS Active+Spares
Tu-95 MS6	Bear H6	31	1984	ALCM	6 x ?	6,500-10,500	186
				Bombs	? x ?		
Tu-95 MS16	Bear H16	31	1984	ALCM	16 x ?	6,500-10,500	496
				Bombs	? x ?		
Tu-160	Blackjack	13	1987	ALCM	12 x ?	10,500-13,200	156
				SRAM	? x ?		
				Bombs	? x ?		
TOTAL 10(BULL) 09(SIPRI)		75					838
SUB-STRATEGIC							
Tu-22M-3	Backfire	124 07(SIPRI)	1974	ASM	2 x ?	4,800-7,000	Some
				Bombs	? x ?		
Su-24	Fencer	400 07(SIPRI)	1974	Bombs	2 x ?	2,100-3,000	Some
TOTAL 09(BULL) 09(SIPRI)		-524					650
FRANCE							
STRATEGIC							
Mirage 2000N		60	1988	ASMP	1 x 300	2,750	50
Rafale F3		0	(2009)	ASMP	1 x ?	2,000	0
TOTAL 09(SIPRI) 08(BULL)		60					50
SUB-STRATEGIC							
Super Etendard		24	1978	ASMP	1 x 300	650	10
Rafale MK3		0	(2010)	ASMP	1 x ?	2,000	0
TOTAL 09(SIPRI) 08(BULL)		24					10

NAME/ DESIGNATION	AKA	NUMBER OF SYSTEMS Active+Spares	YEAR FIRST DEPLOYED	WARHEAD TYPE	NUMBER OF WARHEADS x YIELD (kilotons)	RANGE (km)	TOTAL NUMBER OF WARHEADS Active+Spares
TABLE 2.9 OPERATIONAL NUCLEAR DELIVERY SYSTEMS, 2009-2010							
CHINA							
STRATEGIC							
H-6	Tu-16	20	1965	Bomb	1 x 3,000kg payload	3,100	~20
TOTAL 09(SIPRI)		20					~20
SUB-STRATEGIC							
Q-5	Mig-19	Some	1972-?	Bomb	1 x 1,000kg payload	400	~20
TOTAL 09(SIPRI) 08(BULL)		Some					~20
ISRAEL							
SUB-STRATEGIC							
F-4E-2000	Kurnass	Some	1989	Bomb	1 x 8,480kg payload	2,200	Some
F-16A/B/C/D	Fighting Falcon	205	1980	Bomb	1 x 5,400 kg payload	2,500	Some
F-15I	Thunder	25	1997	Bomb	1 x 10,400 kg payload	2,500	Some
TOTAL 09(SIPRI) 08(SIPRI)		>230					Some
INDIA							
SUB-STRATEGIC							
Jaguar IS/IB	Shamsher	131 07(WIKI)	1979	Bomb	1 x 4,760 kg payload	1,600	Some
MiG-27M	Bahadur	165 07(WIKI)	1982	Bomb	1 x 3,000 kg payload	1,000	Some
Mirage 2000H	Vajra	40 07(WIKI)	1998	Bomb	1 x 6,300 kg payload	1,850	Some

NAME/ DESIGNATION	AKA	NUMBER OF SYSTEMS Active+Spares	YEAR FIRST DEPLOYED	WARHEAD TYPE	NUMBER OF WARHEADS x YIELD (kilotons)	RANGE (km)	TOTAL NUMBER OF WARHEADS Active+Spares
TOTAL 09(SIPRI) 08(BULL)		336 07(WIKI)					Some
PAKISTAN							
SUB-STRATEGIC							
F-16A/B	Fighting Falcon	32	1983	Bomb/ Babur LACM	1 x 4,500kg payload	1,600	Some
Mirage 2000-5		Some	2002	Bomb	1 x 4,000kg payload	2,100	Some
Q-5	MiG-19	Some	1980s	Bomb	1 x 1,000kg payload	1,200	Some
TOTAL 09(BULL) 09(SIPRI)		>32					Some
NORTH KOREA							
SUB-STRATEGIC							
H-5	Il-28	80	1950	Bomb	1 x 3,000kg payload	2,100	Some
TOTAL 09(SIPRI)		80					Some
SLCM							
UNITED STATES							
Tomahawk	TLAM-N	325	1984	Single	1 x 5-150	2,500	(100)
TOTAL 09(BULL) 09(SIPRI)		325					100
RUSSIA							
SS-N-9	Siren	Some	1972	Single	1 x 200	110	Some
SS-N-12	Sandbox	Some	1959-1960	Single	1 x 350	550	Some
SS-N-19	Shipwreck	Some	1980	Single	1 x 500	550	Some
SS-N-21	Sampson	Some	1984	Single	1 x 200	2,400	Some

TABLE 2.9 OPERATIONAL NUCLEAR DELIVERY SYSTEMS, 2009-2010

NAME/ DESIGNATION	AKA	NUMBER OF SYSTEMS Active+Spares	YEAR FIRST DEPLOYED	WARHEAD TYPE	NUMBER OF WARHEADS x YIELD (kilotons)	RANGE (km)	TOTAL NUMBER OF WARHEADS Active+Spares
SS-N-22	Sunburn	Some	1980	Single	1 x 320kg payload	120	Some
TOTAL 09(SIPRI) 08(BULL)		Some					276
ISRAEL							
Turbo-Popeye 3		Some	2000	Single	1 x 200kg payload	1,500	Some
TOTAL 04(IISS)		Some					Some
ALCM							
UNITED STATES							
AGM-868		1,140	1982/ 1991	Single	1 x 900-1,400kg payload	2,500	Some
AGM-129		460	1990	Single	1 x 5-200	3,500	Some
TOTAL 08(SIPRI) 08(BULL)		1,600					Some
RUSSIA							
AS-4	Kh-24 Kitchen	Some	1964	Single	1 x 1,000	310	Some
AS-15A	Kh-55 Kent	Some	1971	Single	1 x 200-250	2,500	Some
AS-15B	Kh-55SM Kent	Some	1986	Single	1 x 200-250	3,000	Some
AS-16	Kh-15 Kickback	Some	1980	Single	1 x 350	150	Some
TOTAL 09(SIPRI) 08(BULL)		Some					Some
FRANCE							
ASMP		Some	1985	Single	1 x 300	250	Some

TABLE 2.9 OPERATIONAL NUCLEAR DELIVERY SYSTEMS, 2009-2010

NAME/ DESIGNATION	AKA	NUMBER OF SYSTEMS Active+Spares	YEAR FIRST DEPLOYED	WARHEAD TYPE	NUMBER OF WARHEADS x YIELD (kilotons)	RANGE (km)	TOTAL NUMBER OF WARHEADS Active+Spares
TABLE 2.9 OPERATIONAL NUCLEAR DELIVERY SYSTEMS, 2009-2010							
TOTAL 08(SIPRI) 08(BULL)		Some					Some
CHINA							
	DH-10	150-350	2007	Single	1 x ?	>2,000	Some
TOTAL 09(SIPRI) 08(BULL)		150-350					Some
PAKISTAN							
Babur	Haft-7	Some	2007	Single	1 x 500kg payload	700	Some
Ra'ad	Haft-8	Some	(>2009)	Single	?	350	0
TOTAL 09(SIPRI)		Some					Some
MISSILE AND AIR DEFENSE SYSTEMS							
RUSSIA							
STRATEGIC DEFENSIVE SYSTEMS							
51T6	SH-11 Gorgon	0	1989	Single	1 x 1,000	350	0
53T6	SH-08 Gazelle	68	1986	Single	1 x 1,000 / 10	80	68
S-300	SA-10/20 Grumble	1,900	1980	Single	1 x low yield	5-150	630
TOTAL 10(BULL) 09(BULL) 09(SIPRI)		733					701
UNITED STATES							
STRATEGIC DEFENSIVE SYSTEMS							
GBI missiles		25					0
Aegis BMD cruisers		3					0

TABLE 2.9 OPERATIONAL NUCLEAR DELIVERY SYSTEMS, 2009-2010							
NAME/ DESIGNATION	AKA	NUMBER OF SYSTEMS Active+Spares	YEAR FIRST DEPLOYED	WARHEAD TYPE	NUMBER OF WARHEADS x YIELD (kilotons)	RANGE (km)	TOTAL NUMBER OF WARHEADS Active+Spares
Aegis BMD destroyers		7					0
TOTAL 08(SIPRI)		35					0
SUB-STRATEGIC DEFENSIVE SYSTEMS							
PAC-3 missiles		546					0
TOTAL 08(SIPRI)		546					0

ACM advanced cruise missile
AKA also known as
ALCM air-launched cruise missile
ASM air-to-surface missile
MIRV multiple independently targetable re-entry vehicles
ICBM intercontinental ballistic missile
IRBM intermediate-range ballistic missile
SRBM short-range ballistic missile
SLBM submarine-launched ballistic missile
SLCM submarine-launched cruise missile
LACM land-attack cruise missile
GBI ground-based interceptors
BMD ballistic missile defense
PAC-3 Patriot advanced capability-3

SOURCES: 10(BULL), 09(BULL), 09(SIPRI), 08(BULL), 08(WIKI), 04(IISS)

TABLE 2.10 OPERATIONAL NUCLEAR WARHEADS, STRATEGIC, 2009-2010, 10(BULL), 09(BULL), 09(SIPRI), 08(BULL)

OBS	COUNTRY	ICBM	IRBM	SLBM	ALCM/ BOMBS	TOTAL
1	Russia	1,090		576	838	2,500
2	U.S.	500		1,152	316	1,968
3	France			240	60	300
4	China	40	94	12	40	186
5	U.K.			160		160
6	Israel	Some				Some
7	India					
8	Pakistan					
9	N. Korea					

ALCM air-launched cruise missile
ICBM intercontinental ballistic missile
IRBM intermediate-range ballistic missile
SLBM submarine-launched ballistic missile

TABLE 2.11 OPERATIONAL NUCLEAR WARHEADS, SUB-STRATEGIC, 2009-2010, 10(BULL), 09(BULL), 09(SIPRI), 08(BULL)

OBS	COUNTRY	SRBM	SLCM	AIR DEFENSE	AIRCRAFT	TOTAL
1	Russia		700	698	650	2,000
2	U.S.		100		400	500
3	Israel	-40-50	Some		-40-50	80-100
4	Pakistan	-35-45			-35-45	70-90
5	India	-30-40			-30-40	60-80
6	N. Korea				6-10	6-10
7	China	Some			Some	Some
8	France					0
9	U.K.					0

SLCM sea-launched cruise missile
SRBM short-range ballistic missile

OBS	COUNTRY	STOCKPILE 10(BULL), 09(BULL), 08(BULL), 09(SIPRI), 07(SIPRI)	DELIVERABLE 10(BULL), 09(BULL), 08(BULL), 09(SIPRI), 07(SIPRI)	DELIVERABLE 08(IISS)
1	Russia	12,000	4,600	
2	U.S.	8,600-9,600	2,468	
3	France		300	
4	China		240	
5	U.K.	-180	160	
6	Israel		80-100	-200
7	Pakistan		70-90	
8	India		60-80	
9	N. Korea		6-10	

TABLE 2.12 OPERATIONAL NUCLEAR WARHEADS, *TOTAL STRATEGIC AND SUB-STRATEGIC*, 2009-2010

Note: The discrepancy between IISS and other sources for Israel may be explained by the following:

"Israel's nuclear weapons are not believed to be fully operational under normal circumstances" (Bulletin of the Atomic Scientists, article "Nuclear Notebook: Worldwide deployment of nuclear weapons, 2009").

As Zbigniew Brzezinski stated on Book TV in 2009, Israel has acquired a second-strike capability.

TABLE 2.13 STATES POSSESSING, PURSUING OR CAPABLE OF ACQUIRING WEAPONS OF MASS DESTRUCTION, 2010

STATE	NUCLEAR ENERGY	URANIUM ENRICHMENT	PLUTONIUM PRODUCTION	NUCLEAR WEAPONS	CHEMICAL WEAPONS	BIOLOGICAL WEAPONS	MISSILE TECHNOLOGY
Algeria	Possessing			Pursuing			Pursuing
Argentina	Possessing		Possessing	Capable			
Armenia	Possessing		Possessing				
Australia				Capable	Capable	Capable	Capable
Belarus				Capable			
Belgium	Possessing		Possessing				
Brazil	Possessing	Pursuing	Possessing	Capable		Capable	Possessing
Bulgaria	Possessing						
Burma					Pursuing		
Canada	Possessing		Possessing				
Chile					Capable	Capable	
China	Possessing	Possessing	Possessing	Possessing	Possessing	Possessing	Possessing
Cuba	Possessing		Possessing				
Czechia							
Ethiopia					Pursuing		
Egypt					Possessing	Possessing	Pursuing
Finland	Possessing		Possessing				
France	Possessing	Possessing	Possessing	Possessing	Possessing	Capable	Possessing
Germany	Possessing	Possessing	Possessing	Capable	Capable	Capable	Capable
Hungary	Possessing		Possessing				
India	Possessing	Possessing	Possessing	Possessing	Possessing	Possessing	Possessing

Country							
Indonesia					Pursuing		
Iran	Pursuing	Possessing			Possessing	Possessing	Possessing
Israel	Possessing	Possessing	Possessing	Possessing	Possessing	Possessing	Possessing
Japan			Possessing	Capable	Capable	Capable	Possessing
Kazakhstan				Capable	Capable	Capable	
Laos					Pursuing	Pursuing	
Libya					Pursuing	Pursuing	Pursuing
Lithuania	Possessing		Possessing				
Mexico	Possessing		Possessing				
Netherlands	Possessing		Possessing				
North Korea	Possessing	Possessing	Possessing	Possessing	Possessing	Possessing	Possessing
Pakistan	Possessing	Possessing	Possessing	Possessing	Possessing	Possessing	Possessing
Romania	Possessing		Possessing				
Russia	Possessing	Possessing	Possessing	Possessing	Possessing	Possessing	Possessing
Saudi Arabia				Pursuing	Pursuing	Pursuing	Pursuing
Serbia				Pursuing	Capable		
Slovakia	Possessing		Possessing				
Slovenia	Possessing		Possessing				
South Africa	Possessing		Possessing	Capable	Capable	Capable	Capable
South Korea	Possessing		Possessing		Capable	Capable	Possessing
Spain	Possessing		Possessing				
Sudan					Pursuing		
Sweden	Possessing		Possessing				

TABLE 2.13 – STATES POSSESSING, PURSUING OR CAPABLE OF ACQUIRING WEAPONS OF MASS DESTRUCTION, 2010

STATE	NUCLEAR ENERGY	URANIUM ENRICHMENT	PLUTONIUM PRODUCTION	NUCLEAR WEAPONS	CHEMICAL WEAPONS	BIOLOGICAL WEAPONS	MISSILE TECHNOLOGY
Algeria	Possessing			Pursuing			Pursuing
Argentina	Possessing		Possessing	Capable			
Armenia			Possessing				
Australia				Capable	Capable	Capable	Capable
Belarus				Capable			
Belgium	Possessing		Possessing				
Brazil	Possessing	Pursuing	Possessing	Capable			Possessing
Bulgaria	Possessing					Capable	
Burma					Pursuing	Capable	
Canada	Possessing		Possessing				
Chile			Possessing		Capable		
China	Possessing	Possessing	Possessing	Possessing	Possessing	Possessing	Possessing
Cuba	Possessing					Capable	
Czechia			Possessing				
Ethiopia					Pursuing		
Egypt	Possessing		Possessing		Possessing	Possessing	Pursuing
Finland	Possessing		Possessing				
France	Possessing	Possessing	Possessing	Possessing	Possessing	Capable	Possessing
Germany	Possessing	Possessing	Possessing	Capable	Capable	Capable	Capable
Hungary	Possessing		Possessing				
India	Possessing	Possessing	Possessing	Possessing	Possessing	Possessing	Possessing
Indonesia					Pursuing		
Iran	Pursuing	Possessing	Possessing	Possessing	Possessing	Possessing	Possessing
Israel		Possessing	Possessing	Capable	Possessing	Possessing	Possessing
Japan	Possessing	Possessing	Possessing	Capable	Capable	Capable	Possessing

Kazakhstan				Capable			
Laos							
Libya	Pursuing	Pursuing	Pursuing				Possessing
Lithuania					Possessing		Possessing
Mexico		Pursuing	Pursuing		Possessing	Possessing	Possessing
Netherlands			Possessing		Possessing	Possessing	Possessing
North Korea	Possessing	Possessing	Possessing	Possessing	Possessing	Possessing	Possessing
Pakistan	Possessing	Possessing	Possessing	Possessing	Possessing	Possessing	Possessing
Romania	Possessing	Possessing	Possessing		Possessing		Possessing
Russia	Possessing	Possessing	Possessing	Possessing	Possessing	Possessing	Possessing
Saudi Arabia	Pursuing	Pursuing	Pursuing	Pursuing			
Serbia			Capable	Pursuing	Pursuing		
Slovakia					Possessing		Possessing
Slovenia					Possessing		Possessing
South Africa	Capable	Capable	Capable	Capable	Possessing		Possessing
South Korea	Possessing	Capable	Capable		Possessing		Possessing
Spain	Possessing	Possessing	Possessing		Possessing		Possessing
Sudan			Pursuing		Possessing		Possessing
Sweden	Possessing	Possessing			Possessing		Possessing
Switzerland	Possessing	Possessing			Possessing		Possessing
Syria	Pursuing	Pursuing	Pursuing	Possessing	Possessing		Possessing
Taiwan	Pursuing	Pursuing	Pursuing		Possessing		Possessing
Thailand			Pursuing				Possessing
Ukraine		Pursuing	Pursuing	Capable	Possessing		Possessing
Vietnam		Pursuing	Capable	Capable	Pursuing		
United Kingdom	Possessing	Capable	Capable	Possessing	Possessing		Possessing
United States	Possessing	Possessing	Possessing	Possessing	Possessing	Possessing	Possessing

SOURCES: 09(SIPRI), 09(EST), 00(BULL), 04(E), 09(CIA)

3. DEVELOPED MARKET ECONOMIES

TABLE 3.1 GNI PER CAPITA AT MARKET EXCHANGE RATES OF DEVELOPED MARKET ECONOMIES

TABLE 3.1.1 GNI PER CAPITA AT MARKET EXCHANGE RATES OF DEVELOPED MARKET ECONOMIES, YEAR 1970			
OBS	COUNTRY	GPC70	RANK
1	United States whites	5,187	1
2	United States	5,000	2
3	Sweden	4,450	3
4	Canada	3,930	4
5	Switzerland	3,740	5
6	Norway	3,130	6
7	Denmark	3,110	7
8	Australia	3,050	8
9	France	3,010	9
10	Luxembourg	2,870	10
11	Germany	2,850	11
12	Belgium	2,780	12
13	Netherlands	2,760	13
14	Iceland	2,530	14
15	Finland	2,450	15
16	United Kingdom	2,210	16
17	New Zealand	2,180	17
18	Austria	2,060	18
19	Italy	2,020	19
20	Japan	1,920	20
21	Greece	1,700	21
22	Israel	1,660	22
23	Ireland	1,460	23
24	Spain	1,160	24
25	Cyprus	879	25
26	Portugal	860	26
27	Malta	760	27
28	South Korea	270	28

TABLE 3.1.2 GNI PER CAPITA AT MARKET EXCHANGE RATES OF DEVELOPED MARKET ECONOMIES, YEAR 1980			
OBS	COUNTRY	GPC80	RANK
1	Switzerland	17,330	1
2	Sweden	14,040	2
3	United States whites	13,723	3
4	Norway	13,210	4
5	Denmark	12,900	5
6	Iceland	12,890	6
7	Luxembourg	12,400	7
8	Netherlands	11,870	8
9	Belgium	11,820	9
10	United States	11,140	10
11	France	11,040	11
12	Germany	10,800	12
13	Canada	9,720	13
14	Austria	9,630	14
15	Finland	9,470	15
16	Australia	9,130	16
17	Japan	8,920	17
18	United Kingdom	7,180	18
19	Italy	6,890	19
20	New Zealand	6,340	20
21	Greece	5,350	21
22	Ireland	5,210	22
23	Spain	5,160	23
24	Israel	4,560	24
25	Cyprus	4,280	25
26	Malta	3,380	26
27	Portugal	2,720	27
28	South Korea	1,560	28

TABLE 3.1.3 GNI PER CAPITA AT MARKET EXCHANGE RATES OF DEVELOPED MARKET ECONOMIES, YEAR 1990			
OBS	COUNTRY	GPC90	RANK
1	Switzerland	32,530	1
2	Luxembourg	27,910	2
3	Japan	25,300	3
4	Sweden	24,900	4
5	United States whites	24,754	5
6	Norway	24,590	6
7	Finland	23,860	7
8	Iceland	22,870	8
9	Denmark	22,770	9
10	United States	22,080	10
11	Germany	19,500	11
12	France	19,130	12
13	Canada	19,040	13
14	Austria	18,980	14
15	Belgium	17,930	15
16	Netherlands	17,800	16
17	Italy	16,900	17
18	Australia	16,130	18
19	United Kingdom	15,690	19
20	New Zealand	12,150	20
21	Ireland	11,390	21
22	Spain	11,210	22
23	Israel	10,270	23
24	Cyprus	9,000	24
25	Greece	8,170	25
26	Malta	6,780	26
27	Portugal	6,430	27
28	South Korea	5,660	28

OBS	COUNTRY	GPC00	RANK
\multicolumn{4}{c}{TABLE 3.1.4 GNI PER CAPITA AT MARKET EXCHANGE RATES OF DEVELOPED MARKET ECONOMIES, YEAR 2000}			

TABLE 3.1.4 GNI PER CAPITA AT MARKET EXCHANGE RATES OF
DEVELOPED MARKET ECONOMIES, YEAR 2000

OBS	COUNTRY	GPC00	RANK
1	Luxembourg	43,650	1
2	Switzerland	40,270	2
3	United States whites	36,303	3
4	Norway	35,860	4
5	Japan	34,620	5
6	United States	34,410	6
7	Denmark	31,840	7
8	Iceland	30,820	8
9	Sweden	29,280	9
10	Netherlands	26,580	10
11	United Kingdom	25,910	11
12	Austria	25,830	12
13	Germany	25,500	13
14	Finland	25,470	14
15	Belgium	25,360	15
16	France	24,450	16
17	Ireland	23,170	17
18	Canada	22,130	18
19	Italy	20,890	19
20	Australia	20,710	20
21	Israel	17,840	21
22	Spain	15,420	22
23	New Zealand	13,450	23
24	Cyprus	13,440	24
25	Greece	12,560	25
26	Portugal	11,590	26
27	South Korea	9,910	27
28	Malta	9,670	28

TABLE 3.1.5 GNI PER CAPITA AT MARKET EXCHANGE RATES OF DEVELOPED MARKET ECONOMIES, YEAR 2008			
OBS	COUNTRY	GPC08	RANK
1	Norway	87,340	1
2	Luxembourg	69,390	2
3	Denmark	58,800	3
4	Switzerland	55,510	4
5	Sweden	50,910	5
6	United States whites	50,650	6
7	Ireland	49,770	7
8	Netherlands	49,340	8
9	United States	47,930	9
10	Finland	47,600	10
11	United Kingdom	46,040	11
12	Austria	45,900	12
13	Belgium	44,570	13
14	Canada	43,640	14
15	Germany	42,710	15
16	France	42,000	16
17	Iceland	40,450	17
18	Australia	40,240	18
19	Japan	38,130	19
20	Italy	35,460	20
21	Spain	31,930	21
22	Greece	28,400	22
23	New Zealand	27,830	23
24	Cyprus	26,940	24
25	Israel	24,720	25
26	South Korea	21,530	26
27	Portugal	20,680	27
28	Malta	16,690	28

OBS	COUNTRY	GRPCMER	RANK
	TABLE 3.1.6 GROWTH RATES OF GNI PER CAPITA AT MARKET EXCHANGE RATES OF DEVELOPED MARKET ECONOMIES, 1970-2008		
1	South Korea	12.21	1
2	Ireland	9.73	2
3	Cyprus	9.42	3
4	Norway	9.16	4
5	Spain	9.12	5
6	Luxembourg	8.74	6
7	Portugal	8.73	7
8	Austria	8.51	8
9	Malta	8.47	9
10	United Kingdom	8.32	10
11	Japan	8.18	11
12	Finland	8.12	12
13	Denmark	8.04	13
14	Netherlands	7.88	14
15	Italy	7.83	15
16	Greece	7.69	16
17	Belgium	7.57	17
18	Iceland	7.57	18
19	Germany	7.38	19
20	Israel	7.37	20
21	Switzerland	7.36	21
22	France	7.18	22
23	Australia	7.02	23
24	New Zealand	6.93	24
25	Sweden	6.62	25
26	Canada	6.54	26
27	United States whites	6.18	27
28	United States	6.13	28

TABLE 3.2 GDP PER CAPITA AT PPP OF DEVELOPED MARKET ECONOMIES

TABLE 3.2.1 GDP PER CAPITA AT PPP OF DEVELOPED MARKET ECONOMIES, YEAR 1970			
OBS	COUNTRY	GPCPPP70	RANK
1	United States whites	5,106	1
2	United States	4,922	2
3	Switzerland	4,840	3
4	Canada	3,969	4
5	Sweden	3,855	5
6	Luxembourg	3,714	6
7	Denmark	3,523	7
8	Netherlands	3,500	8
9	Australia	3,465	9
10	New Zealand	3,331	10
11	United Kingdom	3,273	11
12	Germany	3,227	12
13	France	3,215	13
14	Norway	3,113	14
15	Italy	3,045	15
16	Belgium	2,989	16
17	Iceland	2,980	17
18	Finland	2,902	18
19	Japan	2,811	19
20	Austria	2,757	20
21	Israel	2,667	21
22	Spain	2,179	22
23	Ireland	1,852	23
24	Greece	1,562	24
25	Portugal	1,454	25
26	Malta	1,276	26
27	Cyprus	1,032	27
28	South Korea	500	28

TABLE 3.2.2 GDP PER CAPITA AT PPP OF DEVELOPED MARKET ECONOMIES, YEAR 1980			
OBS	COUNTRY	GPCPPP80	RANK
1	Switzerland	13,965	1
2	Luxembourg	12,968	2
3	United States whites	12,899	3
4	United States	12,186	4
5	Iceland	12,002	5
6	Canada	11,031	6
7	Sweden	10,578	7
8	Austria	10,550	8
9	Belgium	10,248	9
10	Australia	10,245	10
11	Denmark	9,977	11
12	Netherlands	9,869	12
13	Germany	9,781	13
14	Norway	9,555	14
15	France	9,502	15
16	Italy	9,210	16
17	Finland	9,054	17
18	Japan	8,924	18
19	New Zealand	8,693	19
20	United Kingdom	8,383	20
21	Greece	8,315	21
22	Israel	7,183	22
23	Spain	6,850	23
24	Ireland	6,197	24
25	Portugal	5,243	25
26	Cyprus	5,098	26
27	Malta	4,383	27
28	South Korea	2,634	28

TABLE 3.2.3 GDP PER CAPITA AT PPP OF DEVELOPED MARKET ECONOMIES, YEAR 1990			
OBS	COUNTRY	GPCPPP90	RANK
1	Luxembourg	30,411	1
2	Switzerland	24,755	2
3	United States whites	24,569	3
4	United States	23,064	4
5	Iceland	21,303	5
6	Canada	19,499	6
7	Austria	19,374	7
8	Sweden	19,319	8
9	Japan	18,797	9
10	Belgium	18,700	10
11	Denmark	18,462	11
12	Germany	18,373	12
13	Norway	17,885	13
14	Finland	17,699	14
15	Netherlands	17,624	15
16	Italy	17,595	16
17	Australia	17,331	17
18	France	17,268	18
19	United Kingdom	16,319	19
20	New Zealand	13,982	20
21	Spain	13,330	21
22	Ireland	12,987	22
23	Israel	12,904	23
24	Greece	12,791	24
25	Cyprus	12,467	25
26	Portugal	10,785	26
27	Malta	9,817	27
28	South Korea	8,188	28

TABLE 3.2.4 GDP PER CAPITA AT PPP OF DEVELOPED MARKET ECONOMIES, YEAR 2000			
OBS	COUNTRY	GPCPPP00	RANK
1	Luxembourg	53,651	1
2	Norway	36,130	2
3	United States whites	35,849	3
4	United States	34,606	4
5	Switzerland	31,731	5
6	Netherlands	29,403	6
7	Iceland	28,860	7
8	Denmark	28,829	8
9	Austria	28,773	9
10	Ireland	28,643	10
11	Canada	28,407	11
12	Sweden	27,771	12
13	Belgium	27,560	13
14	Australia	27,433	14
15	United Kingdom	26,072	15
16	Germany	25,945	16
17	Finland	25,670	17
18	Japan	25,619	18
19	Italy	25,595	19
20	France	25,328	20
21	Israel	23,504	21
22	Spain	21,323	22
23	New Zealand	20,809	23
24	Cyprus	20,016	24
25	Malta	18,860	25
26	Greece	18,412	26
27	South Korea	17,219	27
28	Portugal	17,089	28

OBS	COUNTRY	GPCPPP08	RANK
\multicolumn{4}{c}{TABLE 3.2.5 GDP PER CAPITA AT PPP OF DEVELOPED MARKET ECONOMIES, YEAR 2008}
1	Luxembourg	78,922	1
2	Norway	58,714	2
3	United States whites	48,980	3
4	United States	46,350	4
5	Switzerland	42,415	5
6	Ireland	41,850	6
7	Netherlands	40,961	7
8	Canada	39,078	8
9	Australia	38,784	9
10	Austria	37,912	10
11	Sweden	36,961	11
12	Iceland	36,902	12
13	Denmark	36,845	13
14	Finland	36,195	14
15	United Kingdom	35,468	15
16	Germany	35,374	16
17	Belgium	35,238	17
18	Japan	34,129	18
19	France	33,058	19
20	Spain	31,674	20
21	Italy	31,283	21
22	Greece	29,356	22
23	Israel	27,905	23
24	South Korea	27,658	24
25	New Zealand	27,260	25
26	Cyprus	26,919	26
27	Portugal	23,254	27
28	Malta	21,243	28

TABLE 3.2.6 GROWTH RATES OF GDP PER CAPITA AT PPP OF DEVELOPED MARKET ECONOMIES, 1970-2008			
OBS	COUNTRY	GRPCPPP	RANK
1	South Korea	11.14	1
2	Cyprus	8.96	2
3	Ireland	8.55	3
4	Luxembourg	8.38	4
5	Norway	8.04	5
6	Greece	8.03	6
7	Malta	7.68	7
8	Portugal	7.57	8
9	Spain	7.30	9
10	Austria	7.14	10
11	Finland	6.87	11
12	Iceland	6.85	12
13	Japan	6.79	13
14	Belgium	6.71	14
15	Netherlands	6.69	15
16	Australia	6.56	16
17	Germany	6.50	17
18	United Kingdom	6.47	18
19	Israel	6.37	19
20	Denmark	6.37	20
21	France	6.32	21
22	Italy	6.32	22
23	Canada	6.20	23
24	United States whites	6.13	24
25	Sweden	6.13	25
26	United States	6.08	26
27	Switzerland	5.88	27
28	New Zealand	5.69	28

TABLE 3.3 INFANT MORTALITY OF DEVELOPED MARKET ECONOMIES

TABLE 3.3.1 INFANT MORTALITY OF DEVELOPED MARKET ECONOMIES, YEAR 1960			
OBS	COUNTRY	INFMRT60	RANK
1	Sweden	16.0	1
2	Netherlands	16.4	2
3	Iceland	17.4	3
4	Norway	18.6	4
5	Australia	20.4	5
6	Denmark	21.4	6
7	Switzerland	21.7	7
8	Finland	22.0	8
9	New Zealand	22.4	9
10	United Kingdom	22.8	10
11	United States whites	23.1	11
12	France	23.8	12
13	United States	26.0	13
14	Canada	28.2	14
15	Cyprus	29.8	15
16	Japan	30.0	16
17	Belgium	30.1	17
18	Ireland	30.7	18
19	Israel	30.8	19
20	Luxembourg	31.5	20
21	Germany	35.0	21
22	Austria	36.6	22
23	Malta	36.7	23
24	Spain	37.9	24
25	Greece	38.4	25
26	Italy	44.1	26
27	Portugal	80.7	27
28	South Korea	96.0	28

TABLE 3.3.2 INFANT MORTALITY OF DEVELOPED MARKET ECONOMIES, YEAR 1970			
OBS	COUNTRY	INFMRT70	RANK
1	Sweden	11.2	1.0
2	Iceland	12.5	2.5
3	Netherlands	12.5	2.5
4	Norway	13.0	4.0
5	Finland	13.1	5.0
6	Japan	13.3	6.0
7	Denmark	13.7	7.0
8	Switzerland	14.8	8.0
9	France	14.9	9.0
10	New Zealand	16.8	10.0
11	Australia	17.7	11.0
12	United Kingdom	17.8	12.5
13	United States whites	17.8	12.5
14	Canada	18.6	14.0
15	Luxembourg	19.3	15.0
16	Ireland	19.4	16.0
17	Spain	20.0	17.5
18	United States	20.0	17.5
19	Belgium	20.2	19.0
20	Germany	22.0	20.0
21	Israel	24.1	21.0
22	Austria	24.9	22.0
23	Malta	25.7	23.0
24	Cyprus	26.0	24.0
25	Greece	28.3	25.0
26	Italy	30.2	26.0
27	South Korea	41.3	27.0
28	Portugal	53.7	28.0

TABLE 3.3.3 INFANT MORTALITY OF DEVELOPED MARKET ECONOMIES, YEAR 1980			
OBS	COUNTRY	INFMRT80	RANK
1	Sweden	7.1	1.0
2	Finland	7.2	2.5
3	Iceland	7.2	2.5
4	Japan	7.4	4.0
5	Denmark	8.1	5.0
6	Norway	8.3	6.5
7	Switzerland	8.3	6.5
8	Netherlands	8.8	8.0
9	France	10.1	9.0
10	Canada	10.3	10.0
11	Luxembourg	10.8	11.0
12	Australia	10.9	12.5
13	United States whites	10.9	12.5
14	Belgium	12.0	14.5
15	Ireland	12.0	14.5
16	United Kingdom	12.1	16.0
17	Spain	12.4	17.5
18	United States	12.4	17.5
19	Germany	12.6	19.0
20	New Zealand	12.8	20.0
21	Austria	13.8	21.0
22	Italy	14.3	22.0
23	Malta	14.9	23.0
24	Israel	15.8	24.0
25	South Korea	17.0	25.0
26	Greece	17.6	26.0
27	Cyprus	19.8	27.0
28	Portugal	23.1	28.0

OBS	COUNTRY	INFMRT90	RANK
	TABLE 3.3.4 INFANT MORTALITY OF DEVELOPED MARKET ECONOMIES, YEAR 1990		
1	Japan	4.6	1.0
2	Iceland	5.5	2.0
3	Finland	5.6	3.5
4	Sweden	5.6	3.5
5	Switzerland	6.5	5.0
6	Canada	6.8	6.5
7	Netherlands	6.8	6.5
8	Germany	6.9	8.0
9	Norway	7.0	9.0
10	Denmark	7.3	10.5
11	France	7.3	10.5
12	Australia	7.5	13.5
13	Ireland	7.5	13.5
14	Luxembourg	7.5	13.5
15	Spain	7.5	13.5
16	United States whites	7.6	16.0
17	Austria	7.8	17.5
18	United Kingdom	7.8	17.5
19	South Korea	7.9	19.0
20	Belgium	8.5	20.5
21	Italy	8.5	20.5
22	New Zealand	9.0	22.0
23	Cyprus	9.2	23.0
24	Greece	9.4	24.5
25	United States	9.4	24.5
26	Israel	9.5	26.0
27	Malta	9.8	27.0
28	Portugal	11.4	28.0

TABLE 3.3.5 INFANT MORTALITY OF DEVELOPED MARKET ECONOMIES, YEAR 2000			
OBS	COUNTRY	INFMRT00	RANK
1	Iceland	2.9	1.0
2	Japan	3.3	2.5
3	Sweden	3.3	2.5
4	Finland	3.5	4.0
5	Norway	3.8	5.0
6	Luxembourg	4.3	6.0
7	France	4.4	8.0
8	Germany	4.4	8.0
9	Spain	4.4	8.0
10	Austria	4.5	10.5
11	Denmark	4.5	10.5
12	Belgium	4.6	12.5
13	Switzerland	4.6	12.5
14	Italy	4.8	14.0
15	Australia	5.1	15.5
16	Netherlands	5.1	15.5
17	Canada	5.2	17.0
18	Cyprus	5.4	18.5
19	Portugal	5.4	18.5
20	Greece	5.5	20.5
21	Israel	5.5	20.5
22	United Kingdom	5.6	22.0
23	United States whites	5.7	23.0
24	Ireland	5.9	24.5
25	South Korea	5.9	24.5
26	Malta	6.0	26.0
27	New Zealand	6.1	27.0
28	United States	7.1	28.0

TABLE 3.3.6 INFANT MORTALITY OF DEVELOPED MARKET ECONOMIES, YEAR 2008			
OBS	COUNTRY	INFMRT08	RANK
1	Iceland	1.9	1.5
2	Luxembourg	1.9	1.5
3	Sweden	2.3	3.0
4	Japan	2.5	4.0
5	Finland	2.7	5.0
6	Norway	2.9	6.5
7	Portugal	2.9	6.5
8	Ireland	3.0	8.5
9	Italy	3.0	8.5
10	France	3.3	10.5
11	Greece	3.3	10.5
12	Austria	3.4	12.0
13	Cyprus	3.5	13.5
14	Spain	3.5	13.5
15	Israel	3.6	15.0
16	Denmark	3.7	16.5
17	Germany	3.7	16.5
18	Belgium	3.9	18.0
19	Netherlands	4.0	19.5
20	Switzerland	4.0	19.5
21	South Korea	4.7	21.0
22	Australia	4.9	23.0
23	New Zealand	4.9	23.0
24	United Kingdom	4.9	23.0
25	Malta	5.5	25.5
26	United States whites	5.5	25.5
27	Canada	5.7	27.0
28	United States	6.7	28.0

TABLE 3.3.7 DECREASE IN RATES OF INFANT MORTALITY OF DEVELOPED MARKET ECONOMIES, 1960-2008

OBS	COUNTRY	DRIM	RANK
1	Portugal	7.17	1
2	South Korea	6.49	2
3	Luxembourg	6.02	3
4	Italy	5.76	4
5	Japan	5.31	5
6	Greece	5.25	6
7	Spain	5.09	7
8	Austria	5.08	8
9	Ireland	4.96	9
10	Germany	4.79	10
11	Iceland	4.72	11
12	Israel	4.57	12
13	Cyprus	4.56	13
14	Finland	4.47	14
15	Belgium	4.35	15
16	France	4.20	16
17	Sweden	4.12	17
18	Malta	4.03	18
19	Norway	3.95	19
20	Denmark	3.72	20
21	Switzerland	3.59	21
22	Canada	3.39	22
23	United Kingdom	3.26	23
24	New Zealand	3.22	24
25	United States whites	3.03	25
26	Australia	3.02	26
27	Netherlands	2.98	27
28	United States	2.87	28

TABLE 3.4 LIFE EXPECTANCY OF DEVELOPED MARKET ECONOMIES

TABLE 3.4.1 LIFE EXPECTANCY OF DEVELOPED MARKET ECONOMIES, YEAR 1960			
OBS	COUNTRY	LIFEXP60	RANK
1	Norway	73.550	1
2	Netherlands	73.393	2
3	Iceland	73.249	3
4	Sweden	73.006	4
5	Denmark	72.177	5
6	Israel	71.684	6
7	Switzerland	71.313	7
8	New Zealand	71.237	8
9	Canada	71.133	9
10	United Kingdom	71.127	10
11	Australia	70.817	11
12	United States whites	70.700	12
13	Belgium	70.368	13
14	France	70.240	14
15	United States	69.771	15
16	Ireland	69.693	16
17	Germany	69.543	17
18	Italy	69.124	18
19	Spain	69.109	19
20	Luxembourg	68.929	20
21	Greece	68.850	21
22	Finland	68.820	22
23	Cyprus	68.655	23
24	Austria	68.586	24
25	Malta	68.554	25
26	Japan	67.666	26
27	Portugal	63.442	27
28	South Korea	54.151	28

TABLE 3.4.2 LIFE EXPECTANCY OF DEVELOPED MARKET ECONOMIES, YEAR 1970			
OBS	COUNTRY	LIFEXP70	RANK
1	Sweden	74.649	1
2	Norway	74.088	2
3	Iceland	73.969	3
4	Netherlands	73.586	4
5	Denmark	73.343	5
6	Switzerland	73.020	6
7	Canada	72.700	7
8	Spain	72.027	8
9	France	72.009	9
10	United Kingdom	71.973	10
11	Japan	71.950	11
12	Greece	71.842	12
13	United States whites	71.700	13
14	Italy	71.559	14
15	New Zealand	71.273	15
16	Israel	71.213	16
17	Belgium	71.211	17
18	Ireland	71.093	18
19	Australia	71.019	19
20	United States	70.807	20
21	Cyprus	70.773	21
22	Germany	70.459	22
23	Luxembourg	70.338	23
24	Finland	70.180	24
25	Malta	70.120	25
26	Austria	69.891	26
27	Portugal	67.420	27
28	South Korea	61.247	28

TABLE 3.4.3 LIFE EXPECTANCY OF DEVELOPED MARKET ECONOMIES, YEAR 1980			
OBS	COUNTRY	LIFEXP80	RANK
1	Japan	76.092	1.0
2	Netherlands	75.743	2.0
3	Sweden	75.741	3.0
4	Norway	75.672	4.0
5	Switzerland	75.459	5.0
6	Spain	75.349	6.0
7	Canada	75.078	7.0
8	Cyprus	74.551	8.0
9	United States whites	74.400	9.0
10	Greece	74.359	10.0
11	Australia	74.334	11.0
12	France	74.180	12.0
13	Denmark	74.102	13.0
14	Italy	73.943	14.0
15	Iceland	73.876	15.5
16	Israel	73.876	15.5
17	United Kingdom	73.676	17.0
18	United States	73.659	18.0
19	Finland	73.440	19.0
20	Belgium	73.247	20.0
21	Malta	72.936	21.0
22	New Zealand	72.829	22.0
23	Luxembourg	72.704	23.0
24	Ireland	72.665	24.0
25	Germany	72.626	25.0
26	Austria	72.424	26.0
27	Portugal	71.386	27.0
28	South Korea	65.802	28.0

OBS	COUNTRY	LIFEXP90	RANK
	TABLE 3.4.4 LIFE EXPECTANCY OF DEVELOPED MARKET ECONOMIES, YEAR 1990		
1	Japan	78.837	1.0
2	Sweden	77.537	2.0
3	Canada	77.377	3.0
4	Switzerland	77.242	4.0
5	Australia	76.995	5.0
6	Greece	76.939	6.0
7	Netherlands	76.878	7.0
8	Italy	76.859	8.0
9	Spain	76.838	9.0
10	France	76.745	10.0
11	Iceland	76.607	11.5
12	Israel	76.607	11.5
13	Norway	76.537	13.0
14	Cyprus	76.517	14.0
15	United States whites	76.100	15.0
16	Belgium	75.968	16.0
17	United Kingdom	75.880	17.0
18	Austria	75.530	18.0
19	Malta	75.498	19.0
20	New Zealand	75.378	20.0
21	United States	75.215	21.0
22	Germany	75.207	22.0
23	Luxembourg	75.193	23.0
24	Finland	74.813	24.0
25	Denmark	74.805	25.0
26	Ireland	74.583	26.0
27	Portugal	73.663	27.0
28	South Korea	71.295	28.0

TABLE 3.4.5 LIFE EXPECTANCY OF DEVELOPED MARKET ECONOMIES, YEAR 2000			
OBS	COUNTRY	LIFEXP00	RANK
1	Japan	81.076	1.0
2	Switzerland	79.681	2.0
3	Sweden	79.648	3.0
4	Italy	79.522	4.0
5	Canada	79.237	5.0
6	Australia	79.234	6.0
7	Spain	78.966	7.0
8	Iceland	78.954	8.5
9	Israel	78.954	8.5
10	France	78.910	10.0
11	New Zealand	78.637	11.0
12	Norway	78.604	12.0
13	Cyprus	78.483	13.0
14	Malta	78.200	14.0
15	Austria	78.042	15.0
16	Greece	77.988	16.5
17	Netherlands	77.988	16.5
18	Germany	77.927	18.0
19	Luxembourg	77.873	19.0
20	United Kingdom	77.861	20.0
21	Belgium	77.624	21.0
22	Finland	77.501	22.0
23	United States whites	77.300	23.0
24	United States	77.034	24.0
25	Denmark	76.754	25.0
26	Ireland	76.541	26.0
27	Portugal	76.517	27.0
28	South Korea	75.855	28.0

TABLE 3.4.6 LIFE EXPECTANCY OF DEVELOPED MARKET ECONOMIES, YEAR 2008			
OBS	COUNTRY	LIFEXP08	RANK
1	Japan	82.588	1
2	Switzerland	82.162	2
3	Italy	81.945	3
4	Iceland	81.575	4
5	France	81.520	5
6	Australia	81.395	6
7	Sweden	81.237	7
8	Spain	81.088	8
9	Israel	81.002	9
10	Canada	80.965	10
11	Norway	80.741	11
12	Luxembourg	80.525	12
13	Austria	80.448	13
14	Netherlands	80.401	14
15	New Zealand	80.151	15
16	Belgium	80.110	16
17	Germany	80.089	17
18	Greece	79.963	18
19	United Kingdom	79.903	19
20	Ireland	79.857	20
21	South Korea	79.833	21
22	Finland	79.792	22
23	Cyprus	79.661	23
24	Malta	79.641	24
25	Portugal	79.250	25
26	Denmark	78.700	26
27	United States whites	78.655	27
28	United States	78.439	28

\multicolumn{4}{c}{TABLE 3.4.7 GROWTH RATES OF LIFE EXPECTANCY OF DEVELOPED MARKET ECONOMIES, 1960-2008}
OBS	COUNTRY	GRLE	RANK
1	South Korea	0.81	1
2	Portugal	0.46	2
3	Japan	0.42	3
4	Italy	0.36	4
5	Spain	0.33	5
6	Austria	0.33	6
7	Luxembourg	0.32	7
8	Malta	0.31	8
9	Greece	0.31	9
10	France	0.31	10
11	Cyprus	0.31	11
12	Finland	0.31	12
13	Switzerland	0.30	13
14	Germany	0.29	14
15	Australia	0.29	15
16	Ireland	0.28	16
17	Belgium	0.27	17
18	Canada	0.27	18
19	Israel	0.25	19
20	New Zealand	0.25	20
21	United States	0.24	21
22	United Kingdom	0.24	22
23	Iceland	0.22	23
24	Sweden	0.22	24
25	United States whites	0.22	25
26	Norway	0.19	26
27	Netherlands	0.19	27
28	Denmark	0.18	28

TABLE 3.5 HEALTH EXPENDITURES OF DEVELOPED MARKET ECONOMIES

TABLE 3.5.1 TOTAL HEALTH EXPENDITURES OF DEVELOPED MARKET ECONOMIES AS PERCENT OF GDP, YEAR 2007			
OBS	COUNTRY	HLTGDP	RANK
1	United States	15.7	1.0
2	France	11.0	2.0
3	Switzerland	10.8	3.0
4	Germany	10.4	4.0
5	Austria	10.1	5.5
6	Canada	10.1	5.5
7	Portugal	10.0	7.0
8	Denmark	9.8	8.0
9	Greece	9.6	9.0
10	Belgium	9.4	10.0
11	Iceland	9.3	11.0
12	Sweden	9.1	12.0
13	New Zealand	9.0	13.0
14	Australia	8.9	15.0
15	Netherlands	8.9	15.0
16	Norway	8.9	15.0
17	Italy	8.7	17.0
18	Spain	8.5	18.0
19	United Kingdom	8.4	19.0
20	Finland	8.2	20.0
21	Israel	8.0	21.5
22	Japan	8.0	21.5
23	Ireland	7.6	23.0
24	Malta	7.5	24.0
25	Luxembourg	7.1	25.0
26	Cyprus	6.6	26.0
27	South Korea	6.3	27.0

OBS	COUNTRY	PUBHLT	RANK
\multicolumn{4}{l}{TABLE 3.5.2 PUBLIC HEALTH EXPENDITURES OF DEVELOPED MARKET ECONOMIES AS PERCENT OF TOTAL HEALTH EXPENDITURES, YEAR 2007}			

TABLE 3.5.2 PUBLIC HEALTH EXPENDITURES OF
DEVELOPED MARKET ECONOMIES AS PERCENT OF
TOTAL HEALTH EXPENDITURES, YEAR 2007

OBS	COUNTRY	PUBHLT	RANK
1	Luxembourg	90.9	1.0
2	Denmark	84.5	2.0
3	Norway	84.1	3.0
4	Iceland	82.5	4.0
5	Netherlands	82.0	5.0
6	Sweden	81.7	6.5
7	United Kingdom	81.7	6.5
8	Japan	81.3	8.0
9	Ireland	80.7	9.0
10	France	79.0	10.0
11	New Zealand	78.9	11.0
12	Malta	77.5	12.0
13	Germany	76.9	13.0
14	Italy	76.5	14.0
15	Austria	76.4	15.0
16	Finland	74.6	16.0
17	Belgium	74.1	17.0
18	Spain	71.8	18.0
19	Portugal	70.6	19.0
20	Canada	70.0	20.0
21	Australia	67.5	21.0
22	Greece	60.3	22.0
23	Switzerland	59.3	23.0
24	Israel	55.9	24.0
25	South Korea	54.9	25.0
26	Cyprus	45.6	26.0
27	United States	45.5	27.0

TABLE 3.6 TAXES AS SHARE OF GDP OF DEVELOPED MARKET ECONOMIES

TABLE 3.6.1 TAXES AS SHARE OF GDP OF DEVELOPED MARKET ECONOMIES, YEAR 1970			
OBS	COUNTRY	TAXGDP70	RANK
1	Sweden	43.4	1.0
2	Denmark	40.4	2.0
3	Austria	38.5	3.0
4	Belgium	38.3	4.0
5	Israel	38.2	5.0
6	Netherlands	37.7	6.0
7	France	37.4	7.0
8	Norway	37.3	8.0
9	Germany	37.2	9.0
10	United Kingdom	35.6	10.0
11	Finland	33.0	11.0
12	Canada	31.3	12.0
13	Luxembourg	30.8	13.0
14	Ireland	30.7	14.0
15	United States	28.9	15.0
16	Iceland	28.1	16.0
17	Italy	27.9	17.0
18	New Zealand	26.6	18.0
19	Australia	25.4	19.0
20	Switzerland	23.8	20.0
21	Greece	21.6	21.0
22	Portugal	20.9	22.5
23	Spain	20.9	22.5
24	Malta	20.0	24.0
25	Japan	19.7	25.0
26	Cyprus	18.5	26.0
27	South Korea	17.5	27.0

TABLE 3.6.2 TAXES AS SHARE OF GDP OF DEVELOPED MARKET ECONOMIES, YEAR 1980			
OBS	COUNTRY	TAXGDP80	RANK
1	Sweden	50.6	1.0
2	Denmark	48.1	2.0
3	Belgium	47.4	3.0
4	Netherlands	45.9	4.0
5	Norway	45.8	5.0
6	Austria	44.5	6.0
7	Germany	43.9	7.0
8	France	43.6	8.0
9	Finland	38.4	9.0
10	Israel	37.4	10.0
11	Luxembourg	36.2	11.0
12	United Kingdom	35.1	12.0
13	Ireland	33.1	13.5
14	New Zealand	33.1	13.5
15	Italy	32.4	15.0
16	Iceland	31.8	16.0
17	Switzerland	30.8	17.0
18	Canada	30.3	18.0
19	United States	30.0	19.0
20	Spain	29.1	20.0
21	Portugal	27.9	21.0
22	Australia	27.7	22.0
23	Japan	25.6	23.0
24	Greece	25.1	24.0
25	Cyprus	22.4	25.0
26	Malta	21.6	26.0
27	South Korea	18.7	27.0

OBS	COUNTRY	TAXGDP90	RANK
\multicolumn{4}{c}{TABLE 3.6.3 TAXES AS SHARE OF GDP OF DEVELOPED MARKET ECONOMIES, YEAR 1990}			
1	Sweden	63.1	1
2	Norway	55.5	2
3	Denmark	54.6	3
4	Finland	53.3	4
5	Netherlands	49.6	5
6	Austria	49.4	6
7	New Zealand	48.7	7
8	France	47.0	8
9	Belgium	45.5	9
10	Canada	43.0	10
11	Germany	41.7	11
12	Italy	41.5	12
13	Ireland	40.1	13
14	United Kingdom	39.4	14
15	Spain	38.7	15
16	Iceland	38.3	16
17	Israel	37.4	17
18	Luxembourg	35.7	18
19	Portugal	34.5	19
20	Japan	34.0	20
21	Australia	33.7	21
22	United States	32.8	22
23	Switzerland	31.5	23
24	Greece	30.9	24
25	Malta	28.0	25
26	Cyprus	27.5	26
27	South Korea	23.1	27

TABLE 3.6.4 TAXES AS SHARE OF GDP OF DEVELOPED MARKET ECONOMIES, YEAR 2000			
OBS	COUNTRY	TAXGDP00	RANK
1	Sweden	60.7	1
2	Norway	57.7	2
3	Denmark	55.5	3
4	Finland	55.3	4
5	Austria	50.3	5
6	France	50.1	6
7	Belgium	49.1	7
8	Germany	46.4	8
9	Netherlands	46.1	9
10	Italy	45.3	10
11	Canada	44.1	11
12	Iceland	43.6	12
13	Greece	43.0	13
14	New Zealand	41.2	14
15	United Kingdom	40.3	15
16	Portugal	40.2	16
17	Israel	40.1	17
18	Luxembourg	39.1	18
19	Spain	38.1	19
20	Switzerland	37.6	20
21	Ireland	36.2	21
22	Australia	36.1	22
23	United States	35.8	23
24	Malta	33.4	24
25	Cyprus	32.5	25
26	Japan	31.4	26
27	South Korea	29.3	27

TABLE 3.6.5 TAXES AS SHARE OF GDP OF DEVELOPED MARKET ECONOMIES, YEAR 2008			
OBS	COUNTRY	TAXGDP08	RANK
1	Norway	60.5	1
2	Sweden	54.0	2
3	Denmark	52.9	3
4	Finland	51.9	4
5	France	49.6	5
6	Belgium	48.2	6
7	Austria	47.4	7
8	Iceland	47.1	8
9	Netherlands	46.0	9
10	Italy	45.9	10
11	New Zealand	45.1	11
12	Portugal	44.1	12
13	Germany	43.4	13
14	United Kingdom	41.9	14
15	Greece	40.4	15
16	Canada	39.9	16
17	Luxembourg	38.3	17
18	Spain	38.2	18
19	Israel	36.8	19
20	Cyprus	36.6	20
21	South Korea	35.7	21
22	Australia	35.5	22
23	Malta	35.2	23
24	Japan	35.0	24
25	Ireland	34.0	25
26	United States	33.3	26
27	Switzerland	29.4	27

TABLE 3.6.6 GROWTH RATES OF TAXES AS SHARE OF GDP OF DEVELOPED MARKET ECONOMIES, 1970-2008			
OBS	COUNTRY	GRTX	RANK
1	Portugal	2.92	1
2	South Korea	2.56	2
3	Norway	2.52	3
4	Cyprus	2.49	4
5	Greece	2.40	5
6	Spain	2.26	6
7	Iceland	2.19	7
8	New Zealand	2.18	8
9	Japan	2.09	9
10	Italy	2.09	10
11	Finland	2.09	11
12	Malta	2.06	12
13	Denmark	1.34	13
14	France	1.32	14
15	Australia	1.27	15
16	Sweden	1.13	16
17	Belgium	1.07	17
18	Canada	1.00	18
19	Austria	0.96	19
20	Netherlands	0.90	20
21	Luxembourg	0.88	21
22	Switzerland	0.76	22
23	United Kingdom	0.70	23
24	Germany	0.68	24
25	United States	0.54	25
26	Ireland	0.40	26
27	Israel	-0.16	27

Appendix: Methodology and Definitions

Selection of Indicators

These parameters were first assembled to illustrate the comparative position of the countries of the world. The aim was to select indicators that were:

- few in number;
- important;
- available for the maximum number of countries;
- statistically reliable;
- independent of the technological and industrial level of the countries.

Missing data was projected with the help of regressions.

Definition of Principal Component 1

I have used "Principal Component 1" for the definition of several indexes.

Principal component analysis is a multidimensional technique for studying the interrelationship between several quantitative variables. For a given set of data with p numerical variables, p principal components can be computed. Each principal component is a linear combination of the initial variables with coefficients equal to the eigenvector of the correlational or covariational matrix. The eigenvectors are typically selected to have a length of one. The principal components are sorted in descending order of characteristic values, which are equal to the variation of the components. Principal components have a number of useful properties; among them are:

- The first principal component accounts for the greatest variation of any linear combination of observed variables of the unit length.
- In geometrical terms, a j-dimensional linear subspace of the first j principal components provides the best possible arrangement of data points measured as the sum of squares of the perpendicular distances from each point to the subspace.[1]

---

1. Mathematics: SAS Institute, Inc. (1988), Kiyosi (2000), Kotz (1985).

DEFINITION OF THE ECONOMIC QUALITY-OF-LIFE INDEX

I computed an Economic Quality-of-Life Index as Principal Component 1 of the four economic indicators of the quality of life given in this yearbook:

log(GPC)	logarithm of GNI per capita at market exchange rates
log(GPCPPP)	logarithm of GDP per capita at purchasing power parities
log(INFMRT)	logarithm of infant mortality
log(max(LIFEXP) – LIFEXP)	logarithm of the difference between maximum life expectancy and life expectancy in the country in question (in 2006, the maximum life expectancy was that of women of Andorra at 86.61 years)

DEFINITION OF THE HUMAN RIGHTS INDEX

In an attempt to give an estimate of the level of human rights, I computed a human rights index as Principal Component 1 of four indicators of the political quality of life:

SCINTX	the index of societal integration
CPR	the index of civil and political rights
HDX	the human development index
GINI	GINI coefficient of income inequality

DEFINITION OF THE ECONOMICO-POLITICAL QUALITY-OF-LIFE INDEX

I computed an Economico-Political Quality-of-Life Index as Principal Component 1 using the four economic and the four political (human rights) indicators of the quality of life described above.

DEFINITION OF GROSS NATIONAL INCOME AT MARKET EXCHANGE RATES

The Gross Domestic Product is the most frequently used indicator of national productivity. It represents the total value of products and services produced.

GNI (or gross national product, in the terminology of the 1968 United Nations System of National Accounts) measures the total domestic and foreign value added claimed by residents. GNI comprises GDP plus net receipts of primary income (compensation of employees and property income) from nonresident sources.[2]

The GDP or GNI, which is recorded in terms of the national currency, has to be translated into a single currency to enable international comparison. GNI per capita at market exchange rates provides GNI data translated into U.S. dollars on the basis of the market exchange rate. In addition to the actual ratios among the buying powers of different currencies, the market rate is based on a number of other factors. From the point of view of actual buying power, the market typically overestimates the discrepancies in the income earned in different countries. (See also GDP at purchasing power parities.)

In instances where there was a choice between sources, priority was given to data from the World Bank, since it uses a more advanced procedure for computing the exchange rate, smoothing fluctuations in the market exchange rate.

---

2 Economics: Finfacts.

In cases where values were missing, the following regression was used:

$$\log(\text{GPC}) = \text{REG}(\log(\text{GPCPPP}))$$

where

log(GPC)	logarithm of GNI per capita at market exchange rates
log(GPCPPP)	logarithm of GDP per capita at purchasing power parities
Number of observations	212
Correlation coefficient	0.97

DEFINITION OF INFANT MORTALITY

The indicator of infant mortality is computed from number of deaths during the first year of life per 1000 thousand live births. This is one of the most important indicators used, since it indirectly measures the state of health care, transportation, communications, and level of culture of the given country (this list can be extended indefinitely).

In cases where values were missing, the following regression was used:

$$\log(\text{INFMRT}) = \text{REG}(\log(\text{GPC}))$$

where

log(INFMRT)	Logarithm of infant mortality
log(GPC)	Logarithm of GNI per capita at market exchange rates
Number of observations	230
Correlation coefficient	0.87

DEFINITION OF LIFE EXPECTANCY

Life expectancy is probably the most accurate single indicator of the quality of life in a given country. It sums up in one number all the natural and social stresses that affect an individual.

In cases where the data are taken from the Encyclopedia Britannica, I used the arithmetic mean of the life expectancies of men and women.

In cases where values were missing, the following regression was used:

$$\log(\max(\text{LIFEXP}) - \text{LIFEXP}) = \text{REG}(\text{GPC}, \log(\text{INFMRT}))$$

where

log(max(LIFEXP) – LIFEXP)	Logarithm of the difference between maximum life expectancy and life expectancy of this country
GPC	GNI per capita at market exchange rates

log(INFMRT)	Logarithm of infant mortality
Number of observations	230
Correlation coefficient	0.93

DEFINITION OF GROSS DOMESTIC PRODUCT AT PURCHASING POWER PARITIES

Typically the GDP is translated into U.S. dollars. The market foreign currency exchange rate, however, does not necessarily reflect differences in actual purchasing power in different countries. The use of purchasing power parities is designed to eliminate this distortion. Purchasing power parities indicate how many currency units are needed in one country to buy the amount of goods and services that can be purchased for a currency unit in another country.

In cases where values were missing, the following regression was used:

$$\log(GPCPPP) = REG(\log(GPC))$$

where

log(GPCPPP)	Logarithm of GDP per capita at purchasing power parities
log(GPC)	Logarithm of GNI per capita at market exchange rates
Number of observations	220
Correlation coefficient	0.98

DEFINITION OF THE SOCIETAL INTEGRATION INDEX

The index of societal integration is an indicator of the intensity of open political life. It is computed as a coefficient of heterogeneity of a parliament (legislature) of a country, under the condition that party seats in the parliament (legislature) are obtained as a result of competitive elections. This indicator can have values between 0 and 1; zero means that all seats in the parliament (legislature) belong to one party or that there are no competitive elections; it approaches 1 if every person in the parliament (legislature) is his own party.

The concept of integration was introduced by Emile Durkheim in his work *Suicide*[3]. Durkheim interpreted integration as a function of the intensity of social communication. I interpreted this conception on the societal level, defining societal integration as the intensity of non-trivial exchanges of information at the highest level of society. I provide a purely structural definition of exchange of information, defining it as a number between 0 and 1 of equal to the probability of interparty (i. e., political party) dialogue in society. As a measure of interparty exchange of information, I took the probability of interparty communication in parliament (the legislative body):

$$SCINTX = \sum_{i=1}^{X} P_i \left(1 - P_i\right)$$

---

3 Sociology: Durkheim (1993).

where

| P(i) | the proportion of members of party number (i) in parliament (the legislative body) |
| X | the total number of political parties in parliament (the legislative body). |

Data about the distribution of seats among parties is taken from an open CIA publication. This indicator can be considered objective because no ruling party would give seats in the parliament (legislature) to the opposition willingly. The introduction of this indicator into the formula for computing the human rights index is based on the concept that the condition of political institutions (and the degree to which they can be called democratic) is closely related to the human rights.

DEFINITION OF THE CIVIL AND POLITICAL RIGHTS INDEX

The index of civil and political rights is subjective. As such I used index of freedom of the press. It is taken from the publication of the Freedom House based in New York. For the sake of objectivity it should be noted that the Freedom House in the view of many observers is biased in favor of the United States, especially taking into account the drastic change of the political climate in America since the attacks of September 11, 2001. And in the cases of certain foreign countries, it gives absurdly high or absurdly low ratings. The advantage of this indicator is that it is available for all countries in question and is computed annually.

In cases where values were missing, the following regression was used:

$$CPRX = REG(\log(GPC), SCINTX)$$

where

CPRX	the index of civil and political rights
log(GPC)	Logarithm of GNI per capita at market exchange rates
SCINTX	the index of societal integration
Number of observations	199
Correlation coefficient	0.68

DEFINITION OF THE HUMAN DEVELOPMENT INDEX

The human development index is an objective indicator. It is the average of the level of income per capita in purchasing power parities, level of education, and level of health care. It is computed annually by a well-respected UN program. The introduction of this indicator into the formula for computing the human rights index is based on the idea that socio-economic rights are part of human rights. Some right-wing lawyers in the U.S. consider the socio-economic rights a bad concept for a well-developed law-abiding state, because it is allegedly difficult to conduct the judicial process if socio-economic rights are recognized as full-blown rights. Even if we agree that there is some truth in this assertion and that there are difficulties for a strict judicial process that would take socio-economic rights as real rights, nevertheless, outside the U.S. socio-economic rights are commonly recognized as a lawful component of human rights. This can be seen, for example, from the Universal Declaration of Human Rights adopted by the UN in 1948.

In cases where values were missing, the following regression was used:

HDX = REG(GPCPPP, log(GPCPPP), INFMRT, LIFEXP)

where

HDX	The human development index
GPCPPP	GDP per capita at purchasing power parities
Log(GPCPPP)	Logarithm of GDP per capita at purchasing power parities
INFMRT	Infant mortality
LIFEXP	Life expectancy
Number of observations	180
Correlation coefficient	0.99

DEFINITION OF GINI COEFFICIENT OF INCOME INEQUALITY

The fourth component of human rights index is Gini coefficient of income inequality. This indicator is computed as an integral of distance between equal distribution and the observed distribution of income in a given country. Its values range between 0 and 100; 0 signifies that observed distribution of income is equal, and 100 signifies that all income of the country belongs to one person. The idea of inclusion of Gini coefficient is based on an observation that formal judicial rights are only a potential that can be realized in a specific social context, and that the bigger the inequality, the more difficult it is for an average person of a given society to insist on his or her formal judicial rights. Thus in countries with developed market economies, the price of good lawyers is dictated by material possibilities of the top of the society. For example, in the social context of the U.S., an average person often simply cannot afford a good lawyer. Because of this it is possible to say that for the realization of formally proclaimed judicial rights, a person should possess a certain material potential. The less inequality there is in a country, the more formal judicial rights are realized.

In cases where values were missing, the following regression was used:

GINI = REG(log(GPC), log(INFMRT))

where

GINI	Gini coefficient of income inequality
log(GPC)	Logarithm of GNI per capita at market exchange rates
log(INFMRT)	Logarithm of infant mortality
Number of observations	163
Correlation coefficient	0.53

DEFINITION OF POPULATION

Population of a country includes all residents regardless of legal status or citizenship — except for refugees not permanently settled in the country of asylum, who are generally considered part of the population of their country of origin. The values shown are midyear estimates.[4]

Definition of Armed Forces Personnel

Armed forces personnel are active duty military personnel, including paramilitary forces if the training, organization, equipment, and control suggest they may be used to support or replace regular military forces.[5]

Definition of Military Expenditures

Military expenditures data are primarily based on the World Bank data. They are taken from Stockholm International Peace Research Institute (SIPRI) and are derived from the NATO definition, which includes all current and capital expenditures on the armed forces, including peacekeeping forces; defense ministries and other government agencies engaged in defense projects; paramilitary forces, if these are judged to be trained and equipped for military operations; and military space activities. Such expenditures include military and civil personnel and social services for personnel; operation and maintenance; procurement; military aid (in the military expenditures of the donor country). Excluded are civil defense and current expenditures for previous military activities, such as veterans' benefits, demobilization, conversion, and destruction of weapons.[6]

Definition of Operational Offensive Nuclear Delivery Systems

I follow the definition of the International Institute for Strategic Studies and the Bulletin of the Atomic Scientists.

Definition of Operational Nuclear Warheads

Here, I include strategic and sub-strategic operational warheads aligned to an in-service delivery system, excluding artillery shells and mini-nukes.[7]

Definition of the States Possessing, Pursuing or Capable of Acquiring Weapons of Mass Destruction

The main part of this data is taken from the Bulletin of the Atomic Scientists[8] for 2000. The original data of the Bulletin also includes information about WMD programs in Iraq. This information is now thoroughly discredited and therefore is not included. It is worth noting that anybody who looked at military budgets by countries in the beginning of the 2000s would have noticed that Iraq's military expenditures were less than the military expenditures of most countries in the Middle East. Such a person would have considerable doubt that Iraq was economically capable to sustain WMD programs. Similarly, the same table from Bulletin of the Atomic Scientists lists poor countries, like Ethiopia, Laos and Sudan, as pursuing WMD programs. It is highly doubtful that these impoverished countries have the socio-economic wherewithal to pull off the weaponizing of dangerous biological and chemical substances.

Conversely, I concluded that all countries which have nuclear power plants should be considered to some degree capable of acquiring nuclear weapons. The list

---

4 Economics: The World Bank (1).
5 Economics: The World Bank (1).
6 Economics: The World Bank (1).
7 Military: International Institute for Strategic Studies.
8 Military: Bulletin of the Atomic Scientists.

of such countries is available from Encyclopedia Britannica[9] for 2002 and the CIA[10] for 2006.

I also decided that such highly developed economic powers as United Kingdom, France, Japan, and Germany, should be capable of acquiring the whole range of WMD. In the case of Japan and Germany, which have nuclear power plants, it is reasonable to believe that they have the capability also for biological, chemical, and missile technology. In the case of United Kingdom and France, which are acknowledged by the Bulletin of the Atomic Scientists as nuclear, chemical and missile powers, I think they are also capable of biological weapons. Based on the information about launches of satellites by Japan and Brazil, I consider these two countries as actually possessing the missile technology.

Definition of Developed Market Economies

In section 3, I used data for the period since 1960/1970 for 23 original member countries of the Organization for Economic Co-Operation and Development (excluding Turkey, which is too poor to be compared to the other OECD countries) plus other countries, which also have high per capita GDP and are democracies and for which there exists relevant historical data for the period since 1960/1970 (Cyprus, Israel, Malta, and South Korea qualify for this criteria).

Definition of the Scope of Data for Developed Market Economies

In the tables presented in section 3, I have attempted to look at certain theories popular in the U.S. (and possibly also in the former centrally planned economies of Central and Eastern Europe). I considered, for example, the recent debates about health care reform in the U.S.

Some of the arguments against health care reform in the U.S. are:

1) The U.S. has fewer social programs than other countries and this gives it an advantage in economic competition.

2) The U.S. has the best system of health care in the world, so why to disrupt it?

3) The U.S. has the most economically effective system of health care and social efforts to improve it may only destroy it, creating an ineffective bureaucracy (a variant of the preceding thesis).

4) The current American economic model with lower taxes and lesser social programs provides for faster economic growth and a better quality of life.

5) Even if health care reform could produce better social/economic results, it presents a risk (in the form of a putative socialist order) to freedoms in the U.S. It would be better to remain the freest country in the world.

For item number 5, I refer the reader to the political quality-of-life indicators presented in section 1. For items 1 through 4, the relevant statistics for the developed market economies are presented in section 3.

Definition of Total Health Expenditures

Total health expenditure is the sum of public and private health expenditure. It covers the provision of health services (preventive and curative), family planning activities, nutrition activities, and emergency aid designated for health but does not include provision of water and sanitation.[11]

---

9 Economics: Encyclopedia Britannica.

10 Economics: Central Intelligence Agency.

11 Economics: The World Bank (1).

Definition of Public Health Expenditures

Public health expenditure consists of recurrent and capital spending from government (central and local) budgets, external borrowing and grants (including donations from international agencies and nongovernmental organizations), and social (or compulsory) health insurance funds.[12]

Definition of Taxes as Share of GDP

Taxes refer to general government sector, which is a consolidation of accounts for the central, state, and local governments plus social security.[13]

Definition of Growth Rates of Taxes as Share of GDP

Growth rates of taxes as share of GDP are defined as such relative growth rates, which cause the observed changes of taxes as share of GDP. The corresponding formula for computation is

$$
\begin{aligned}
GRTX = (((\,100\,/\,(\,100 - TAXGDP_1\,) \\
* (\, TAXGDP_1 / TAXGDP_0\,) \\
- (\,TAXGDP_1 / 100\,)\,) \\
** (\,1\,/\,N\,) - 1\,) * 100
\end{aligned}
$$

where

GRTX	growth rates of taxes as share of GDP
TAXGDP0	taxes as share of GDP at the beginning of the period
TAXGDP1	taxes as share of GDP at the end of the period
N	number of years in the period

---

12 Economics: The World Bank (1).
13 Economics: U.S. Bureau of Census (1).

References

Reference

Encyclopedia Britannica (1983) *The New Encyclopedia Britannica*, 15th edition, in 30 Volumes, Chicago

Law

Freedom House, *Freedom of the Press: A Global Survey of Media Independence*, Rowman & Littlefield Publishers, Inc., New York, annual

Sociology

Durkheim, Emile (1993) *Suicide: A Study in Sociology* (Translated by John A. Spaulding and George Simpson), Routledge, London

Military

Bulletin of the Atomic Scientists

International Institute for Strategic Studies, *The Military Balance*, Oxford University Press, annual

Stockholm International Peace Research Institute, *SIPRI Yearbook: Armaments, Disarmament and International Security*, Oxford University Press, annual

Union of Concerned Scientists

Economics

Central Intelligence Agency, *The World Factbook*, annual

Encyclopedia Britannica, *Book of the Year*, annual

Eurostat Press Office, *Tax Burden and Structure of Taxes*, annual

Finfacts, http://www.finfacts.com/biz10/globalworldincomepercapita.htm

Israel Finance Ministry, Press Releases

Maddison, Angus (1995) *Monitoring the World Economy, 1820-1992*, OECD, Paris

_____ (2001) *The World Economy: A Millennial Perspective*, OECD, Paris

_____ (2003) *The World Economy: Historical Statistics*, OECD, Paris

_____ (2007) *Contours of the World Economy, 1–2030 AD*, Oxford University Press, New York

Mitchell, B.R. (2003)(1) *International Historical Statistics: Africa, Asia and Oceania, 1750–2000*, Palgrave Macmillan, London

_____ (2003)(2) *International Historical Statistics: Europe, 1750–2000*, Palgrave Macmillan, London

_____ (2003)(3) *International Historical Statistics: The Americas, 1750–2000*, Palgrave Macmillan, London

OECD, *Revenue Statistics*, Paris, annual

The World Bank (1989-1994) *World Tables*, annual, The John Hopkins University Press

_____ (1995) *World Data 1995*. World Bank Indicators on CD-ROM

_____ (2008) *World Development Indicators Online*

U.S. Agency for International Development, *U.S. Overseas Loans and Grants [Greenbook]*, http://qesdb.cdie.org/gbk/index.html

U.S. Bureau of the Census (1) *Statistical Abstract of the United States*, annual

_____ (1975) *Historical Statistics of the United States, Colonial Times to 1970*, Vols 1 and 2, Washington, D.C.

United Nations Development Programme, *Human Development Report*, annual, Oxford University Press, New York

Mathematics

Itô, Kiyosi, Ed. (2000) *Encyclopedic Dictionary of Mathematics*, by the Mathematical Society of Japan, The MIT Press, Cambridge, Massachusetts

Kotz, Samuel, Norman L. Johnson, Eds. (1985) *Encyclopedia of Statistical Sciences, Vols. 1-9*, John Wiley & Sons, New York

SAS Institute Inc. (1988) *SAS/STAT User's Guide, Release 6.03 Edition*, Cary, North Carolina